GREAT SYMPHONIES
How to Recognize and Remember Them

ALSO BY
SIGMUND SPAETH

The Common Sense of Music
The Art of Enjoying Music

GREAT SYMPHONIES

HOW TO RECOGNIZE AND REMEMBER THEM

By
SIGMUND SPAETH

GARDEN CITY PUBLISHING CO., INC.
Garden City, New York

PRINTED IN THE UNITED STATES OF AMERICA

PREFACE

WHEN this book was begun, it was intended primarily for children, and the Foreword for Grown-ups was written chiefly as a guide to parents and teachers who might be interested. But the author soon discovered that adult music-lovers, and particularly the confessed laymen, were enormously enthusiastic over the possibility of securing an informal, non-technical introduction to the most important symphonies, particularly with the promise of simple aids to remembering the outstanding tunes or themes.

So the book, which began in the spirit and atmosphere of childhood, gradually grew up, just as a child may grow up with a symphony. Its later pages do not hesitate to use words that at first were carefully avoided. Their meaning should be entirely clear by that time, and there is a Glossary at the back which will give whatever additional information is needed.

The materials of this book are definitely scheduled for inclusion in a future school course, but

are meanwhile made available for the general
reader by insistent request. It is suggested that
the book be used often in connection with an
actual hearing of the music, at least by the
novice, outside of a preliminary acquaintance
with the tunes, which any amateur can play ade-
quately. A very practical piano edition is the
Analytic Symphony Series, edited by Percy
Goetschius, and published by the Oliver Ditson
Company. Phonograph records of all the symphonies in this book are available and will be
found listed at the back. Miniature scores can
also be found in most libraries, so there is no lack
of equipment for the serious student or teacher.
Now go on and read the Foreword.

Sigmund Spaeth

FOREWORD FOR GROWN–UPS

THIS has nothing to do with your actual age. You might be musically grown up at eight, like Mozart, or you might be eighty years old and still a child so far as music is concerned.

The object of this Foreword is to explain the book to all those who are already music-lovers by nature or experience and to any other people who by reason of their general intelligence may be considered adults. Some of these people may object to certain things in this book, or possibly to its whole basic idea, and if they came right out and expressed their opinions honestly, it might not be a bad thing.

It is easy enough to say that symphonies are instrumental music, and, with a few striking exceptions, were never meant to be sung. That is perfectly true. The only excuse for setting words to the most important symphonic tunes is that the music will be most easily remembered that way.

The idea is not a new one at all. It has been

applied to all kinds of information, such as the names of the Presidents of the United States and the Kings of England, the alphabet and multiplication table, and the important dates of history. Many of the proverbs and maxims of the world are in rhyme, simply because the verse form impresses them clearly on the human memory, and if you add music, memorizing becomes still easier.

One of the chief reasons why people in general are not familiar with the great symphonies may be found in the fact that they cannot remember the tunes. Often they are entirely unaware that there *are* such tunes. They hardly know what a symphony really is, and think of it merely as a mass of complicated music, difficult to play and equally difficult for the listener to appreciate.

Therefore, quite apart from putting the tunes of great symphonies into a form that is easily remembered, this book may claim to make the whole structure and purpose of symphonic music somewhat clearer to the average listener. There are plenty of good books about the symphonies, but they are mostly for people who have had considerable concert experience or have made a technical study of music.

How many people know that "sonata form" is nothing more than an elaboration of the familiar principle of "statement, contrast and reminder" found in practically every song, from "He's a Jolly Good Fellow" to Foster's "Old Folks at Home"?* How many are aware that this form is characteristic of the first movements of practically all symphonies, sonatas, concertos and string quartets, besides appearing in many other kinds of music? How many realize even so simple a fact that a complete symphony must have four movements or sections?

For such people this book should serve as the most painless of introductions to symphonic literature; but it should also have its uses for the thousands who already have a smattering of musical knowledge, and even for that limited number of well-grounded music-lovers and musicians who could fairly claim exemption from the sugar-coated pills of cultural doctoring.

It is aimed quite definitely at all students and teachers of the so-called "appreciation of music" (which has already been changed to "enjoyment" by most sane and progressive educators), and can be used without hesitation or hauteur by classes from the grade schools all the way up to college. For the individual enthusiast, or the general reader mildly interested in knowing more about music, this book should prove entertainingly acceptable. Somebody can generally be found to play the melodies, which are purposely given without accompaniment and in the simplest

*See the author's "The Art of Enjoying Music," pp. 93–125.

and most convenient keys. (The original keys are always indicated, but obviously they will frequently be impossible for average voices.)

Credit for the germ of this whole idea really belongs to Miss Mabelle Glenn, of Kansas City, one of our outstanding educators in the field of music, who some years ago asked the author to prepare material of this sort for a convention of Music Supervisors in her home town. The setting of words to instrumental themes has also figured prominently in the work of Walter Damrosch, Ernest Schelling, and other musicians who specialize in children's programs, while choruses and glee clubs all over the world are familiar with vocal adaptations of music originally written for instruments.

No justification or apology is really necessary, therefore, although there may be those who will find fault with the details of wording here and there. The following rules have generally governed the creation of these symphonic texts:

1. They must be easily singable, fitting the natural accents of the notes and the spirit of the melody.

2. They must be simple and direct enough to appeal to children, but not so silly as to offend intelligent adults.

3. They should if possible draw some attention to the composer, or the character of the symphony, or both.

In this connection there is a horrible memory of one musical educator who undertook to analyze Beethoven's Fifth Symphony for an audience of children in New York. For the opening four notes, definitely described by the composer as representing "Fate knocking at the door," this gentleman used the words "I've lost my hat!"

Without undue arrogance, it may be assumed that no such desecration has been committed in this volume. Wherever a composer has given any clear indication of his meaning (as Beethoven did many times), the intention has been followed as far as possible. The actual words of Schiller's *Ode to Joy*, used by Beethoven in the Finale of his Ninth Symphony, are of course translated literally, as is the Russian folk-song of the *Birch Tree*, employed by Tschaikowsky in the closing movement of his Fourth. These two examples alone should dispose of the possible contention that symphonic melodies are *per se* unsingable.

It is true that some themes are badly adapted to vocal treatment, and when such cases present apparently insuperable difficulties, the subjects have either been passed by with a mere descriptive comment, or whittled down to their most vocal and hence most memorable passages. When a theme appears in several ways, as is often the case, it has been considered permissible to select the most practical version, even if this did not always coincide with its first statement. The main object, after all, is to supply the reader or student with something that will make the best tunes of symphonic music stand out in his memory so that they are easily recognizable whenever the symphonies are heard.

To try to cover the whole symphonic literature in this book, or even all the significant works in that form, would have been absurd. The symphonies included are those most likely to be heard on concert programs or over the air, and this list covers most of the masterpieces in the history of this climax of absolute music, whose importance surely requires no argument. Sibelius, Rachmaninoff, Richard Strauss, Mahler, Bruckner and many others had to be omitted, including some excellent modern composers of England and America, partly because their presence would make this book too bulky, and partly because their works are generally too complex for such treatment. (Restrictions of copyright would also affect the situation at times.)

The chronological order is a natural one, for Haydn supplies the simplest material for singing, as well as the clearest outlines of form, with his followers gradually elaborating the principles that he laid down. By the time Brahms and Tschaikowsky are reached, the memorizing and singing of symphony tunes should be a thoroughly easy and perhaps a fairly pleasant process.

CONTENTS

CONTENTS

GREAT SYMPHONIES
How to Recognize and Remember Them

BEGINNING WITH PAPA HAYDN

THE WORD "symphony" comes from two Greek words and really means nothing more than "sounding together." You find the "sym" also in words like "sympathy" and "symmetry," and the "phony" part occurs in "telephone" (sounding far off), "microphone" (small-sounding) and "megaphone" (large-sounding). (Maybe the slang word "phony" comes from the same root, meaning something that sounds better than it is.)

So a symphony is just a piece of music that a lot of people play together, and a symphony orchestra is an orchestra large enough to play such a piece, which generally needs at least sixty or seventy players, and perhaps more.

From the time of Franz Joseph Haydn, who lived from 1732 to 1809, and is called "the father of the symphony," this form of music has become more and more recognized as a most important kind of composition. A symphony is supposed to have four parts, or "movements," and each of

1

these parts has at least one and probably two or more melodies that are quite easy to remember.*

The composer does things with these tunes, like a playwright or a novelist working with his characters, so every symphony really has a musical plot, in which each movement is like an act in a play. The tunes often get all mixed up, even turned upside down. They are given to different instruments in the orchestra, sometimes faster, sometimes slower. But generally it all comes out right in the end, like any good story.

Symphonies are instrumental music, and very seldom have words of their own. They are called "pure" or "absolute" music because they have no special title or program or story. They are known simply by their number and their key, as a rule, and they try to express feelings and moods that everybody can share, but such things are not easy to put into words. A song or an opera is really an easier kind of music to write than a symphony, because the words do so much to make the composer's meaning clear to the listener.

In this book there are words which anybody can learn to sing, and these words will make it easier to remember the tunes, and perhaps also something about the composers and the symphonies themselves. Since Haydn was the first com-

---

*The ancestor of the symphony was the classic suite, which merely put together a succession of dance tunes.

poser who wrote real symphonies, he is the best one for a start, if you want to know something about this kind of music.

They called him "Papa Haydn," not because he was the father of the symphony (which was not really known until later), but because he had a fatherly way with music and with everybody who listened to it. (Pronounce his name "hide'n," as in "hide'n go seek.") His pieces generally sounded happy and contented and cheerful, and they were not hard to understand. Haydn liked to play jokes, and many of these are in his music.

He once wrote a *Toy Symphony,* in which most of the instruments are toys, like rattles and cuckoo-calls and whistles and little tin trumpets. Almost any group can learn to play this symphony, so long as there is one good pianist and one good violinist to do the important parts.

Another famous musical joke of Papa Haydn was his *Farewell Symphony,* in which he made each player blow out a candle and stop playing, one at a time, until there were only two left, and finally they blew out their candles too, and the symphony was over.

HAYDN'S SURPRISE SYMPHONY

But the best known of all the Haydn jokes is in the *Surprise Symphony,* which he wrote in

1792, nearly a hundred and fifty years ago. The surprise comes in the second movement, and it is a very loud chord, played suddenly after a soft and peaceful melody. Haydn said that this would wake up all the people who had fallen asleep during the symphony. But if you listen to the first movement, you will find very little reason to fall asleep, for it is lively, joyful music that anybody would like to hear.

There is a slow Introduction, which is itself a sort of joke, for Haydn does not mean to be serious at all. After seventeen measures, he suddenly starts a merry tune that could be fitted with words like this:

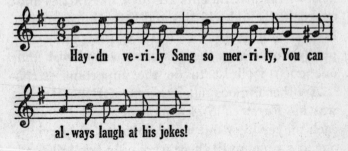

Hay-dn ve-ri-ly Sang so mer-ri-ly, You can

al-ways laugh at his jokes!

He plays all sorts of musical tricks with this tune, until he has reached the eightieth measure, when he brings in a second tune, a little softer, a little sweeter, and a little gentler than the first. They are both introduced by the stringed instruments (violins, etc.), and the second one might have these words:

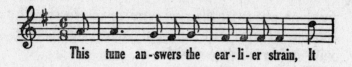

This tune an-swers the ear-li-er strain, It

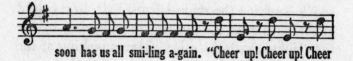

soon has us all smi-ling a-gain. "Cheer up! Cheer up! Cheer

up!" That is its hap-py re-frain!

After this tune has been played once, it is repeated, with the flute playing the same notes as the first violins, and then going into a little duet with the oboes, which sound like someone singing through his nose.

The development or plot of this opening movement is mostly about the first tune, which goes around in all sorts of disguises, till at last it comes back very softly and timidly, as if it wanted to be forgiven for running away. The orchestra makes a lot of noise in welcoming it back, and finally there is a contest, in which the strings play the first tune again, and then the wood-wind instruments (flute, oboes, bassoons) play it their way. Then they all do the same sort of thing with the second tune, as a reminder, for it really has not had much attention, compared with the first tune. Before anything more can be done about it, the orchestra seems to say, in unison, "Time's up!" and pulls down the curtain with a few closing chords.

Now comes the second act, or movement, which contains the main surprise. It starts right in with this tune, played slowly and softly by the first violins, with the other players picking at the strings instead of using the bow, for an accompaniment:*

Papa Haydn wrote this tune, And a chord is coming soon,

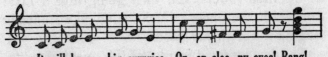

It will be a   big surprise, Op-en slee-py eyes! Bang!

The "bang" really comes after this little tune has been played twice, the second time even softer than the first, so that the loud chord would actually be both a surprise and a shock, especially to anyone who might have gone to sleep, as Papa Haydn said.

This is the only tune in the second movement of the *Surprise Symphony,* although it runs a little longer than just the few notes above. The

---

*Haydn used this same tune in *The Seasons,* to represent a whistling ploughboy.

trick that Haydn plays is to write "variations," that is, extra notes and musical decorations, which dress up the tune in such ways that it sounds different, although it is really always the same tune. This happens eight times altogether, and you never grow tired of the tune, because the variations make each reminder seem fresh and new.

The third movement of Haydn's *Surprise Symphony* is a Minuet, which was originally a rather slow and stately dance, with three beats to a measure, like a slow waltz. People danced the Minuet in the powdered wigs and elaborate costumes of what we call "colonial days," and it was popular all over Europe, as well as in America.

Haydn calls this movement *Menuetto,* by which he means to show that it is faster than a regular Minuet. It really is much too fast for such a dance, and the very first tune makes this quite clear:

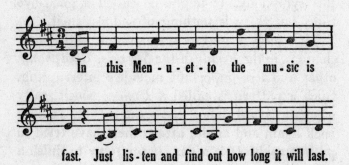

In this Men - u - et - to the mu - sic is
fast. Just lis - ten and find out how long it will last.

7

Haydn wrote this melody one tone higher, which would be a little too high to sing, and where we have the words "fast" and "last" he had the violins play a chord, with its top note an octave higher. He went on a little further with the tune too, but this is the most important part.

The Minuet in a symphony generally has a regular form, like this: The first tune is repeated, note for note. Then comes a second tune, which is also repeated, and then the first tune again. After that there is a third tune, called the *Trio,* in two parts, each repeated. Finally the first and second tunes are played through once more, which finishes the Minuet. If you can remember the first tune, especially in this *Menuetto,* that is really enough.

By the time you reach the last movement, or *Finale,* in the *Surprise Symphony,* you feel that you already know Haydn quite well. He starts again with one of those jolly tunes that make you forget he was all of sixty years old when he wrote this symphony. It might be called a good-bye tune, but there is nothing of sadness in it.

This tune is played seven times, with slight changes, in the *Finale* of the *Surprise Symphony,* other and less important melodies interrupting. Such a pattern is called a *Rondo,* which really means a round dance, the same melody coming back again and again, after others have tried to push it aside. It is a gay, happy way to finish a

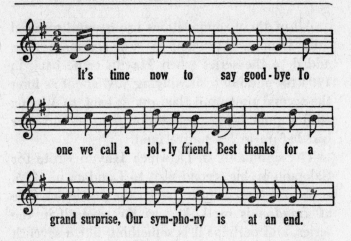

It's time now to say good-bye To one we call a jol-ly friend. Best thanks for a grand surprise, Our sym-pho-ny is at an end.

symphony, and many other composers used *Rondos* in their symphonies after Haydn's time. In fact, they all took him as a model, and built on the foundations that he created, making the symphony gradually more and more elaborate, like a cathedral that starts with a few simple arches and becomes after many years a wonderful piece of architecture.

HAYDN'S LONDON SYMPHONY

In 1791, when Haydn was already nearly sixty years old, he came to London for the first time, at the invitation of a concert manager named Salomon. During his visit of a year and a half in London, Haydn wrote six great symphonies, as ordered by Salomon, including the *Surprise*.

9

All of these compositions are generally called "the London symphonies," and six more were added to the series when Haydn came back in 1794 for another visit, staying just about as long the second time, and then going back to Vienna with a much bigger reputation than he had ever had before in his native land.

The symphony in D, which Haydn wrote for Salomon on his second visit to London, in 1795, is the one that is meant when the particular title of *London* is used. It was the seventh in the series, and perhaps it is something like a seventh son. At any rate it is a beautiful symphony, and we are lucky to have it, so that we still hear it played to-day.

Haydn begins it with a slow Introduction, just as he did in the *Surprise Symphony*. But this Introduction starts very loud, as if trumpets were blowing a signal to begin some great ceremony. The whole orchestra takes part in these first few notes, which might be sung in this way:

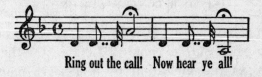

Ring out the call!   Now hear ye all!

The lower strings then seem to ask "What shall we do next?", using the same pattern of rhythm three times, but timidly, with uncertain little answers from the first violins higher up. So the

whole orchestra gives the trumpet call again, this
time in major key, instead of minor, as it was
at the start. The strings are still uncertain, and
it is only after a third loud signal, immediately
echoed very softly, that the orchestra seems able
to get together on a real tune. This tune is in
D major, and it seems to express the gaiety of
London life, the smart uniforms of the Guard
at Buckingham Palace, and the British love of
outdoor games and sports, at which they have
always done so well. This first real tune might be
sung thus:*

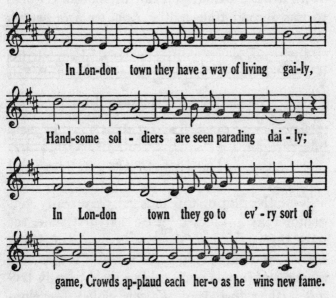

In Lon-don town they have a way of living gai-ly,

Hand-some sol - diers are seen parading dai - ly;

In Lon-don town they go to ev' - ry sort of

game, Crowds ap-plaud each her-o as he wins new fame.

*Does this sound something like the "good-bye" tune in the
Finale of the *Surprise Symphony?* See p. 9.

This leads to all kinds of excitement, with the whole orchestra making loud comments on the tune, which is really a very good one. "Let's hear it again in a different key," says Haydn. "Perhaps you'll like it better that way." At least it sounds just as good, but this time the second half of the melody trails off in a different direction, and there is a lot more arguing in the orchestra before a new tune suddenly turns up. This begins like a dialogue, and could have something to do with London Bridge, which has been famous for so many years in a nursery rhyme. With a little fixing, you can fit the same words to this second tune in the *London Symphony:*

Now the plot of this musical play really gets going. Haydn takes a bit of that first tune, the part that comes on the words "way of living gaily," and puts it into all sorts of keys, with all sorts of instruments taking their turn in trying it their own way. This is called "development" and pretty soon you are very familiar with that "way of living gaily." You are glad to be reminded of the original tune, as you first heard it, especially with the flute adding a little counter-melody of its own, higher up, for the second half.

The orchestra has its final argument, and there is a timid return to the "way of living gaily" idea, by the strings. Then the clarinets and oboe give a last suggestion of the second tune, which has been almost overlooked in the excitement. The last eighteen measures emphatically approve of the "way of living gaily," and the movement ends with chords and three final octaves that leave you in no doubt at all about the key, which was D major.

Now comes the second movement, which is slower, and changing the key to G major. After the lively bustle of the first movement, this sounds as though London had arrived at the end of a hard day, with everybody about ready to go home. It starts with a lovely melody, which can be sung thus:

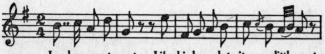

London goes to rest,   Like birds each to its own little nest;

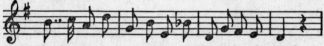

London goes to sleep, and naught disturbs her slumber deep.

This melody is repeated, and followed by a second strain that more or less imitates it. Then Haydn begins experimenting, seeming always to begin the same tune, but always working it out differently, and letting the orchestra add more and more in the way of decoration. Finally he is satisfied just to sound the first four notes in different ways, and lets the movement end with orchestral ornaments, which are very pretty and restful.

The third movement of this *London Symphony* is a *Menuetto,* the same as in the *Surprise.* The time is again faster than a regular Minuet, but you can easily think of gay Englishmen at the time of George I, II or III dancing in this lively fashion. They had the right sort of costumes too. If the rhyme for this tune seems pretty terrible, excuse it, please.

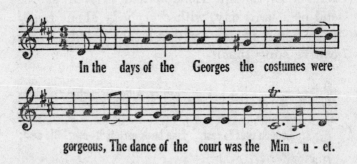

In the days of the Georges the costumes were gorgeous, The dance of the court was the Min - u - et.

That tune is played twice through without any change, and then comes a second tune which is very similar, with another repetition of the main melody, and a trilling surprise finish. The *Trio,* which always completes a Minuet, has a two-tone pattern, alternating with scale passages in the strings, which are really too fast for words. You could use tra-la-las and sing it this way:

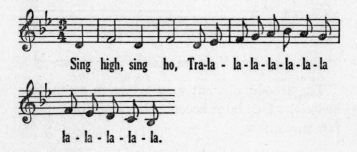

Sing high, sing ho, Tra-la - la - la - la - la - la - la

la - la - la - la - la.

This is repeated and then goes into a second part in which the two-tone melody and the scale passages are played at the same time, instead of alternately, first by wood-wind and then with strings also. A short interlude reminds you of the "sing high, sing ho" for the last time, and back goes the whole orchestra to a repetition of the first two parts of the *Menuetto,* in the regular fashion. You can't help feeling gay at the finish.

Now there is only the *Finale* left, and for this Haydn takes us out into the country. The movement starts in the bass, with a sustained octave in the horns, like the sound of a bag-pipe. Over this droning bass, the fiddles play a regular country tune that seems to laugh out loud.

Country folks Have their jokes, Gaily playing and dancing,

Bag-pipes drone, Merry tone, Country life is en-tranc-ing!

The accompaniment soon brings in a countermelody, which later becomes the main tune for a few measures.

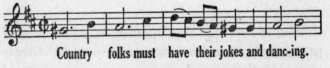

Country folks must have their jokes and danc-ing.

That little scale on "have their jokes" seems to fascinate Haydn, and he experiments with it in several ways, first treble, then bass. Finally the full orchestra shows us a scale that is a scale, and the strings fill in with a slow melody that might be sung:*

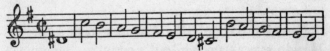

You can't be always prancing, Music is much more than dancing

*The key has been changed from D to G, to make it singable.

In spite of this warning, the orchestra flings about pieces of the first tune until you agree that it simply must be repeated entire. This inspires Haydn to do a bit of developing, by working snatches of the first tune against the familiar scale passages, until you again hear the slow interlude of the strings. This leads to a recapitulation or final reminder of that important country dance tune with which the movement opened, and after a while this is heard again, rather heavily, in the bass, as though the English peasants were coming down hard with their hobnailed boots. The slow interlude is also repeated, this time with the flute playing scales up against it. There seems to be some doubt for a while just what Haydn prefers of all this material, but after a few more scales, he gives his vote to the country dance tune, growing gradually softer, until there is nothing left to do but play a few loud chords in D major, in case you have forgotten that that is the key of the *London Symphony*. Probably you are sorry it is over.

HAYDN'S CLOCK SYMPHONY

Another of the symphonies written by Haydn in London has the title of *The Clock,* and you will see why when you get to the second movement. Its key is D major and it was composed in 1794.

17

The *Clock Symphony* follows Haydn's habit of a slow Introduction, which is this time in minor key, based on a rising scale. This scale turns into a cheerful major mood at the start of the first real theme, a fast (*Presto*) tune that makes you feel no time can be lost in getting the clock under way.

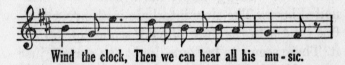

Let's hurry with Haydn to wind the clock,

Wind the clock, Then we can hear all his mu-sic.

The orchestra makes plenty of noise after this melody has been introduced, but after a while Haydn seems to try for something a little different. With the same general rhythmic pattern, in 6-8 time, he searches for a second melody, not too far removed from the first, like this:

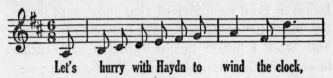

Keep winding and winding and wind-ing, Soon

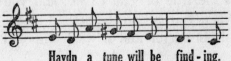

Haydn a tune will be find-ing.

This leads to more noise, and finally a downward scale takes us back to the first melody for a repetition. The middle part of the movement ("development") experiments with different ways of winding the clock, taking the first tune apart and putting it together again.

In the last part of the movement ("recapitulation") Haydn reminds us of both the first and the second melody, arriving at his biggest climax, and finally going into a conclusion (*Coda*) which brings back the first tune, to lead into D major chords at the finish.

It is in the second movement that the title of *The Clock* is made clear. It begins with a realistic tick-tock accompaniment, which runs right along under a charming melody that permits these words:*

Tick-tock-tick-tock! Hear the tick-tock sound on high, The

clock is tel-ling ev'-ry-one how time goes by.

There is an interruption by a noisy passage in minor key, but the tune calmly returns, played by the first violins, while the ticking accompani-

*The key is transposed from G to C, for vocal convenience.

ment is carried by only one flute and one bassoon, over two octaves apart. After a long pause, the clock begins to tick again, this time in the second violins. Before the end of the movement you hear the main melody played by the full orchestra, which makes you realize how fine it is, far beyond anything an actual clock could do.

With everything evidently in working order, Haydn relaxes in the third movement, which is of course a *Menuetto*. Its first tune is quite danceable, a bit faster than a Minuet, and of a distinctly romantic character.*

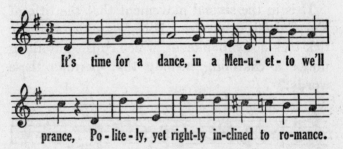

It's time for a dance, in a Men-u-et-to we'll prance, Po-lite-ly, yet right-ly in-clined to ro-mance.

This goes through the regular Minuet form until the *Trio* is reached. It begins with a drone bass (just repeating the major chord), over which the flute plays a lively set of scales, which might as well be whistled, without any words:

*The original key of D becomes G for singing.

At one point it sounds as if the harmony were wrong, and some people might easily think the orchestra was making a mistake. But Haydn evidently meant it that way, and when the *Trio* repeats, he changes it so that everybody can stop worrying.

The *Finale* of Haydn's *Clock Symphony* expresses a vote of confidence in the continued march of time, of which the radio and movies have long been reminding us. The main melody runs sturdily ahead, with four fast beats to a measure, mostly following the scale.*

Time goes on to a very fast and hap-py beat,

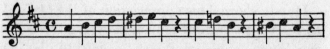

Night or dawn, it nev-er will ad-mit de-feat.

Haydn builds on this until he reaches another key, in which he uses the first three notes of the tune as though he meant to turn them into a new melody. But actually, just before getting back to his main melody, he brings in a little special tune, like this:

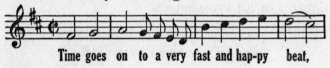

That's the way to wind a clock, wind a clock, wind a clock.

*The second line is sung an octave lower than Haydn's notes.

21

There is another noisy episode in minor key, and then the first melody turns up again with unexpected decorations and the effect of a fugue. (See Glossary.) After the whole orchestra has done its part to remind us of this solid tune, it is given a final statement, very simply and quietly, like a farewell. Its last five notes are repeated, just as people do when they are saying good-bye, and then Haydn runs away into his closing chords, as if he felt a little ashamed of growing so sentimental. It all makes a very human finish to one of the most human and delightful of all symphonies.

HAYDN'S OXFORD SYMPHONY

While Haydn was living in London for the first time, he was given the degree of Doctor of Music by Oxford University. That is one of those honors that do not necessarily mean much, but in Haydn's case it did, because Oxford is a great English university, and Haydn was a great musician. Don't be deceived, however, when you hear someone called "Doctor." It would be a mistake, as a rule, to trust him with a cut finger.

Haydn showed his appreciation of the Oxford degree by tossing off a symphony for the occasion. Some people say it was too hard to play, so this older symphony, written in 1788, was substituted. The key of this *Oxford* symphony is G major.

It begins with an Introduction, as usual, but this Introduction has more of a melody of its own than Haydn is in the habit of writing. It might be sung to these words:

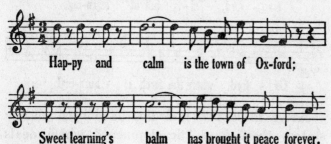

Hap-py and calm is the town of Ox-ford; Sweet learning's balm has brought it peace forever.

This scholarly and beautiful opening soon turns into a more boisterous *Allegro,* which literally means "happy." Its first tune might be sung thus:

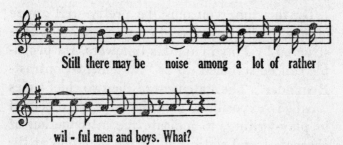

Still there may be noise among a lot of rather wil - ful men and boys. What?

(But no Englishman would be satisfied with one "What?" He would almost certainly say "What? What?")

There is a second tune that is heard fairly soon, which might also refer to the charming town of Oxford:

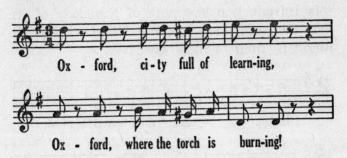

Ox - ford, ci - ty full of learn-ing,

Ox - ford, where the torch is burn-ing!

After these two melodies have been clearly stated, there is a "development" which deals mostly with the first *Allegro* tune. This tune comes back completely in its original key, by way of reminder, and finally a short *Coda,* or "tail-piece," leads to conventional G-chords for a finish.

By this time you must be pretty well aware of how the first movement of a symphony is constructed by Haydn and his followers. Its principle can be summed up as "Statement-Contrast-Reminder." The statement of the two chief tunes is called "exposition," and the same word is used in play-writing, to indicate the introduction of characters and setting up of the situation at the start. But the characters in a symphony are tunes, so they are introduced by their composer under the same title of "exposition."

The contrasting material corresponds to the plot of the play. There must be some conflict, some suspense, some uncertainty, or else a symphony or a play will become monotonous and uninteresting. The composer supplies this contrast, or suspense, by "developing" his two principal tunes in what is sometimes called a "free fantasia." He breaks them in pieces, takes them into various keys, turns them over to different instruments, perhaps even turns them upside down. Technically this is the most interesting part of a symphonic movement, and the greater the composer, the more he is able to accomplish in this "development" section.

But finally he wants to remind his hearers of the most important tunes, of which the average ear might easily lose track in the course of this elaborate "development." So he first brings back his main tune, generally in its original key, and then the second tune also, but in a different key. This reminder is called "recapitulation," and corresponds to the happy ending. Finally he may add a *Coda,* just to bring the movement to a close. (Sometimes this *Coda* becomes very important, as you will see later.)

The whole form of such a movement (which you find almost always at the start of a symphony, and sometimes also in the later movements) is called "sonata form." It is used in the

25

first movements of sonatas, concertos, quartets, etc., as well as in symphonies, and it is just as well to be on the look-out for it in every symphony mentioned in this book. (The word *sonata* really means nothing more than a "sound-piece," one that is played by instruments, as distinguished from a *cantata,* which is meant to be sung. A symphony is a sonata for orchestra instead of for a single instrument. A concerto is a sonata for a solo instrument with orchestral accompaniment.)

After this interlude of technical explanation, which fits in with the scholarly town of Oxford, let's get back to the *Oxford Symphony* itself. The slow movement (*Adagio*) is written in the key of D. Its main melody, played by the stringed instruments, could be sung like this:

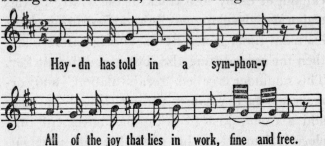

Hay - dn has told in a sym-phon-y

All of the joy that lies in work, fine and free.

It is repeated, with the addition of a flute part, and then Haydn experiments with it in various ways, once suggesting it in minor key. He finally gives us some loud music in D minor, for a slight contrast, using repeated notes, but without any outstanding melody. There is an interlude by the wood-wind, and then he goes back to his main tune, finally ending the movement very softly.

The *Menuetto* is again faster than a real Minuet, starting with the full orchestra, and repeating its first melody, which sounds like this:

In a Hay-dn Men-u - et - to the

music goes a little fast, Sometimes it runs along like

an - y song, But still a Hay - dn Men - u -

et - to, go - ing on and on and nev - er

stopping till it gets to where it has to end at last.

By this time you also know that the regular form of a Minuet is an opening melody, repeated, followed by an answering melody, also repeated, then a *Trio* in two sections, each of which is also repeated, and then a return to the two sections of the Minuet itself, this time played without repetition. (The *Trio* gets its name from the fact that it was originally played by three instruments.)

The *Trio* of this Minuet has the bassoons and trumpets imitating a curious syncopation or ragtime effect, that was suggested in the second section of the Minuet itself. This syncopation, which produces artificial accents by anticipating or delaying the real beat, continues in the bassoons and lower strings, and you hear some funny jumping octaves, as if the Oxford scholars were forgetting their dignity and playing leap-frog in caps and gowns.

The *Finale* (*Presto*) carries this idea still further. Its main melody is like a real college song, and it has no dignity at all.

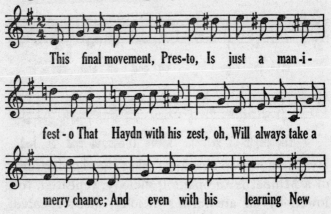

This final movement, Pres-to, Is just a man-i-
fest-o That Haydn with his zest, oh, Will always take a
merry chance; And even with his learning New

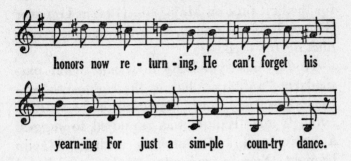

honors now re - turn - ing, He can't forget his

yearn-ing For just a sim-ple coun-try dance.

(You can sing three G's on the same level for the last measure, if you wish.) The cellos now do the octave jumps, and these even get into the melody at times. In fact, this movement is *full* of octaves. Haydn soon tries the same tune in minor key. There is some development, and then a reminder of the whole tune, in major. The solo flute starts a charming passage for the wood-wind, and this is followed by a dialogue between these instruments and the strings. When the end of the symphony seems to have been reached, the flute jumps in once more with a snatch of the main tune, which the strings answer impatiently for the last time. The orchestra agrees *fortissimo* that the end has come. There are three loud chords in G, and the *Oxford Symphony* is over.

HAYDN'S MILITARY SYMPHONY

The symphony known as *Military* was the eleventh of the series that Haydn composed for Salomon and the English public. It was played for the first time on May 12th, 1794, in Hanover Square Room, London, with the composer conducting the orchestra.

To-day this symphony does not sound particularly "military," but in the eighteenth century almost any music that used the bass drum, cymbals and triangle was supposed to suggest a brass band and marching soldiers. Haydn brought these instruments into his second and fourth movements, so the symphony becomes technically military, if you do not take your wars too seriously.

The Introduction starts with a beautiful slow melody, which was later imitated by Bizet in *Carmen* and Puccini in *La Tosca,* both very good operas. Haydn wrote it in G major, which is the key of this symphony. But that is too high for singing, so let's put it into the closely related key of D, like this:

Softly on tip-toe comes A tune that will soon turn to drums.

The Introduction treats this tune in several interesting ways, ending on a sustained chord. Then comes the first real theme (tune) of the opening movement, which seems to show the influence of the introductory tune. It makes a very nice and gentle military song, like this:*

*The key is still transposed to D.

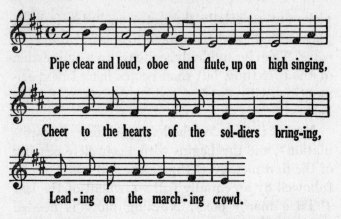

Pipe clear and loud, oboe and flute, up on high singing,

Cheer to the hearts of the sol-diers bring-ing,

Lead - ing on the march - ing crowd.

The orchestra experiments quite a while with
this material, and finally starts it again, but this
time it works out quite differently. There is even
a hint of minor treatment, but the strings interrupt this with a little *staccato* accompaniment
(short, brittle notes) and then bring in a new
tune, which is decidedly gay:*

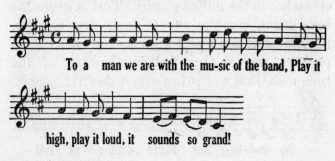

To a man we are with the mu-sic of the band, Play it

high, play it loud, it sounds so grand!

The development or plot of the movement
begins with this tune in a new key, and Haydn

*The transposition is now from D to A.

picks out especially the notes on "play it high, play it loud" and tries them in a lot of different ways. Then he suddenly switches to a suggestion of the first tune, but soon comes back to experimenting with the last, which he seems to like better.

Now it is time for the happy ending (recapitulation), and this begins with a complete hearing of the first melody ("Pipe clear and loud," etc.), followed by an equally full statement of the last ("To a man," etc.). Nothing more is needed except a *Coda,* or "tail," which sounds mostly like the last tune, but finally goes into scales and chords, just to let you know that the movement is over.

The second movement of Haydn's *Military Symphony* starts with a marching tune which the composer borrowed from France, where they specialize in the military spirit. This is where the bass drum, cymbals and triangle first come in prominently, but it still sounds very innocent, so perhaps we are justified in thinking of the tune with these words (an octave down):

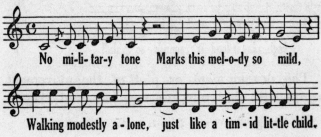

No mi-li-tar-y tone   Marks this mel-o-dy so   mild,

Walking modestly a-lone,   just   like a   tim-id lit-tle child.

The whole movement is taken up with this one melody, which at one time is played in minor key, and finally broken into pieces. Suddenly the trumpet plays a fanfare, very much like the one that Mendelssohn later used to start his exit *Wedding March.* There is a big *crescendo* (gradually increasing in volume), starting with the rolling drums, and bringing in the whole orchestra very loud, before Haydn decides to stop with one of his regular sets of major chords.

A gay and lively whistling tune begins the third movement, which is a *Menuetto,* as usual with Haydn. It might be remembered by these words:*

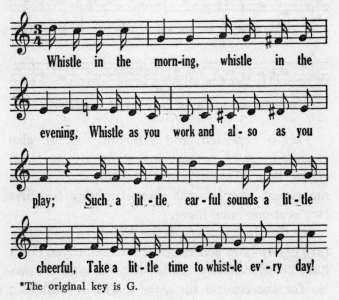

Whistle in the morn-ing, whistle in the evening, Whistle as you work and al - so as you play; Such a lit - tle ear - ful sounds a lit - tle cheerful, Take a lit - tle time to whist-le ev' - ry day!

*The original key is G.

This catchy tune is played twice through, and then there is a section, also played twice, which is quite similar, turning the whistling figure into short scales, and also using the chromatic notes (half a tone apart) in other scale forms.

Now comes the *Trio,* which is regularly the second part of a Minuet, and its skipping tune could be sung this way:

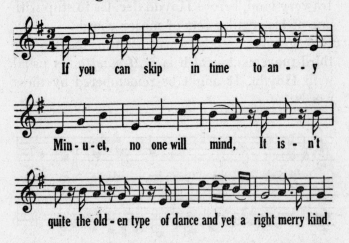

If you can skip in time to an - - y
Min - u - et, no one will mind, It is - n't
quite the old - en type of dance and yet a right merry kind.

This is repeated, and a second section, also repeated, gives various imitations of its tune. After that Haydn returns to the start of the movement and lets the orchestra play the first two sections once more.

By the time you reach the *Finale* of this *Military Symphony* you are fairly sure that you don't have to give it any really war-like significance. So for the closing tune, we might as well sing words that show that nobody's afraid of the big, bad soldiers. This isn't meant as a suggestion of the best way to stop wars, but probably the horses wouldn't mind:

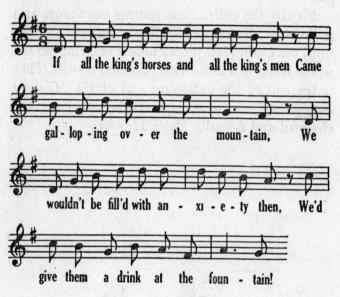

If all the king's horses and all the king's men Came gal-lop-ing ov-er the moun-tain, We wouldn't be fill'd with an-xi-e-ty then, We'd give them a drink at the foun-tain!

This lively tune is played through twice, and then Haydn begins to play with the first few notes, trying them in different keys, especially the part that says "and all the king's men." He keeps this up for quite a while, until you are so used to the galloping rhythm that you will never be afraid of a horse or a soldier again.

Even with only this one tune for material, Haydn manages to give plenty of development or plot to the movement. He lets the violins play soft, hesitating chords, and then suddenly interrupts them with a loud drum-beat; but you feel that this is just a joke, and no one is going to get hurt.

Finally the entire tune returns once more and gallops in all directions (like a western movie) until the *Coda* (tail-piece) insists on bringing the whole thing to a close with two loud chords. That is the end of the galloping and of the *Military Symphony,* and a very good place to leave the cheerful and friendly Papa Haydn.

THE MIRACULOUS MOZART

WOLFGANG AMADEUS MOZART, who lived only
from January, 1756, to December, 1791, proved
in those few years that he was perhaps the greatest natural genius that music has ever known.
(Please pronounce the z in his name as if it were
ts. The o is long, as in "mole.")

When he was only three years old, the little
Mozart, instead of just banging on the keyboard,
like so many other children, had found out for
himself how to make pleasant sounds on the
harpsichord (which was the piano of its day),
and his father, Leopold Mozart, himself a fine
musician, began to give him lessons immediately.
At the age of four the boy was already able
to play the violin and harpsichord well, and at
six he had composed and published a whole set
of violin sonatas.

He was still only six years old when his father
took Wolfgang and his sister Marianne on a
concert tour which was a sensational success.
The little boy must have been very lovable and

charming, and he remained that way all his life, even when things turned out badly for him.

Mozart wrote his first symphonies when he was eight, and at fourteen his opera, *Mitridate,* was produced successfully in Milan. He took some lessons from Haydn, to whom he first gave the nickname of "Papa," but soon Haydn was learning more from Mozart than he could ever have taught him.

For about twenty years Mozart produced a steady flow of operas, symphonies, songs, and chamber music (sonatas, quartets, etc.), living mostly in Vienna, but also visiting Paris, Munich and other cities, including his native Salzburg, in Austria. He was handicapped by poverty and the jealousy of people who should have been his friends, and, like so many geniuses, he was not at all a practical man. He died in Vienna when he was only thirty-five years old, leaving an unfinished *Requiem* which had been ordered by a mysterious stranger, and at which he worked until his health failed him. Mozart wrote more than forty symphonies in his short life, and of these the three greatest were all composed within a single year (1788). Two of them are known only by their keys (E-flat and G minor) and the last (and perhaps the finest) is called *Jupiter.* Probably the most popular of these three great Mozart symphonies, however, is the one in G minor, and this is certainly the easiest with which to become acquainted.

MOZART'S G MINOR SYMPHONY

This symphony is full of melody of the most delightful sort, and it also has some excellent dramatic touches, for Mozart loved the theatre, and was at his best in the operatic style of music; so it is natural that he should also put drama into his best symphonies.

You will immediately notice an important difference between this Mozart symphony and any of those by Haydn already discussed. Mozart uses no Introduction at all. He starts right in with one measure of accompaniment that leads immediately into his first tune. It is a very happy tune, full of laughter and fun:*

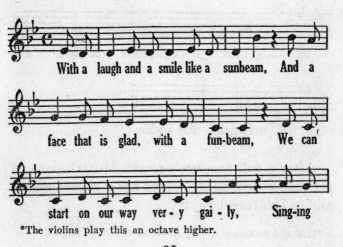

With a laugh and a smile like a sunbeam, And a face that is glad, with a fun-beam, We can start on our way ver-y gai-ly, Sing-ing

*The violins play this an octave higher.

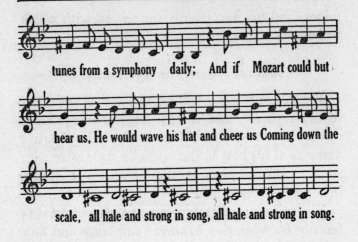

tunes from a symphony daily; And if Mozart could but

hear us, He would wave his hat and cheer us Coming down the

scale, all hale and strong in song, all hale and strong in song.

This begins to repeat itself at once, but changes quickly, to go into a new melody, like this:

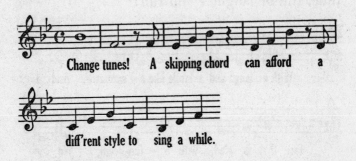

Change tunes! A skipping chord can afford a

diff'rent style to sing a while.

After a full measure's pause, Mozart gives us his real second theme, which has a slower effect, and in a different key:*

*It is still necessary to sing an octave below the original.

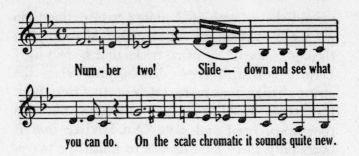

Num - ber   two!   Slide —   down and see what

you can do.   On the scale chromatic it sounds quite new.

Mozart now experiments with the notes that carry the words "with a laugh and a smile," playing two of them very slowly against the repeated pattern of three. A lot of fast work by the strings leads to a chord which brings back the minor key of the start, and everything is repeated right up to the same chord. But the second time it leads to a series of chords in the wood-wind, and the real development begins.

This development deals chiefly with the opening tune, turning it over to various instruments and getting all sorts of surprising effects with its few notes. A series of questions and answers in the wood-wind finally arrives at a complete reminder of this important theme, in its original key (recapitulation). There is a return also of the little connecting melody ("Change tunes"), but in a new key, and after this has been discussed by the whole orchestra, we also hear the

41

second theme again ("Number two"), this time in minor instead of major key. Mozart goes through some of the same tricks that he had used before, but with fresh details, and when the strings make one more attempt to bring back the whole first tune, the orchestra puts its foot down hard and says "No." After that it takes only three loud chords to finish the movement.

The second movement of Mozart's symphony in G minor (*Andante*) begins with a slow theme which is really two melodies overlapping. The top voice stays on one note in each measure (six times), gradually getting higher, while a lower voice has a counter-melody that keeps this effect from growing monotonous. But Mozart keeps on reminding you of that regular beat of six eighth-notes to a measure, and in time you get the impression of people walking, which is what *Andante* really means. It might be expressed like this in words:

With slow stately tread We are moving ahead And the

world is outspread, As if waiting to say hel-lo. We

an - swer,   we   an-swer,   with

"Come on, lead us, come on, lead us, Tell us where we shall go!"

This idea is carried on until a short second melody appears, which might be considered a series of echoes, based on the first, and with a similar meaning.

Lead us! Lead us!   Where do we go? Where do we go?

The development of this movement starts with the rhythmic walking effect, which is gradually decorated more and more by little two-note figures that have already been prominent. Soon there is a reminder of the whole theme as it was at the start of the movement (recapitulation), and in due time the little second theme is also heard again, with everything ending quietly and beautifully.

Now comes a Minuet (*Menuetto*) of the sort that Mozart was especially good at writing. It starts robustly in G minor (the key of the symphony) and its first part could be sung thus, although the instruments carry the melody an octave higher after the sixth measure:

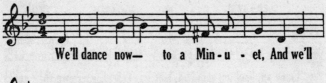

We'll dance now— to a Min-u-et, And we'll

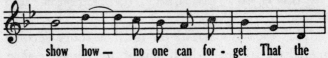

show how— no one can for-get That the

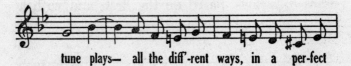

tune plays— all the diff'-rent ways, in a per-fect

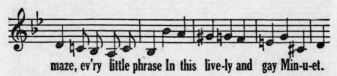

maze, ev'ry little phrase In this live-ly and gay Min-u-et.

The second section of the Minuet imitates the first, again with the effect of two melodies harmonizing with each other. For the *Trio* Mozart goes quietly into G major, with a fascinating dance tune like this:

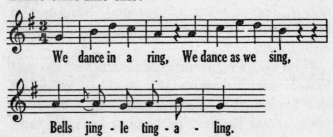

We dance in a ring, We dance as we sing,

Bells jing-le ting-a-ling.

There is an imitation of this also, with bass
and treble voices answering each other, and making interesting contrasts between the strings and
the wind instruments.

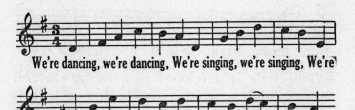

We're dancing, we're dancing, We're singing, we're singing, We're
dancing, we're dancing and singing to - geth - er.

Finally the whole movement goes back to the
start and runs through the *Menuetto,* as usual.

In the *Finale,* Mozart introduces a new dance
rhythm, so light and dainty that it seems no
human feet could keep time to it. Beethoven
admitted that he used this tune for the third
movement of his fifth symphony (see p. 96) but
by a change of rhythm and key he made it sound
entirely different. We shall have to depend upon
tra-la-las for the fast notes of Mozart's dancing
Finale, and try to remember it this way:*

With fair-y foot-steps danc - ing, Tra - la

*Part of this had to be put down an octave.

la - la - la - la - la - la - la - la - la, This music is en-

trancing, Tra - la - la-la - la - la-la-la - la-la - la.

This tune is developed in a noisy, cheerful
fashion, until a gentler, contrasting melody is
introduced by the strings:*

"A - way away, away, fol - low me!" — we

hear the voice of Mo - zart call · · ·

ing, And so we sing — our voic-es ris - ing and

fall - ing, From morn till close of day.

This also receives some noisy comments from
the whole orchestra, and after a while a section

*This is transposed from B-flat to E-flat.

of development begins, using mostly the first seven notes of the opening tune ("With fairy footsteps dancing"). This gives Mozart a chance for further dialogues between the strings and the wind instruments, and it is remarkable how much he does with those few tones.

The whole melody finally returns, in its original key (G minor), and we also hear the second tune again, but with distinct alterations. There are some heated arguments in the orchestra, which insists on staying in the minor key, and that is exactly what happens, with two quick chords and a good, solid G in octaves at the finish.

MOZART'S SYMPHONY IN E-FLAT

This symphony has been called Mozart's "swan song." It is by no means close to his actual death, but its lyric qualities make it more of a real song than either the G minor or the *Jupiter*. It differs from the others of this group of three also in having an Introduction, which was a regular habit with Haydn, but much less so with Mozart and Beethoven. This Introduction, in E-flat, begins with big chords, suggesting the words:

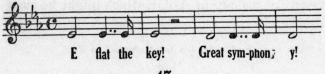

E flat the key!   Great sym-phon y!

The first real melody comes after twenty-five measures have been played. It is in triple time, and still in E-flat, although this key has to be put down to B-flat if you want to sing it easily:

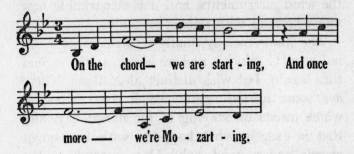

On the chord— we are start - ing, And once more —— we're Mo - zart - ing.

The nearest thing to a second melody is a little passage that stands out like this:*

Mo - zart goes right on in a trip - le rhy-thm.

You hear it imitated in the development of this movement, along with some little two-note figures that remind you of the first movement of Mozart's G-minor symphony (see p. 39). But the main melody comes back soon and the movement ends cheerfully on E-flat chords.

The slow movement (*Andante*) starts with a beautiful melody in A-flat, which might be sung thus:

*Now the key of B-flat has to be changed to F.

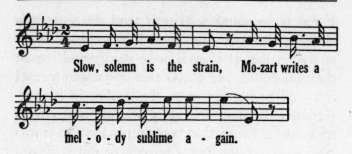

Slow, solemn is the strain, Mo-zart writes a

mel - o - dy sublime a - gain.

There is a second half to this melody, with a slightly different ending, and then the entire eight measures are repeated. A second section varies the same tune, with decorative tones running in pairs, as in the slow movement of the G minor symphony, and after this has been repeated there is a transition, by way of the wood-wind, to a new melody of a more cheerful character:

Strings change the air, All—— must do their share.

There is a short development of the first theme, which finally returns in its complete form, but without repetition. Then the second tune also comes back, this time in a new key, and after much interesting treatment of all this material, the movement ends abruptly with two very loud chords.

The third movement of Mozart's symphony in

E-flat is, as usual, a Minuet, and this time it is close to the style and pace of the actual dance of that name. It is even more sturdy and robust than the Minuet of the G minor symphony, and it would be impossible to find a flaw in its perfect melodic line. The only trouble is it covers such a wide range that you simply have to transpose some of the tones an octave down if you want to sing it. But it really seems worth bothering to that extent, and it is not at all a difficult tune to remember.

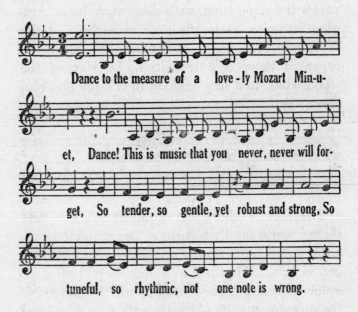

Dance to the measure of a love - ly Mozart Min-u-

et, Dance! This is music that you never, never will for-

get, So tender, so gentle, yet robust and strong, So

tuneful, so rhythmic, not one note is wrong.

This is only the first section of the Minuet, which repeats in the regular way, and then goes into a second section that imitates the first and then literally echoes it, with a different ending.

But the *Trio* is in quite a different mood, very gentle and sweet, as though a gentleman were apologizing to a lady for having been slightly rude to her. You will find a very similar melody at the start of the slow movement in Mozart's *Jupiter* symphony (see p. 53) and you may also notice the influence of this tune on Beethoven, in his fifth symphony (see p. 91).

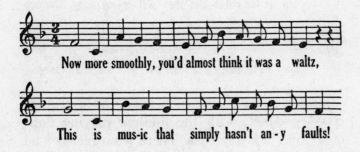

Now more smoothly, you'd almost think it was a waltz,

This is mus-ic that simply hasn't an-y faults!

The second half of this *Trio* is just as lovely as the first, bringing in a dulcet connecting melody. Finally the gentle mood disappears, and the robust Minuet returns for its closing reminder.

The last movement of Mozart's E-flat symphony, *Allegro,* is almost too fast to sing. It rushes along like a brook, and if you have a lively tongue perhaps you can keep up with it. In any case, the spirit is right. (The notes are an octave lower than Mozart wrote them.)

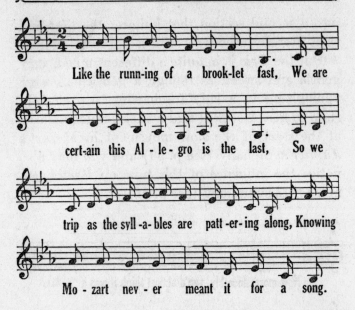

Like the runn-ing of a brook-let fast, We are
cert-ain this Al - le - gro is the last, So we
trip as the syll -a- bles are patt -er- ing along, Knowing
Mo - zart nev - er meant it for a song.

This rushing theme soon goes into a regular
country dance, with the fiddlers playing furi-
ously over a heavy bass. There is no real second
theme, although snatches of counter-melody pop
up here and there, and after a general repetition,
Mozart begins a development of the first tune,
paying attention mostly to the fast scale passages ("like the running of a brook"). He then
reminds us of the entire melody, along with the
counter-snatches, and by that time you should
really know the running of that brook by heart.
The end of the symphony is quite funny, for the
brook seems to have been silenced by very loud
broken chords, played by the full orchestra; but

the little scale passage pokes its head in once more in the treble and once in the bass, as if saying "I told you so," and you have to laugh because you would never think that such a big symphony could be over so suddenly.

This is the third and last, and perhaps the greatest, of the three symphonies that Mozart wrote in the year 1788, just three years before his untimely death. (Actually these three great symphonies were written within a period of six weeks, between June 26 and August 10, an amazing proof of the speed and ease with which this unique genius composed his music.)

The name of *Jupiter* was given to this symphony by an admirer, not by Mozart himself. But it fits fairly well, because of the nobility and grandeur of its ideas, which might easily refer to Olympian Jove himself.

The key of the *Jupiter* symphony is C major, the boldest, most uncompromising of them all, needing no sharps or flats for its regular progression. Perhaps Beethoven paid Mozart a compliment by writing his own *first* symphony in the same key, and using it also for the triumphant *Finale* of his fifth. (Brahms later put the big marching melody of *his* first symphony into C major, so it seems a favorite for expressing the sublime in music.) There is even a suggestion of the *Jupiter* opening in Beethoven's first *Allegro* theme (see p. 64). Mozart starts right in with a solid announcement of the key by the full orchestra, as though a crowd of worshippers were calling on Jupiter himself, in an ancient ceremony.

This confident, courageous call is balanced by two pleading measures, as if the supplicants to Jove were not at all sure of their ground. The whole theme might be sung like this:

There is much noisy comment on this, with Jupiter seemingly undecided whether to throw a thunderbolt or to receive his mortal visitors. In time the opening theme is repeated softly, with a counter-melody above it, in the woodwind, and soon this counter-melody, which is little more than a scale, receives attention from the full orchestra. Some more blustering chords lead to the second theme of the movement, which sounds as though Jupiter were answering in comforting tones, encouraging mortals to approach his throne. At the same time it is a charming tune.

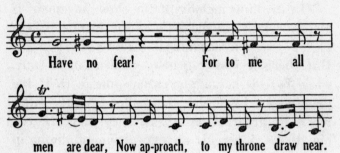

Have no fear! For to me all

men are dear, Now ap-proach, to my throne draw near.

This leads to various comments by the orchestra, which gradually turn into a chattering little tune, as though the people themselves were discussing Jupiter's attitude. Perhaps they are saying things like this:

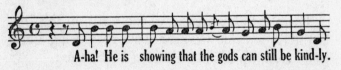

A-ha! He is showing that the gods can still be kind-ly.

The development, which begins shortly, deals first with this chattering motive, but later also takes up the opening theme and its countermelody. By the time Mozart is ready to remind us of the entire tune (recapitulation), he is back in the original key of C major, but this time he puts the counter-melody of the downward scale into C minor. The real second tune also returns, but now it is in C major instead of G, as before. Finally we hear even the chattering motive in C, and the movement ends with plenty of scales and chords in the same unforgettable key.

The opening melody of the slow movement is closely related to the *Trio* of the Minuet in the E-flat symphony, as indicated above (see p. 51).* But there it was a gentle, good-natured tune, while here it has a portentous sound, as if the people were beginning to wonder whether Jupiter is as great, after all, as they had believed him to be. There is an expression of doubt in the opening notes, followed by a definite exclamation, and this occurs twice, thus:

Ev - en Jove may fail! Ha!   Ev-en Jove turns pale! Ha!

There is much orchestral comment on this too, but after a while we hear some reassuring tones that make up a second melody, like this:

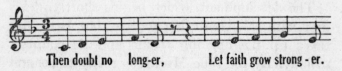

Then doubt no   long-er,   Let faith grow strong - er.

*See also Beethoven's use of this idea, p. 99.

The development is mostly ornamental, and you are hardly aware of the melodic undercurrents until the first slow tune comes back, this time with running decorations added. The reassuring strain is also heard again ("Then doubt no longer," etc.), this time in F major, the key in which the movement started. When the whole thing is almost over, Mozart seems to remember a bit of the first melody that he had almost forgotten, and then closes very simply and softly, with nothing more to say.

The Minuet of the *Jupiter* symphony starts with a reminiscent little tune, and if you listen carefully you realize that you heard something very much like it in the second theme of the G minor symphony (see p. 41). Perhaps that is the best way to remember it.

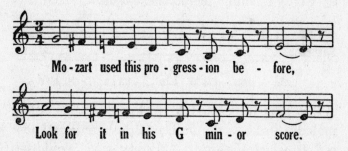

Mo-zart used this pro-gress-ion be-fore,
Look for it in his G min-or score.

The second section of this Minuet seems satisfied with breaking up this opening tune and imitating it in various ways, rather different from the conventional style. The *Trio* seems to say "Amen" four times, but with cheerful violin passages in between, to remind you that you are not in church after all. It carries this idea still further with chords over a lively accompaniment, and finally admits that it is time to repeat the actual Minuet.

Mozart's *Jupiter* symphony has a *Finale* that is practically unique in music of this kind. It is mathematically as complicated as anything outside of Bach, but its materials are so vivid and real that it never sounds like a mere problem of musical arithmetic. The whole movement can be considered a great mixed chorus in praise of Jupiter, and by this time we are ready to believe that this god is something more than a pagan Jove, perhaps with the religious significance of the great Jehovah Himself. So we can give Mozart's opening theme the words:

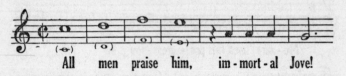

All   men   praise   him,   im-mort-al   Jove!

After that it is hard to pick out a distinctive melody. But a little phrase of three notes stands out, to which the words "Mighty Jove" could be fitted, and later, where you would expect a second tune, three different notes suggest the words "We praise him." These two patterns fill out the movement until it is time for the development, which takes up the first melody, but soon adds the other materials.

Migh - ty Jove!   We praise him!

It is still some time before you hear the opening theme as it was in the beginning, and even then it is extended in various directions. The three-tone figures, "Mighty Jove" and "We praise him," are also heard again in several ways.

But it is the *Coda,* or tail-piece, that is really the most remarkable portion of this entire *Jupiter* symphony. A fascinating series of harmonies leads up to what is actually a five-part fugue. (A fugue is literally a flight of tunes, one chasing the other, all harmonizing in what is known as counterpoint.) Mozart uses not only the main theme and the subordinate three-tone patterns, but adds two other melodic lines that have scarcely been noticeable so far. The effect is astonishing, and even if you are unaware of the technical mastery that is being displayed, you cannot help feeling that this is truly a chorus of praise, worthy to stand beside the great vocal choruses of Bach, Handel and Beethoven at their best.

So with triumphant chords in C major the *Jupiter Symphony* ends, leaving us to wonder what this genius, Wolfgang Amadeus Mozart, might not have accomplished if he had lived beyond his middle thirties. These three symphonies alone are a monument to his command of absolute music. His like will not be seen again.

THE CLIMAX OF BEETHOVEN

HAYDN and Mozart were both great composers, but to-day it almost seems that they were mere forerunners of Ludwig van Beethoven, one of those supreme masters that art produces all too seldom. Beethoven was born at Bonn on the Rhine in 1770 and died in Vienna in 1827. Pronounce his name Bay-toe-ven, accenting the first syllable.

Beethoven's early compositions show the decided influence of Haydn and Mozart. The first of these actually gave him some lessons, and the second was quick to recognize his genius, and to supply him with ideas (in some cases definite melodies, as Beethoven himself admitted).

But Beethoven did not have the sunny disposition of either of his forerunners. He was a harsh, crabbed soul, suffering from deafness after he was thirty years old, misunderstood by most people, and fiercely independent of social conventions and artificialities. Yet he had a strong sense of humor (a bit rough at times), and could be entirely pleasant with those he knew well and liked.

Beethoven's music is far more serious than

that of either Haydn or Mozart. He tried to express the sorrows and problems of life as well as its joys, and he was not interested in merely writing technically correct and pretty compositions. He may be called the first romantic composer, because he broke away from the classic idea of mere beauty of form, and insisted that music could and should express far more than this. Without Beethoven, modern music would have been impossible, and in his later works he actually used harmonies that prove him to have been a hundred years ahead of his time. He wrote nine symphonies, one opera (*Fidelio*), a great quantity of chamber music (quartets, trios, etc.), concertos, overtures and incidental music for plays, some songs and choral works, and a number of sonatas for the piano and the violin, which are among the finest of their kind. There are those who consider Beethoven the greatest of all composers, and certainly, with Bach and Brahms, he forms a triumvirate of the supreme creators of absolute music, with whom only Wagner, on the dramatic side, can fairly be ranked. He brought the sonata form, and particularly the symphony, to a climax of effectiveness which may never be surpassed.

BEETHOVEN'S FIRST SYMPHONY

It is only natural that Beethoven's early works should sound very much like the music of Haydn and Mozart, who were his models. Yet even in his first symphony, which was not completed until the year 1800, he shows decided touches of originality and independence. He had the habit of jotting down his musical ideas in a note-book which he carried with him, and these sketches show that he was working on this symphony a long time before it was ready for performance. It is a mistake to think that inspirations come to composers as they sit at the piano, idly fingering the keys. They get a basic idea (such as Beethoven always recorded in his note-book) and then work it out slowly and carefully until they know it is as right as they can make it. The definition of genius as "the infinite capacity for taking pains" applies to Beethoven perhaps better than to any other creative artist in the history of the world.

This first symphony follows Haydn's habit of a slow Introduction, and the opening notes, by the full orchestra (an octave higher), sound like a proclamation to the listening public:

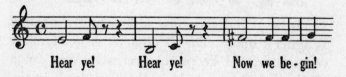

Hear ye!   Hear ye!   Now we be-gin!

This Introduction does not last long. You soon hear the first real tune, in C major, the key of the symphony, which may remind you of the opening of Mozart's *Jupiter Symphony,* in the same key:*

Here's number one, and you know there will be nine before the

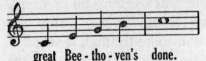

great Bee - tho - ven's done.

The second tune comes in fairly soon, in the key of G major, which is a close relative of C:

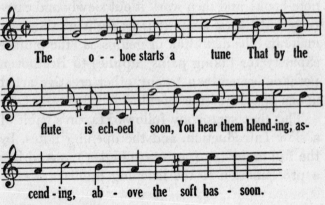

The o - - boe starts a tune That by the

flute is ech-oed soon, You hear them blend-ing, as-

cend - ing, ab - ove the soft bas - soon.

(You may find this tune influencing a part of Wagner's opera, *Die Walkuere,* a good many years later.) It keeps the orchestra busy for a while, and then you hear the first tune again, also in G, with echoes.

This entire section (the exposition) is re-

*See p. 54.

peated, with its second ending going right into the "development" or "free fantasia." In this contrasting part of the first movement, the material is taken from the opening tune, which is treated in many interesting ways. When the recapitulation (reminder) arrives, it naturally begins with this same tune, complete in its original key of C major. The second tune also comes back in this key, and after some more individual effects, the movement closes with a *Coda* that is more elaborate and brilliant than in the Haydn-Mozart fashion.

The opening melody of the second movement may remind you a little of the corresponding part of Mozart's G minor symphony. But Beethoven's tune is really more lively in character, and even though it uses Mozart's trick of harmonizing with itself (which is characteristic of the fugal style of counterpoint), it has plenty of originality. It should not be taken too slowly, for Beethoven marks it *Andante Cantabile con Moto,* which means that it moves along with a singing quality. It could be sung thus:

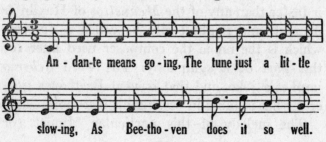

An - dan-te means go - ing, The tune just a lit - tle

slow-ing, As Bee-tho - ven does it so well.

There is a second tune which answers the first, and hardly needs any words of its own.

It is this theme that supplies most of the material for the development, especially its first four notes.

With the recapitulation, the first tune returns, this time with a running accompaniment of short (*staccato*) notes. The second tune also comes back, with the regular change of key, and there are some interesting drum rhythms before Beethoven arrives at another fairly elaborate *Coda,* ending with a violin-horn dialogue which gives a final reminder of those important pairs of notes that have been heard so often in this slow movement.

The third movement of Beethoven's first symphony is called a Minuet (or *Menuetto*), but it is faster than any of the *Menuettos* of Haydn or Mozart, and might easily be called a *Scherzo,* which is the name the composer used later for this part of a symphony. The word *Scherzo* implies a joke, and that is what Beethoven generally has in mind in writing his fast movements.

The melody of this particular Minuet (or

Scherzo) is interesting because it follows the notes of the scale right on up. So it might be best to remember it by that characteristic:*

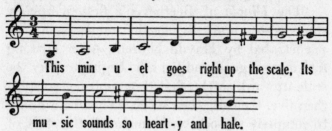

The second part of the Minuet imitates this scale tune, rhythmically, and after both sections have been repeated, we arrive at the conventional *Trio.* But Beethoven is satisfied to use just a succession of chords to start this *Trio,* after which the violins interrupt with more scale passages. It might be sung like this, since it starts in the wind instruments:

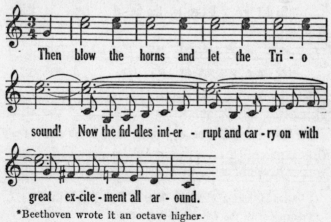

*Beethoven wrote it an octave higher.

The second part of the *Trio* is similar, and it works on the first chords a bit before going back to the two-part Minuet as usual.

The *Finale* of Beethoven's first symphony starts with a musical joke that might have been perpetrated by Haydn himself. After striking a G octave, good and loud, he begins to play the scale upward, softly, first three notes, then four, then five, then six, then seven. When he is ready to complete the octave, he makes it the start of his first tune, a very lively and cheerful one, which sticks to the spirit of Haydn that has been so evident in this whole symphony. The second part of the tune is more wistful, and has in it something of a farewell mood. Here is how the whole tune might be sung:*

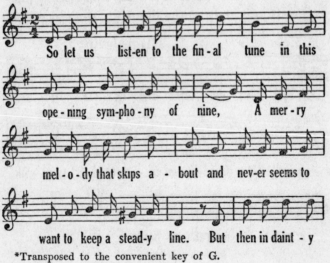

So let us list-en to the fin-al tune in this ope-ning sym-pho-ny of nine, A mer-ry mel-o-dy that skips a - bout and nev-er seems to want to keep a stead-y line. But then in daint - y

*Transposed to the convenient key of G.

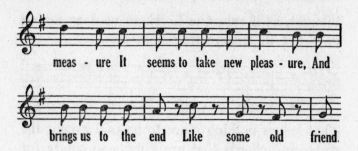

meas - ure It seems to take new pleas - ure, And

brings us to the end Like some old friend.

This runs along like a merry little brook until it is time for a second tune, which goes like this (using the second violin part, for convenience):

Keep it sing-ing and ring-ing, More simp-le pleas-ure bring-ing.

A passage of rag-time (syncopation) leads to a series of false starts, which finally arrive at a complete repetition of the first part.

The development which follows combines the musical ideas of the first and second themes, using the upward scale of the first and the two opening tones of the second. But the scales become more and more prominent, as usual, and it is only when the recapitulation starts that the entire first tune is clearly heard again. The second tune comes back in the key of F, following the custom, though not too slavishly. Again Beethoven uses a long *Coda,* and in this one he introduces a short march, as a sort of afterthought, as if someone to whom you are saying good-bye kept repeating politely:

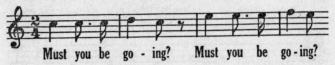

Must you be go - ing? Must you be go - ing?

That leaves nothing more to be said except the scales and chords that are always so handy for the finish of a symphony. Beethoven doesn't mind being conventional at the end. For his first symphony he has written a very good one.

BEETHOVEN'S SECOND SYMPHONY

Beethoven took his time in writing his symphonies, preparing them very carefully from the notes that he was always making in his little book. He was two years or more at the gradual creation of his second symphony, finishing it in 1802, although it was not performed until April, 1803, in Vienna.

This is a much more important work than the first symphony, giving still greater proofs of its composer's originality and independence. It is true that he starts again with the conventional Introduction, in the manner of Haydn, but it is far more elaborate than those early forms and has an unusual independence of material. Since this symphony is in the key of D major, it is natural for Beethoven to start with that note, played very loud by the full orchestra in octaves.

But immediately the wood-wind enters almost
timidly, as though uncertain what might happen.
This contrast of commanding noise and doubtful
courage might be summed up in these words:

Attend, and be not fearful, Our theme will soon be cheerful.

The long Introduction finally leads right into
the first fast tune, played in the bass by the
cellos. Nowadays it would suggest words of this
sort:

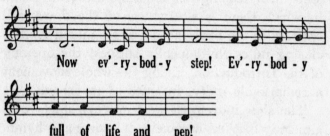

Now ev'-ry-bod-y step! Ev'-ry-bod-y

full of life and pep!

This music becomes louder and more complicated, until Beethoven is ready for a second tune,
introduced softly by the clarinet:

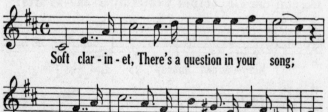

Soft clar-in-et, There's a question in your song;

With no re-gret Vi-o-lins bring the answer a-long.

This really develops into quite a march theme, and it serves, with snatches of the Introduction and the first tune, to carry the movement up to the point of repetition, where in time the contrasting section (development) begins. This deals largely with the "everybody step" of the first tune, so that this little passage has become quite familiar by the time Beethoven starts his recapitulation with the entire theme. The second tune now also appears in the key of D, and again there is a lot of emphasis on the "everybody step" idea, leading to a long and elaborate *Coda,* in which there is a new use of the downward scale, with the little fast passages mixed in. The closing notes rhythmically suggest the opening of the Introduction, giving the whole movement a remarkable unity, in spite of its length.

The slow movement (*Larghetto*) starts with a melody that has become well known as a hymn. (It appears in hymn-books with the title of *Alsace,* although it is admitted that the composer was Beethoven.) For most of this tune we can use the actual words by Isaac Watts:

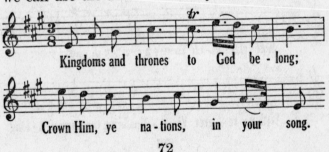

Kingdoms and thrones to God be-long;

Crown Him, ye na-tions, in your song.

But this second movement of Beethoven's second symphony contains so much melody that there seems no limit to it. An answer to the opening theme is worth remembering, also with the words of the Watts hymn:

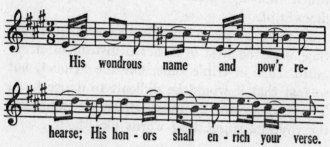

His wondrous name and pow'r re- hearse; His hon - ors shall en - rich your verse.

(In the hymn, this immediately follows the first part of the tune, but Beethoven repeats each part, using different endings.)

Then there is a subordinate theme which Schumann later imitated and which could be sung like this:

Then praise the Lord in joy - ful song, Ye peo - ple that to Him be - long.

The middle section (development) puts the main melody into minor key, and then carries it through many fascinating harmonies and decorations. There is a recapitulation of all the tunes, and this time the *Coda* is quite short, simply suggesting a change in the opening melody, which nobody but Beethoven would have thought of.

In the third movement Beethoven for the first time uses the title of *Scherzo* instead of *Menaetto*. It is in triple time, like the Minuet, but so fast that it would be difficult to dance to it. The drums come in unexpectedly to emphasize the rhythm, suggesting words like this:*

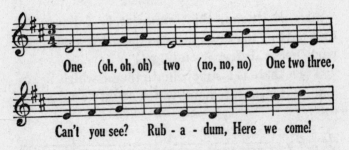

Beethoven sticks to the old outlines of the Minuet form, even though he has discarded the name, and this opening tune has an immediate answer which imitates it and finally repeats it.

There is a *Trio* too, starting with a short melody like this (again transposed an octave down):

*The parts have to be put into the same octave for singing.

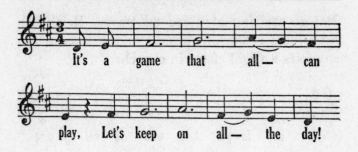

It also has a second section, like the *Trio* of a Minuet, with both parts repeated before the first two sections of the *Scherzo* return, giving the movement a very lively finish.

The beginning of the *Finale* is not easy to sing, although it shows that all the orchestral instruments are now working in harmony. You can try it this way:

Before arriving at a second theme, Beethoven introduces a solemn melody in the bass, which suggests a fugal chant in church:

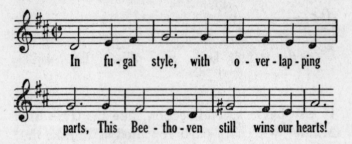

In fu-gal style, with o - ver - lap - ping parts, This Bee - tho - ven still wins our hearts!

The real second tune is also largely in the bass, with various instruments sharing it, using mostly chord tones:

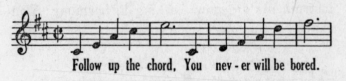

Follow up the chord, You nev - er will be bored.

The movement goes through the regular processes of development and recapitulation, but always with the stamp of the greater Beethoven, who has already gone far beyond any of his forerunners, and is now on the verge of producing some of the greatest symphonies in the whole literature of music. There is a long *Coda,* in which the solemn bass melody plays an important part, with echoes of the first tune right up to the finish.

BEETHOVEN

From his second to his third symphony,
Beethoven's music took a tremendous step for-
ward. The *Eroica,* as he himself called it, is far
in advance of anything he had written up to the
time of its completion, in 1804. Some authori-
ties think it is the best of all the nine symphonies,
and Beethoven himself indicated that it was his
favorite.

This was in spite of a deep disappointment
that came with its composition. The "hero" indicated by the title of this third symphony (*Eroica*)
was Napoleon Bonaparte. But when Napoleon
declared himself Emperor of France, Beethoven
realized that his hero was only a selfish human
being after all. In his rage he almost destroyed
the whole symphony. The manuscript in Vienna
shows that he tore a hole in the page where the
name of Napoleon had stood. On the title-page,
he wrote in Italian: "Composed to celebrate the
memory of a great man." But whether we think
of this symphony as relating to Napoleon, or to
heroes in general, it remains a great work of
genius, and heroic thoughts are unmistakable in
the music. The key is E-flat, and the symphony
begins with two major chords by the full orchestra, after which the cellos immediately play the
opening theme. This melody seems to go into
the clouds, with no definite ending. It is made

77

of the tones of the bugle, immediately suggesting the character of a military hero. (Strangely enough, the same tune, note for note, appears in Mozart's childhood opera, *Bastien et Bastienne*.) It might be interpreted as the announcement of the hero's arrival, addressed to the actual instruments of the band:

Bugles, drums, the con-quer-ing he - ro comes!—

It is not long before another melody is heard, this time sung by the oboe and the strings in turn, and in a softer, sweeter style:

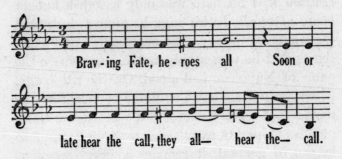

Brav-ing Fate, he-roes all Soon or

late hear the call, they all— hear the— call.

There are other suggestions of melody, and the heroic music carries on richly until it is time to repeat the entire exposition.

The development immediately uses material from both the important themes, but gradually concentrating more and more on the first bugle progression, which stays mostly in the bass. The second tune has its share of attention, and both finally return in their complete forms, with a change of key for the second. There have been surprisingly original touches again and again in this first movement of the *Eroica* symphony, and perhaps the climax of originality comes in the *Coda,* which is more important than any that Beethoven has yet written. What was once literally a "tail-piece" is now a vital part of the whole symphonic structure, with material that both sounds and is actually brand new.

In the second movement Beethoven does another completely original thing by writing a funeral march; and it is one of the greatest funeral marches ever composed. You could never mistake its meaning, even without words. Try it this way:

Muf-fled drums tell a he-ro's end - ing,

Slow steps, mourners wending, Raise not the head, The

eyes are closed, the he - ro is dead, cold and dead.

There is a second part to this funeral march, which sounds a little more optimistic, although it is still in a sorrowful mood:

Then start life a - new, Real heroes are

all, all too few, al - as!

The funeral march contains still another melody, this time in C major, instead of the C minor of the start. It might be sung thus:

Fall in   line! Why continue to mourn and   pine?

(Later you will find the first seven notes, in the same key, at the start of the triumphant *Finale* of Beethoven's fifth symphony, so it is logical to give them the same words here, especially as the music indicates a more courageous spirit, as compared with the funeral march itself.) There is a section of development, with snatches of the main melody, and then a lengthy reminder of the whole march, with new touches of rhythmic decoration. At the very end, Beethoven breaks up the minor melody, as though it were being heard through stammering sobs, a poignantly dramatic effect.

After all this melancholy, the *Scherzo* sounds almost as cheerful as its name would suggest. It is in a fast triple time, starting very softly, and giving the oboe a piping little tune, clearly indicating the happier side of the heroic life.

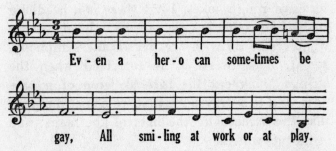

Ev - en a her - o can some-times be gay, All smi - ling at work or at play.

This gay triple rhythm, which hardly needs a melody to make it effective, continues until a *Trio* is reached, and this is obviously a hunting call, played by the horns, with soft answers from the strings:

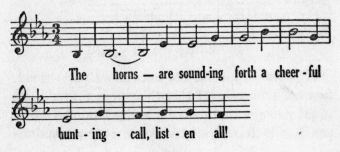

The horns — are sound-ing forth a cheer - ful hunt - ing - call, list - en all!

With these two melodic ideas, the third movement of the *Eroica* runs it course, helter skelter, as if trying desperately to get away from the grave-yard of the funeral march. Perhaps it is merely whistling in the dark, as even a hero does at times.

At least this *Scherzo* has put Beethoven into a good-humored mood for his *Finale,* which starts out as though it were going to be just a series of rough jokes. First there is a headlong rush of Introduction, that seems to have nothing whatever to do with the key of the symphony, E-flat. This oversight is corrected when the strings pluck out the bare skeleton of a bass part, and it is only later that we come to realize that this is actually the bass of the main tune of the movement.

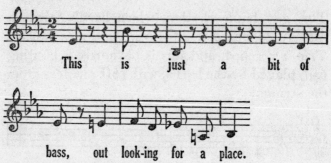

It is thereupon played once more with broad, sustained tones, and this time goes into a little fugal passage that calls for a repetition. Beethoven finally tries his bass theme over an accompaniment of the triplets that ran wild in the *Scherzo,* and after all these experiments, he suddenly embarks on the tune for which we have been waiting,—a satisfied, lilting, joyous tune, that mocks at death and heroes alike. It is introduced by the oboe, with a running accompaniment in which that familiar bass theme is now firmly established.*

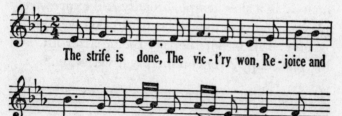

The strife is done, The vic-t'ry won, Re-joice and

sing, Let praise of he-roes ring!

There is a short middle part to this tune, by way of contrast, but it comes back with a dainty ending, in imitation of the start:

Let prais-es ring, Re-joice and sing!

But Beethoven still cannot resist worrying that bass theme, and he tries it again in a variety of ways until he gets back to his main melody in a new key, with variations.

*This melody was taken by Beethoven from his own *Prometheus,* and he had already written a set of *Variations* and a *Fugue* for pianoforte, using the same material.

Another experiment with the bass leads to still another version of the happy melody, this time quite simply played, in C major, with a touch of minor at the end. Then, after a lot more orchestral excitement, with the bass theme still struggling to hold its own, Beethoven introduces the master stroke of the whole movement. Without warning he suddenly lets us hear the main melody in a slow tempo, broadly and expressively played, and it sounds so beautiful that we wonder whether this is not the real theme after all, and the fast, happy version merely a variation.*

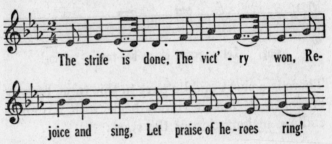

The strife is done, The vict'-ry won, Re-
joice and sing, Let praise of he-roes ring!

Before we can make up our minds about this, we hear it again, loudly played by the brass instruments in the bass, with drum effects. By this time it is fairly clear that this is a heroic tune after all, fit to express every phase of the courageous life.

This leaves only the *Coda,* which again is profoundly thoughtful, as almost always with

*This is as the strings play it. The wood-wind has it an octave higher.

Beethoven. The full orchestra finally rushes into a *Presto* conclusion, shaking out the remaining scraps of melody with violent rhythmic attacks, and at last landing triumphantly on the same E-flat chords that had been heard at the start of the symphony, a heroic finish to a heroic piece of music.

BEETHOVEN'S FOURTH SYMPHONY

After writing the tremendous *Eroica,* Beethoven seems to have been willing to take a breathing spell. In some ways his fourth symphony is a let-down. Yet it is typically Beethoven, and represents technically a still further advance toward the sublime inspirations of his last years.

People had been telling Beethoven that he ought to write music like that of Haydn and Mozart. They called him a madman, and talked about his eccentricities and musical heresies very much as we do to-day about the extremes of modernism. So he evidently thought he would show them that he could write a symphony in the style of Haydn and Mozart, without losing the Beethoven individuality. That is just about what the fourth symphony turned out to be. It has no "program," no story to tell, or picture to paint. It is pure music, in the classic style, and it supplies a satisfactory interlude between the dramatic intensities of the heroic third and the fateful fifth. It was completed in 1806, and its key is B-flat major.

Beethoven's fourth symphony goes back to the old-fashioned idea of an Introduction, in slow time. But this Introduction has an independent mood, similar to that of the *Leonore Overture, No. 3.* The strings pick their way slowly and carefully down a series of octaves, and then the violins softly ask a timid question:

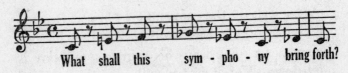

What shall this sym - pho - ny bring forth?

After much wavering, the answer is given in favor of a light-hearted tune, and when it arrives, there is no questioning its gaiety:

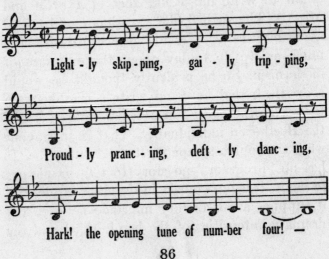

Light - ly skip - ping, gai - ly trip - ping,

Proud - ly pranc - ing, deft - ly danc - ing,

Hark! the opening tune of num-ber four! —

Beethoven experiments with this in the bass as well as the treble, and then lets the bassoons and the oboe play a little conversational game, with the flute also putting in its word:

Just a lit-tle wood-wind al-ter-na-ting thus.

This is really enough melody for the whole movement, although Beethoven introduces some more octaves to fill in the gaps. The middle section (development) concentrates on the skipping notes of the first tune ("Lightly skipping, gaily tripping"). Then a remarkable modulation starts a very soft drum roll, over which the strings play little snatches of scales (an effect later used dramatically by Wagner in his *Ride of the Valkyries*) and gradually this increases in volume until the full orchestra is playing the skipping tune again.

The wood-wind conversation is also heard again, in a new key, with the octaves filling in as before. This time the *Coda* is short, more in the style of Mozart than of Beethoven, using the skipping notes to build chords for a finish, all very easy to follow, and not too serious.

But the second movement, *Adagio*, has the depth of all the slow melodies of Beethoven. It is simple enough, coming right down the scale, something like the hymn tune, *Joy to the World*, or the old Italian *Caro mio ben,* and it might be sung to such words as these:

Slow - ly, A - da - gio, that is the

way Bee - tho - ven wrote it, Ra - ther

sad - ly, and not glad - ly, The mu-sic has a

wist-ful, quite mourn - ful sound.

This beautiful melody alternates with other material of a less tuneful character, with constantly changing decorations, and, after four complete hearings, is echoed in a brief *Coda,* which devotes itself mostly to building up to an E-flat chord, with various instruments dividing the notes, leaving the highest, as usual, to the flute.

In the third movement Beethoven again shows his willingness to compose in the Haydn or Mozart style by using the title of *Menuetto* instead of the *Scherzo* to which we had become accustomed. But this *Menuetto* is after all a *Scherzo,* and a very original one at that. Its melody jumps about unexpectedly, with shifting accents, as if trying to attract the attention of anyone who might have been lulled into restfulness by the slow movement. It might be translated into a rising call, like this:

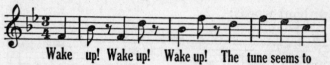

Wake up! Wake up! Wake up! The tune seems to

say, No one can be sleep-ing when day-light is peep-ing.

The *Trio* starts like a country dance, and makes one want to go around and around, like the music itself:*

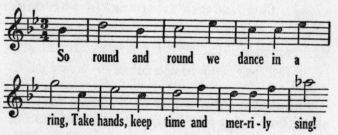

So round and round we dance in a

ring, Take hands, keep time and mer-ri-ly sing!

Beethoven treats these melodies much more freely than was permitted in the conventional

---

*The instrumentation is wood-wind and horns, with echoes from the first violins.

Minuet, keeping to the rustic spirit rather than that of the drawing-room. There is a tiny *Coda,* —just a saucy little phrase by the horns, and one loud final chord.

The start of the *Finale* is not a singable tune, but belongs on the strings, which is just where Beethoven puts it, with perhaps a country fiddler still in mind. The opening notes are enough, without words:

The second tune, however, is slower in the spacing of its notes, and more vocal in character. It is given to the oboe and the flute in turn:*

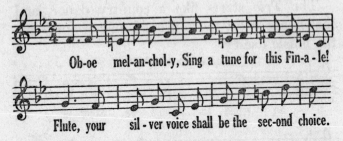

Ob-oe mel-an-chol-y, Sing a tune for this Fin-a-le!

Flute, your   sil-ver voice shall be the sec-ond choice.

The sonata form is followed, with a development that brings in both tunes in interesting fashion and eventually gets back to their complete restatement. The *Coda* is fairly long, and quite brilliant. At the end the violins pause to

*The last part has to be sung in the lower octaves.

study the actual notes of their first theme, and seem to decide that there was nothing much to it after all. Three times they reflectively hang on for a moment. Then the full orchestra rushes in and drowns out the fiddling sequence with half a dozen chords. Beethoven has proved that he could be as Haydnish or Mozartian as anyone could ask, and he is now ready for another gigantic flight of the imagination into realms that no symphony had yet dared to explore.

BEETHOVEN'S FIFTH SYMPHONY

The fifth (in C minor, completed in 1808) is unquestionably the most popular of the nine Beethoven symphonies. This is partly because of its real greatness, combined with definite melodic lines that are not hard to follow, and partly because it represents a clear and interesting program. This plot or story is fascinating to most people, for it deals with the eternal struggle against Fate.

Beethoven himself said of the opening notes of this symphony, "Thus Fate knocks at the door," and there is no mistaking their rhythmic significance. Perhaps it is best to imagine Destiny itself loudly announcing:

I am your Fate! Come, let me in! —

But the four notes might also be interpreted as "Come, let me in" or "Open the door." Take your choice, or think of the phrase merely as the portentous pounding that it is.

The marvel of this Fate motif is the way Beethoven builds from it a complete opening theme, in which, with its extension, the same rhythmic pattern appears no less than forty-five times. It covers so much ground that you cannot possibly sing along with it all the way, but you can imagine the three possible wordings as alternating continuously, like this:

I am your Fate, come, let me in, open the door!—

The horns finally call a halt, to permit ordinary mortals to have their say. But they do it in a very superior and contemptuous fashion:

You can't es - cape your Fate!

The human voice speaks up rather timidly, yet showing no inclination to give in too easily, and this answer provides the second melody for this opening movement of Beethoven's *Fate Symphony:*

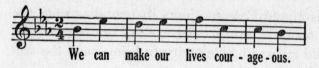

We can make our lives cour-age-ous.

Even as it is uttered, you hear the impatient pounding in the bass, indicating that Fate does not intend to be kept waiting long. But the courageous voice goes serenely on, in spite of the threatening noises, and soon turns the actual Fate motif into a bold challenge:

You may be right, but we shall fight with all our might!

So with shrieking wood-wind and hammering blows the battle is on. The development that follows is a real plot, not just a musical exercise.

The horns again sound their threat, which is defiantly answered by the strings, *fortissimo*. The real struggle begins quietly enough, as though the fighters were trying out their strength, but soon the whole orchestra is in an uproar, dominated by the rhythmic Fate motif. The contemptuous horn call has no effect except to inspire a series of answering chords, musically beautiful, yet in constant conflict.

Fate has all the better of the argument thus far, and the opening theme comes back in full force, with every appearance of victory. A plaintive little interlude by the solitary oboe has no effect, and Fate continues its pounding until the bassoons take up the horn call and permit the mild answer of humanity to bring back the second melody, this time in C major.

There is a long *Coda,* which first gives Fate the advantage, but then also turns the human answer into a new and daring series of chords. Both sides finally seem ready to stop, and with plaintive comments from the pacifist oboe, hovering like a bird above the orchestra, Fate is allowed to shout its final defiance, just as dictators do when they think they have won a war. This battle, however, is far from over.

The second movement is completely human,— a long, sustained song of calm confidence. Fate seems to have retired from the field, and the pounding noises are over. The beautiful melody sung by the violas and cellos might be interpreted in these words:

When the moon ris-es in the sky, and all the

stars of Heav'n are shin-ing clear on high, We

fear no Fate, No task too great, We are mas-ters!

The second part of the melody is even more serenely confident:

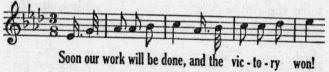

Soon our work will be done, and the vic-to-ry won!

Musically this material goes through a series of variations, a form that has been often used in the slow movements of sonatas and symphonies, and which really means nothing more than a variety of decorations and other treatments applied to the same tune. Each time that you hear either half of Beethoven's slow melody it sounds more elaborate than before, until the tune is almost buried under instrumental ornaments.

There is an interruption of soft chords, giving the clarinet a chance to imitate the first part of the melody quite simply, with suggestions also from the bassoon and flute, and finally all the wood-wind weaving in and out. This leads to further variations, followed by an amazingly original *Coda*. The bassoon starts this with a mocking imitation of the opening melody, over a flippantly dancing bass, and the frightened little squeals of the oboe indicate that there is still trouble ahead. Confidence is restored in one of the most beautiful passages in all music. The close of the melody, which has been played in the same way each time, is suddenly changed by a stroke of genius to a heart-rending expression of human emotion. The whole problem of life seems to be summed up in those few notes. Compare the musical effects, and let your own feelings put them into words if possible:

The third movement of this Fate symphony is a strange substitute for the conventional *Scherzo* or *Menuetto*. It is marked *Allegro* ("cheerful") but starts in a mysterious, unearthly fashion, with a melody that comes from the very depths of the orchestra. You have already heard this melody, note for note, in the *Finale* of Mozart's G minor symphony (see p. 45), but differences of rhythm, tempo and key give it an entirely new effect in the hands of Beethoven. You can almost imagine a battling humanity taking new courage from those who have struggled in the past:

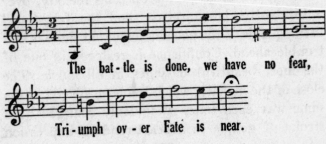

The bat - tle is done, we have no fear,
Tri - umph ov - er Fate is near.

This confident utterance is heard twice, and then the horns break out again with the rhythmic pounding of Fate, which is obviously still far from defeat. This time, with the fundamental beat running in threes, it seems to say:

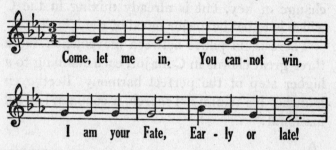

Come, let me in, You can-not win,
I am your Fate, Ear-ly or late!

But the opening melody puts up a staunch resistance, and soon the two are definitely in conflict. The atmosphere of strife is continued in what corresponds to a *Trio,* with the strings playing against each other in a blustering style that needs no words:

The opening melody returns confidently, and when you next hear the Fate rhythm you suddenly realize that those fearsome notes are being satirized, and that there is nothing more to be afraid of. Fate is being led around by the free will of man, like a dancing bear, compelled to perform the tricks taught by his master. In time the triple rhythm becomes a mere mutter in the bass, while a few notes of the opening melody soar higher and higher in preparation for the real song of triumph. The bass cannot wait for the change of key, but is already mixing in the C which is to be the major mood of the *Finale*.

There is no pause between movements. With three great chords in C major, each climbing to a higher step of the perfect harmony, Beethoven launches his triumphal march, a command to all mankind:*

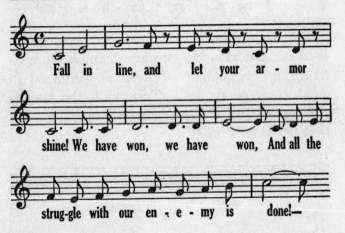

Fall in line, and let your ar - mor shine! We have won, we have won, And all the strug-gle with our en - e - my is done!—

It is mostly chords and scales, in the simplest and barest of all keys, but its effect is irresistible. No other composer has written such a musical expression of triumph.

*Compare the far gentler use of this same idea in the funeral march of the *Eroica,* p. 80.

A second line of melody also starts on the notes of the major chord:*

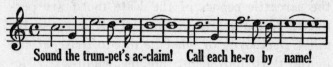

Sound the trum-pet's ac-claim! Call each he-ro by name!

The triumphal march soon becomes a dance, with a new tune introduced to a skipping rhythm, more light-hearted than before:

Come on al - ong, join in the song, fol - low the

crowd, Step-ping in glee, hap-py and free, noi-sy and proud!

Beethoven is so delighted with the whole cele-bration that he generously throws in still another tune, broader and more gloating than the last, as if he were saying:

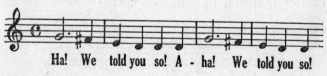

Ha! We told you so! A - ha! We told you so!

The march begins all over again (having passed a given point, as they say), and then the com-

*Compare this with the slow theme of Mozart's *Jupiter Symphony*, p. 56 and also the *Trio* of the Minuet in his E-flat symphony, p. 51.

poser takes time for an actual development, using mostly the skipping dance tune, into which the sarcastic echoes of the Fate motif are permitted to enter after a while. That seems to remind Beethoven of what he did to that pattern in the third movement, and he whimsically decides to repeat some of it. This is another of those bold heresies that this revolutionary genius was constantly thinking up. (Haydn had once tried the experiment, without much success, but to-day it is quite common to find the *Finale* of a symphony including parts of earlier movements. The heresy of one generation becomes the convention of the next.)

The reminder of a defeated Destiny serves chiefly to bring back the main melody of the triumphal march, which is followed gaily by all the other tunes of this astonishing *Finale*. A long *Coda* combines the skipping dance with the broad rhythms of the march itself, and suddenly interrupts itself with an entirely new treatment of earlier material by the bassoon:

Then sound the trump-et's ac - claim!

The flute suggests still another thought along the same line:

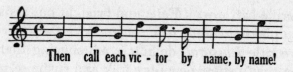

Then call each vic - tor by name, by name!

This finds such favor that the flute finally breaks into a long trill of delight and the orchestra dances shamelessly in great, clumsy chords.

The celebration ends when the "I told you so" theme comes back at top speed, as though the police were scattering the crowd, and, after a hasty reminder of the march tune, Beethoven concentrates on finishing his symphony unmistakably in C major, although it began in C minor. He takes a whole page of music to do it, first alternating the tonic (C) with the dominant (G), and then trying the C major chord at different levels and in various rhythmic combinations. Finally he seems satisfied that everybody must understand by this time, so he hits the chord six times more for good measure, and ends with a solid C over several octaves, shaking his fist as he did on his death-bed, and defying Fate to the last. No wonder the world has become almost hysterically devoted to Beethoven's fifth symphony!

BEETHOVEN'S PASTORAL SYMPHONY

Just as Beethoven rested after his *Eroica,* in producing the lighter and less important fourth symphony, so he again took a breather after his terrific battle with Fate, and brought out a sixth symphony in 1808, in F major, with the descriptive title *Pastoral,* definitely announcing that it dealt with simple country folk and rustic scenes, and giving it a clear "program" throughout.

Actually Beethoven was working on his fifth and sixth symphonies at the same time. They are often called "twins," although entirely different, and when they had their first performance, on the same program, in Vienna, the numbers were reversed, so that the *Pastoral* seemed the earlier of the two. Beethoven later corrected this, and the fifth symphony is rightly considered the older work.

As compared with the tremendous fifth symphony, the *Pastoral* is almost childlike in its simplicity. Yet it is thoroughly effective, and its descriptions and suggestions of Nature have perhaps never been surpassed in music. These are not to be taken too literally. Beethoven himself said that he intended this music "more as an expression of feeling than painting." We are permitted to see the pictures as clearly as we wish, but we cannot and should not lose sight of the pure musical beauty of the whole work.

Beethoven gave a descriptive title to each movement of this sixth symphony. The first is "Awakening of pleasant feelings on arriving in the country." There is no Introduction. Over a droning bass, the strings immediately sing a bit of folk-music that is completely in the pastoral spirit. Beethoven's own hint almost supplies the words:

It's nice to feel so gay And hear the shep-herds play.

There is a second tune that sounds a little like some of the passages in the fifth symphony, but is not really vocal in character:

Another melodic bit might almost be the call of the American robin:

This is followed by more scale material, with the rhythmic pattern of Schubert's later *Military March*. It seems to add to the hospitable welcome of the countryside:

Come far a - way, where the peop-le work and play.

All this is repeated before the development begins. This middle section first works on the little pastoral tune, and then makes much of the "rob-in's call." The recapitulation brings back all the melodic material, with only the first tune in the original key of F, and the *Coda* has the characteristic Beethoven length. It is all delightful music, but with no romantic or dramatic problems to speak of.

The second movement, "Scene by the Brook," is in a slow, 12-8 time, with a rhythmic under-current of the brook's own murmuring, in groups of three. (It might be the actual word "murmur-ing," repeated over and over.) The melody itself might express the admiration of those who see the brook going by. It also has plenty of repetition.

Look!　　　　What a pret-ty　brook!

There is a subordinate melody also, of a more sustained character, introduced by the bassoon, and definitely imitated by Schumann many years later (see p. 163).

Tune —　the bas - soon　to　your mu - sic.

Near the end of the movement, Beethoven deliberately introduces imitations of bird-song, the flute trilling in the manner of the nightingale, while the clarinet plays the two downward notes of the cuckoo, and the oboe fills in with the high monotone of the quail. (This is a German quail, not the American Bob White, whose notes are quite different.) For these bird imitations Beethoven was of course criticized, as usual, but they fit into the music perfectly and form a melodic line of their own.

The third movement, *Allegro,* is clearly a country dance, which Beethoven indicates by the title "Merry Gathering of Country People." The main tune can be sung thus:*

The peas-ants are danc-ing and pranc-ing to-geth-er, The weath-er is noth-ing to them, ha, ha, ha! Now swing your part-ner and don't let her go, A dance in the count-ry is nev-er too slow!

*The second part is an octave down, as in the second violins.

This lively melody, variously treated, goes right into the musical description of a thunder-storm, which really adds an extra movement to the symphony. It is not a very terrifying storm, but it has its dramatic moments. The thunder is first suggested by the drums, and soon we hear the whistling of the wind, both fairly convincing.

There is still no pause as the *Finale* begins, called by Beethoven both "Shepherds' Song" and "Happy and thankful feelings after the storm." The introductory sound of a shepherd's pipe is unmistakable. (Wagner developed the effect far more elaborately in *Tristan und Isolde,* using an English horn instead of Beethoven's clarinet.) Then comes the real song of gratitude, (still an octave down, for singing):

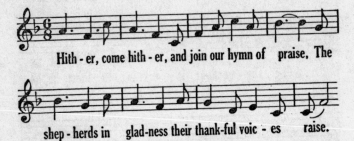

Hith - er, come hith - er, and join our hymn of praise. The

shep - herds in glad-ness their thank-ful voic - es raise.

(The late Ben Greet, in his performances of Shakespeare's *As You Like It,* used an adaptation of this tune to the words of the famous "Come hither" song.)

There are two subordinate snatches of melody,

but the thankful tune is the one that stands out in the entire movement. Even the long *Coda* concentrates on it, showing its close relationship to the shepherds' song of the opening, which the horn finally echoes softly, to be cut off by two crashing chords in F. It is a pleasant ending to a pleasant symphony, which again leads to more important things.

BEETHOVEN'S SEVENTH SYMPHONY

Four years passed before Beethoven produced another symphony, his seventh, in the key of A major. In that time he had made mighty strides as a composer, developing a broader vision and a surer musicianship than any of his earlier works had showed. The seventh symphony was finished in 1812, and had its first performance a year later in Vienna.

This might fairly be called the *Dance Symphony,* not because it makes use of actual dance forms, but because it has a continuous spirit of rhythmic regularity that makes it irresistible. It has been called (by both Wagner and Liszt) "the apotheosis of rhythm," and this description is justified by the animated vitality of at least three of its movements.

There is a long, slow Introduction, however, which seems to promise yet delay all the rhythmic liveliness that is to follow, as though the orchestra were giving the dancers time to gather and choose their partners. But at last there is a definite sound of tuning fiddles, and the time goes into a skipping 6-8 beat, with the repeated note E (the top string of the violin) impatiently suggesting a good place to start the tune. When it finally gets under way, there is a hearty invitation evident in its tones:*

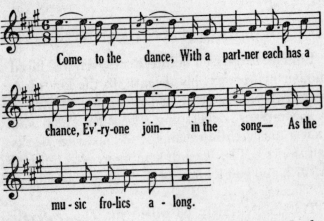

Come to the dance, With a part-ner each has a chance, Ev'-ry-one join— in the song— As the mu-sic fro-lics a - long.

By the time a second melody is reached, the dance is going at top speed. The skipping rhythm continues, for this is no fox-trot or tango, but just a human expression of the instinct to keep time (still sung an octave down):

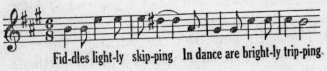

Fid-dles light-ly skip-ping In dance are bright-ly trip-ping.

*Beethoven wrote them an octave higher.

A repetition of all this rhythmic material leads to a section of development, in the regular sonata form that most symphonies use for their opening movements. Here Beethoven shows wonderful ingenuity in his treatment of the lively skipping figure. (He later made it the basis of the great *Scherzo* of his ninth symphony. See p. 124.)

Both tunes return in the traditional recapitulation (reminder), but again there are constant touches of originality, of which the most remarkable is saved for the *Coda*. Here for twenty-two successive measures Beethoven uses a syncopated pattern in the bass, always on the same notes, while the violins sing innocently above. (This ground bass is derived from the start of the first tune.)

Evidently he is having one of his little jokes, and trying to see how long his hearers can stand it. But Weber, a lesser composer of his day, took the joke seriously, and solemnly proclaimed that "Beethoven is now ripe for the madhouse." There were times when such a statement might have meant something, but not in the composition of the seventh symphony.

In the second movement, the dancers rest a while, but "time marches on." The key changes to A minor, the tempo is much slower (although still marked *Allegretto*), and both melody and bass deliberately repeat notes, as if trying to suggest the monotony of time itself.

After a single loud chord of introduction, the main theme goes like this (with violas leading):

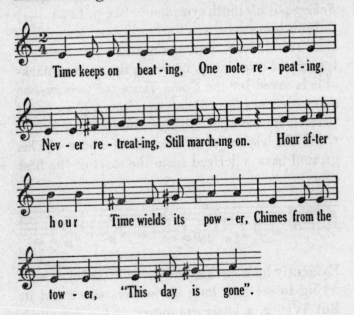

Time keeps on beat-ing, One note re-peat-ing, Nev-er re-treat-ing, Still march-ing on. Hour af-ter hour Time wields its pow-er, Chimes from the tow-er, "This day is gone".

In repeating this melody, Beethoven brings in a counter-tune, which can be sung in harmony with it (using violas and cellos):

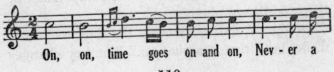

On, on, time goes on and on, Nev-er a

beat is lost from night to earl - y dawn. Long

hours time shall wield its mys - tic pow'rs, Chim-

ing that this day is gone.

The form of this second movement may be considered that of a theme and variations (decorations and alterations), although it also has something of the spirit and outline of a *Rondo,* which was originally a round dance, in which two or more melodies alternated.

Beethoven brings in such an alternating melody in major key, with an accompaniment in triplets, while the bass still hammers at the original rhythmic pattern. Here are some possible words to it:

With time in const-ant mot - ion, It fits 'most

an - y rhyth-mic no - tion.

This tune is heard again in what is really the *Coda,* practically the same as it was before. The remaining measures deal with bits of the main melody, and finally an almost complete quotation once more. At the end the violins defiantly put the accent on the wrong note of the pattern, and a soothing chord by the wind instruments hushes them up for their impertinence.

The third movement is marked *Presto,* faster than the average Beethoven *Scherzo,* and much faster than a Minuet. The dancing has obviously started again, and it is livelier than ever. This is the main tune:

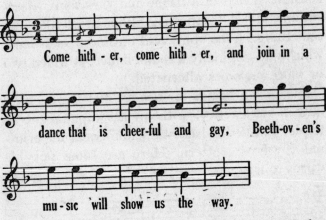

Come hith-er, come hith-er, and join in a dance that is cheer-ful and gay, Beeth-ov-en's mu-sic will show us the way.

There is no need of any further material for quite a while, but in time the music arrives at a *Trio,* which might be interpreted as a breathing-spell. Sing it this way, with deep breaths between phrases (an octave below the clarinets):

Rest awhile,   rest awhile.   Play in mellower style.

With plenty of time devoted to the development of this restful idea, the original dance tune can come back happily for another enthusiastic reception. Relaxation and exercise alternate once more, and when a short *Coda* suggests sitting out the next one, the whole orchestra impatiently cuts the whole thing off with three snapping octaves and two chords.

The *Finale* begins with two rhythmic exclamations that Beethoven imitated later in the *Scherzo* of his ninth symphony. (See p. 124.) Here they lead to a fast 2-4 dance tune that could actually be used for a modern one-step or a double-time fox-trot. It would be hard to sing this at such a rapid tempo, even on a lower level, but you might try whistling it:*

*It has been pointed out by such English writers as Grove and Villiers Stanford that this tune is unmistakably Irish, in fact a "gigantic reel." Beethoven had used the same material in his accompaniment to the Irish song, *Nora Creina,* and the actual notes appear at the end of another Irish tune, *Kitty Coleramie,* which Beethoven had also arranged. The entire seventh symphony may be said to show the influence of the Irish music on which its composer had been working.

It is a helter skelter, confetti-throwing procedure, as if everybody had suddenly decided to march around the tables in a quick lock-step, perhaps popping a few balloons here and there.

There is a snatch of subordinate theme, as if some of the people were calling out:*

Come on a - long, come on a - long, come on a - long!

But this is not allowed to interfere very much with the main dance tune, which keeps whirling and leaping and twisting all over the place, until even the innocent bystander begins to feel exhausted. That is exactly what Beethoven may have intended. He seems to say "If it's dancing you want, I'll show you some dancing that *is* dancing!"

You forget that he is meanwhile going through all the motions of development, recapitulation and *Coda*. Sure enough, it *is* a transfiguration of rhythm, and that is all that your mind has to grasp, as you keep time, inevitably, to this riotous *Finale* of a great symphonic dance.

BEETHOVEN'S EIGHTH SYMPHONY

Following his habit, Beethoven let down again after turning out a tremendous masterpiece in his seventh symphony. The eighth, in F major, was

*But an octave lower than Beethoven wrote it.

composed in the same year, 1812, but it is entirely different in character, going back once more to a style that is reminiscent of Haydn and Mozart.

Yet it is a fine symphony, and by no means an actual step backward, musically or technically. If it had not been preceded by the amazing seventh and followed by the climactic ninth, it might easily stand out as the master-work that it is. Under the circumstances, however, the eighth symphony necessarily suffers a little from neglect, a musical Cinderella which must find a prince of conductors before it is fully appreciated. It is literally a "twin" to the seventh, and this is the second time that Beethoven indulged in such a luxury. (Triplets were possible for Mozart, and quintuplets were nothing strange to Haydn, but the symphonies of those composers were far different from the elaborate and profound inspirations of a Beethoven.)

This eighth symphony opens immediately with a melody of the Haydn-Mozart character, very simple and lovely:*

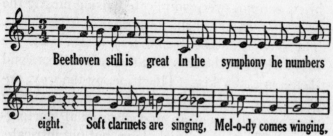

Beethoven still is great In the symphony he numbers eight. Soft clarinets are singing, Mel-o-dy comes winging,

*At the start and finish this is moved down an octave.

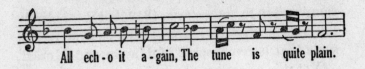

All ech-o it a-gain, The tune is quite plain.

A second tune also sounds quite simple, although it covers too much ground for practical singing. The notes alone should be enough:

The statement or exposition of these two melodies is shorter than is usual with Beethoven, and he seems content to let the music speak for itself, without great elaboration.

The development section is also comparatively brief, and not over-complicated, using mostly the opening measure of the first tune for its material. The recapitulation (reminder) starts with the first melody in the bass, and then gives the second theme in a new key. (This tune, by the way, appears each time in two different keys, changing unexpectedly from an unconventional starting-point.) The *Coda* is fairly long, but not intricate;

concentrating finally on establishing the key of F major, which has been by no means self-evident thus far.

The second movement, *Allegretto Scherzando,* contains one of those musical jokes that Beethoven was fond of perpetrating. He was interested in a famous inventor of the time, Johann Nepomuk Maelzel, a fascinating person, who travelled about the country with a mechanical chessplayer, a robot trumpeter that played Austrian and French cavalry signals as well as other music, and a *Panharmonicon,* which was evidently the ancestor of those machines that still play for you to-day if you put a nickel in the slot. Maelzel, however, is best remembered by his invention of the Metronome, that practical little time-beater, shaped like a pyramid, with its pendulum waving upside down. Those of us who have practiced with a Metronome standing inexorably on the piano may not feel too friendly toward Mr. Maelzel.

Beethoven himself grew a bit tired of him when he found Maelzel taking credit for a lot of things that really did not belong to him, and there was even a lawsuit between them. But at the time of the eighth symphony they were good friends. So Beethoven paid his respects to Maelzel by giving his not too slow movement the rhythmic accompaniment of a Metronome beat and a melody which he himself described as saying "Ta-ta-ta, ta-ta-ta, lieber Maelzel." So why not stick to that idea (but dropping it an octave lower)?

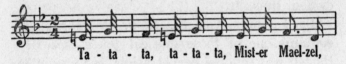

Ta - ta - ta, ta - ta - ta, Mist-er Mael-zel,

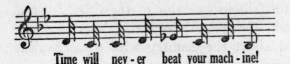

Time will nev-er beat your mach-ine!

(Since Maelzel's machine actually beat time, that is about as bad a joke as Beethoven himself might have made. Notice the rhythmic similarity to the opening of Mozart's G minor symphony, as you find it on p. 39.)

For a second tune Beethoven hands the Maelzel Metronome a bit of rag-time:

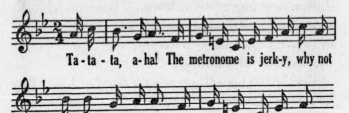

Ta - ta - ta, a-ha! The metronome is jerk-y, why not

fix it, or mix it with mu-sic that is new?

But he evidently decides not to give the machine time actually to get out of order, and the whole movement is quite short, with only a slight development and a quick return to both melodies, full of humor and charm.

With a second movement that was somewhat faster than usual, Beethoven slows up the third to something like the old Minuet tempo (*Menuetto*). It can be sung thus at the start, if you do not hurry too much (again an octave down):

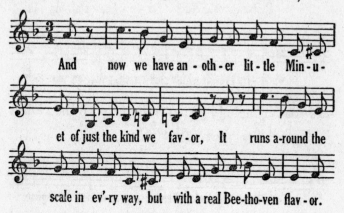

And now we have an-oth-er lit-tle Min-u-et of just the kind we fav-or, It runs a-round the scale in ev'-ry way, but with a real Bee-tho-ven flav-or.

What amounts to a *Trio* begins as follows, with quick, *staccato* triplets in the accompaniment:

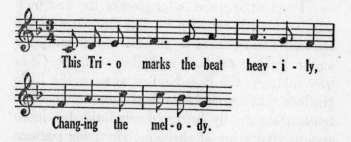

This Tri-o marks the beat heav-i-ly, Chang-ing the mel-o-dy.

A repetition of the Minuet completes the rather short movement.

The *Finale* is in fast time, with the fiddles tim-idly discussing its possibilities at the start:

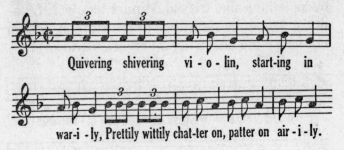

Quivering shivering vi - o - lin, start-ing in

war-i - ly, Prettily wittily chat-ter on, patter on air - i - ly.

A broader melody comes in later, with the violins now showing more confidence.

Play on! The met-ro-nome is gone.

Obviously the orchestra needs no help in keeping time for this final movement. It rushes ahead, with no apparent problems or difficulties. The development uses the latter part of the first mel-ody, making it sound a bit like the close of the familiar *Deutschland ueber Alles,* over and over again. Back come both melodies, with the *Coda* soon playing the broad notes against the little triplets that started the first tune, and these triplets eventually bring to mind the far more serious treatment of the same rhythmic pattern in the Fate symphony, no. 5. (See p. 97.) Finally the horns give this pattern a beautiful echo, and the orchestra runs wild in triple rhythms to a grand finish on wide-spreading F major chords. Beethoven had something on number eight, after all.

BEETHOVEN'S CHORAL SYMPHONY

It is easy to fall into the habit of calling Beethoven's ninth symphony his greatest (and therefore the greatest in history) simply because it was his last and most elaborate. It may even have superseded the fifth in popularity by this time, although this is difficult to judge because of its necessarily limited number of performances. Many people unquestionably go to hear the ninth symphony whenever possible merely because they know they will hear a large chorus and four soloists in addition to the orchestra and are thus fairly sure to get their money's worth, from a material standpoint.

As it happens, the ninth symphony is actually the most mature, the most profound and the most difficult of all the works of its composer (not excepting even the baffling and seldom heard *Missa Solemnis*). But it is not at all likely to be enjoyable to the average listener at a first hearing, or perhaps for several more. Its melodies are not particularly apparent until the choral *Finale* is reached, and then they may suffer by being too obviously beyond the range of the singers. Beethoven had no mercy on the human voice, and he treated his sopranos in particular as though they were mere instruments, with brazen throats and unlimited wind-power.

However the listener may feel about the actual music of Beethoven's ninth symphony, he can hardly help realizing that he is here in the presence of something that had never been attempted before, and certainly has not been equalled since. In the *Eroica,* the fifth and the seventh symphonies, Beethoven seemed to have gone as far as this form of music would permit. He had definitely touched the heights of sublimity in a purely instrumental expression. It required nearly a dozen years more of life and experience to make him realize that there was still something to be said, and that the climax of symphonic music could not be instrumental alone, but must have the aid of words.

At the time of the seventh and eighth symphonies, in 1812, Beethoven was already planning another symphony, in D minor, the actual key of the ninth. His note-books show that he was even then making sketches for such a work, and within a few years he had jotted down much of the material, particularly for the *Scherzo.* But the idea of a choral *Finale* came to him much later, and it was a long time before he decided to use the words of Schiller's *Ode to Joy* for this purpose.

With so long an interval (1812–1823) between the eighth and ninth symphonies, it is natural that even the instrumental movements of the latter should show a decided variation from anything the composer had done before. His whole idea of symphonic structure had changed, and he was no longer bound in any way to the formulas of the past. It is almost impossible here to speak of first and second themes, development, recapitulation, *Coda,* etc. Each movement seems to be several movements in one, as Beethoven's own tempo directions indicate. While the key is D minor, it is some time before this becomes evident, and still longer before anything emerges from the mysterious, groping Introduction that could properly be called a melody. In fact, melody, as Haydn and Mozart used the term, hardly exists in this first movement. After various experiments, the full orchestra suddenly tears at the notes of the D minor chord, covering two octaves, and emerges with this peremptory phrase:

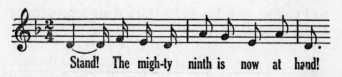

Stand! The migh-ty ninth is now at hand!

There are several other melodic lines, but they do not adapt themselves easily to words, and it is perhaps significant that in this final symphony Beethoven resists the attempt to vocalize his themes until he himself is ready to do so. One little passage in the wood-wind may be worth remembering because of a rather startling reminder that comes in the *Finale* (see p. 132) :

Joy, by fair - est gods in - spired!

For the novice in symphonic music, the *Scherzo* is likely to be the most attractive movement at a first hearing, and it is actually in many ways the most remarkable part of this ninth symphony. Beethoven first states its rhythmic pattern in various ways, using even the kettle-drums alone. (See his similar introductory pattern in the *Finale* of the seventh symphony, p. 113.) When the tune finally gets under way, it proves to be gay and full of humor, although it still has an air of mystery, which is heightened by a fugal treatment (counterpoint). It begins in the second violins, and has to be started an octave lower by human voices:

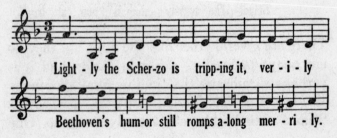

Light - ly the Scher-zo is tripp-ing it, ver - i - ly

Beethoven's hum-or still romps a-long mer - ri - ly.

After a while a countermelody is heard in the wood-wind, over which the faster notes seem to be flashing like jewels:

Like fine pearls glow - ing

This leads directly to a second tune, heavier and more solid than the first, in the manner of a country dance:

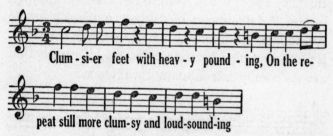

Clum - si-er feet with heav - y pound - ing, On the re-

peat still more clum-sy and loud-sound-ing

There is a section of development, considerable recapitulation, and finally an unexpected *Trio,* which makes a new tune, in D major and 4-4 time, out of the notes of the country dance.

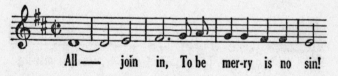

All — join in, To be mer-ry is no sin!

The bassoon accompanies this in a mocking manner, sounding like a series of "Ha ha ha's" in the bass. (Compare this whole effect with the far simpler treatment of a similar idea in the *Trio* of Beethoven's second symphony, p. 75.) This is followed by fugal passages and other development. A *Coda* finishes the movement, which is certainly unlike any other *Scherzo* in symphonic literature.

Now comes a slow movement, *Adagio,* which is also full of originality. The opening melody is clear enough, but by no means obvious, with inner voices playing an important part almost from the outset. It has the initial notes and something of the spirit of Wagner's later *Prize Song,* in *Die Meistersinger,* seeming to express a serene confidence in the fundamental worth of mankind, though troubled by the strife and bitterness that are so common to human experience.

Time will tell if the world has learn'd its les-son well.

A second theme suggests even more of the courageous plodding of those who insist on striving for higher things:

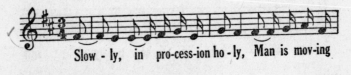

Slow - ly, in pro-cess-ion ho - ly, Man is mov-ing

on-ward and fac-ing dawn-ward!

126

There are variations on the first melody, and finally, in the *Coda,* a new note is sounded, like a trumpet call, indicating that something startling will happen in the *Finale* which is to come, with just a rhythmic suggestion of that old Fate motif, very softly, in the wind-choirs.

This unique *Finale* starts in utter confusion, with all the wind-instruments of the orchestra and apparently all the notes of the scale arguing at the tops of their voices. The question of course is what melody shall be considered fit for the choral climax.

The bass fiddles stop the noise with an indignant speech, exactly like a traffic policeman

What ho!—— Where do we go?

("Who do you think you are?" etc.), and a review of the evidence is in order. A bit of the first movement is suggested, but immediately howled down. Rather timidly the chief melody of the *Scherzo* dances in, but meets with no more success, the kettle-drums dealing the knock-out blows.

Two measures of the slow movement are more favorably received, but after experimenting with some modulation (change of key), the basses again give up in despair. Finally a simple melody is suggested by the wood-wind,* with a note to each beat, and this does the trick. The rest of the orchestra waits in appreciative silence while the bass strings play the complete tune which is eventually to be fitted with words. Schiller's actual text, from his *Ode to Joy,* can be translated here, although it does not appear until later. (The notes are spaced as in the choral version):

Joy, by fair-est gods ins-pired, Maid-en from E-lys-i-um, We, with new amb-i-tion fired, To thy sa-cred shrine have come. Thro' thy spell in bonds su-pern-al, Free and joy-ful once a-gain, All mankind u-nites, fraternal, Where thy gentle wings remain.

The building up of this material from its instrumental to its vocal expression is very gradual.

*This was prophesied in the first movement. See p. 124.

First a mere note or two of harmony is added. Then the upper strings weave a countermelody around it. Finally the full choir of the wood-wind chants it in complete harmony, with the strings marking the time in chords. This time the final measure of the theme continues into what seems an attempt at development, but this is soon cut short by the vociferous reminder of the whole orchestra that human voices were to be introduced.

Sure enough, a baritone soloist enters with soothing words, using the very notes with which the bass viols had previously made their indignant comments. It is a type of singing known as recitative, and not far removed from actual speech.

O friends! No more choic-es! 'Tis time— for voic-es!

The baritone follows his exhortation by singing the accepted melody, which is soon picked up by the lower voices of the chorus, and finally the solo quartet and full chorus alternate in a completely harmonized version. The quartet also gives the theme a highly decorated hearing, and in between these vocal treatments, the orchestra is heard in reminders of its own addition to the melody, with the full chorus reaching a climax of religious chords.

Now comes a most surprising instrumental effect, which in modern terms would rightly be called a "jazzing" of the tune. It is definitely syncopated, with a distortion of the rhythm, the melodic line, and the instrumental coloring, which is entrusted to the curiously unsymphonic combination of brass, wood-wind, triangle, cymbals and drums!*

This effect is repeated, with the solo tenor adding an explosive counter-theme, with these words (the male choral voices later joining him) :

The orchestra experiments further with rhythmic devices, largely triplets, adding a fugal

*This was known in Beethoven's time as "Turkish music."

effect. Then the chorus bursts forth with the complete theme again, using the words of the opening stanza, as above.

There is a pause, and suddenly the male voices of the chorus utter a new and majestic theme:

We em-brace you, count - less mil-lions! This em-brace for all the world!

This is imitated by the full chorus in a remarkable passage of harmony, which soon leads to another fugue, in which the sopranos sing the first tune in a light-hearted skipping rhythm, while the contraltos imitate the majestic theme in even time. The male voices soon join in, with the basses doing the skipping, and the climax comes when the sopranos are made to stay on a high A for thirteen measures, above the lower voices. With further rhythmic experiments by the basses, the chorus finally arrives at a series of soft chords.

A solemn hush precedes the *Coda,* which is introduced by strings and wood-wind. The solo voices gradually work up to a round, in which the chorus also joins, in complicated counterpoint:

Joy,   thou   maid-en from E - lys - i - um!

Just when you are expecting a conventional close, in charming harmonies, the quartet changes the key with a surprising chord and goes into a *cadenza,* or decorative interlude, which is among the loveliest but most difficult passages in the whole symphony.

Another surprising modulation leads to a *Prestissimo* finish, taken at top speed by both voices and instruments, for which the time is first indicated by quick descending octaves. The melody is a compressed version of what was once the majestic masculine theme, with these words:

We embrace you, countless millions, This embrace for all the world!

(Beethoven makes his sopranos sing up to A again, but ordinary people can be satisfied to stay an octave lower on the last two measures.)

One more strange interlude momentarily stops the mad rush of the music, and then the orchestra runs away with the closing measures, apparently quite satisfied, and rightly, with the results of this greatest of all symphonic collaborations between human and instrumental voices.

SCHUBERT'S SINGING
SYMPHONIES

FRANZ SCHUBERT, who outlived Beethoven by only one year (1828), although born in 1797, had very different ideas on the composition of symphonies. Schubert was one of the world's greatest masters of song, yet he would not have dreamed of using actual voices in a symphony. Instead, he made his instrumental melodies sing so definitely and beautifully that they constantly suggest the human voice itself, and are therefore better adapted to words than any since the days of Haydn.

Schubert's life was tragic in its shortness, yet in those brief thirty-one years, fully half of which he spent in significant creative work, he managed to produce an amazing amount of beautiful music, including over six hundred songs, eighteen operas, nine or ten symphonies, sixteen string quartets and a number of other instrumental combinations, a large body of church music, twelve sonatas for the piano and four for the violin, and innumerable smaller pieces of all kinds. He was probably the fastest working, most prolific composer of all time, and belongs permanently among the great masters of the art.

SCHUBERT'S UNFINISHED SYMPHONY

Of the nine (possibly ten) symphonies composed by Franz Schubert, the most popular is unquestionably number seven, in B minor, known all over the world as the *Unfinished Symphony*. It may even be argued that this is the most universally popular piece in the whole symphonic literature.

The fact that it has only two movements (lacking a *Scherzo* and a *Finale*) does not keep it from being a perfect masterpiece, worthy of comparison with the best work of Beethoven, Mozart and Brahms. It does not strive for the gigantic feats of imagination that Beethoven performed with such inward struggle and torment, nor does it show the technical resources of that master musician, or of the more modern Brahmsian style. But within its smaller compass it is an inspired creation from start to finish, and it is perhaps just as well that Schubert did not attempt to finish it.*

The *Unfinished Symphony* was written in

*The sketches that he left for a *Scherzo* do not equal the standards of the two completed movements, and the attempts of others to reconstruct this *Scherzo* have of course been futile and ridiculous.

1822, six years before Schubert's untimely death. No one knows why he did not finish it. (Perhaps he was himself aware that he could not possibly live up to the ideal he had set.) In any case, it would be difficult to find anywhere else in music an instrumental work of this calibre written by a young man of twenty-five!

The Introduction to the *Unfinished Symphony* might really be called its opening tune, for it plays an important part in the later development. It is played in octaves by the bass strings, and might be interpreted thus:*

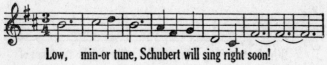

Low,   min-or tune, Schubert will sing right soon!

With four measures marking time as an interlude, another melody is immediately heard, which is really the first theme of the symphony. It is played by oboe and clarinet over quivering strings, and seems to call on Schubert himself for his best efforts:

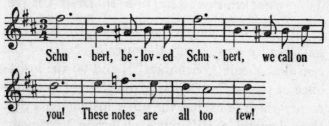

Schu - bert, be-lov-ed Schu - bert,   we call on
you! These notes are   all too   few!

*This is one time when human voices have to sing an octave higher than the instruments, but the key is the same, B minor.

This lovely melody is interrupted by heavy chords from the orchestra, and the horns and bassoons sustain a unison D which leads directly into the second theme, with two measures of syncopated accompaniment for a preface. This is the familiar melody used by Sigmund Romberg for his *Song of Love* waltz, in *Blossom Time,* that charming operetta whose hero was Franz Schubert himself (founded on the German *Dreimaedlerhaus*). It is a tune that irresistibly compels everyone to sing along with the cellos, as they introduce it to the rest of the orchestra.

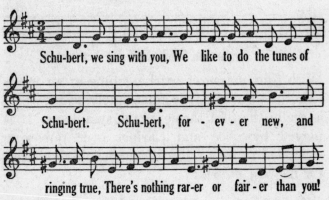

Schu-bert, we sing with you, We like to do the tunes of Schu-bert. Schu-bert, for - ev - er new, and ringing true, There's nothing rar-er or fair - er than you!

The agitated chords that interrupt this unforgettable tune represent the opening notes of the real first theme ("Schubert"), and on the insistence of the orchestra it is given a slight development, which so excites the other instruments that they demand a still more elaborate treatment. Schubert gives it to them in a fascinating series of overlapping imitations, in the wood-wind, applauded by the brass until the softly plucked strings lead back to a repetition from the very start.

The development section starts right in to work on the introductory theme, formerly in B minor, now in E minor. All that one hears of the second theme is an echo of the syncopated accompaniment, and the first is not noticeable until we are almost ready for the recapitulation, when crashing chords again suggest its pattern and make its complete repetition logical in the original key. Horns and bassoons again lead to the cello tune, which is this time in D major instead of G. This recapitulation shows all the best features of the original exposition, remaining loyal to things which simply could not have been better expressed.

A good-sized *Coda* uses the introductory theme as a means of getting back to the key of B minor and staying there. The finish is solid and confident, as it should be with such well made music.

The opening of the slow movement of Schubert's *Unfinished Symphony* has an almost religious sound. In fact it was imitated by some actual sacred music many years later.* The chief melody is this:

O Lord, guide us, we pray Thee.

*The *Sanctus* in Gaul's *Holy City*.

The accompaniment of plucked strings (*pizzi-cato*) and two introductory chords play an important part in the immediate development of this material. Soon Schubert arrives at a second melody, this time sung by the clarinet, and again with a strongly syncopated accompaniment. (The transposition here shows the notes of the actual clarinet part, an octave lower):

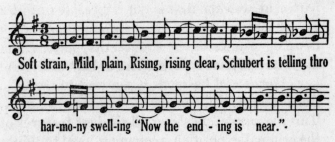

Soft strain, Mild, plain, Rising, rising clear, Schubert is telling thro har-mo-ny swell-ing "Now the end - ing is near."

This also is developed in many ways, including a change to major key. A section of recapitulation brings back both melodies in their entirety, the second now in the key of A minor. The *Coda* surprisingly makes a new melody out of the chords and plucked strings of the two introductory measures, and then picks up two violin interludes for still more surprising modulations into unexpected keys. There is a spirit of resignation at the end, but with every note still echoing some part of the first theme. It is such compactness of technique, added to consistent melodic inspiration, that makes Schubert's *Unfinished Symphony* the great and deservedly popular work that it is.

There is some question as to whether Franz Schubert actually wrote nine or ten symphonies. This is because many of his compositions were discovered only after his death. He worked rapidly, and as soon as he had completed one piece of music, went right on to another.

One of his lesser symphonies, in B-flat, known as number five, deserves to stand between the tonal perfection of the eighth (*Unfinished*) and the dramatic power of the one in C major, variously listed as the seventh or the tenth. (See pp. 143ff.) This fifth symphony was written in less than a month during the autumn of 1816, when Schubert was only nineteen years old. It has a special interest, not only as an example of remarkable precocity, but because it is so definitely in the style of the even more precocious Mozart.

Although eight of Beethoven's nine symphonies had been published by this time, and in spite of the fact that their composer later became literally Schubert's musical god, the young genius seems up to this time to have been entirely unaware of their significance; or perhaps he realized his own technical shortcomings, and deliberately selected the easier model of Mozart until such a time as his own genius might be fully developed.

In any case, Schubert's fifth symphony is well

worth hearing and analyzing, and for a beginner it would be a happy choice as a general introduction to the symphonic form. There is nothing startlingly original about it. The outlines are clear and simple, and the tunes excellent. Moreover it has a robust, popular spirit that places it quite definitely apart from the more aristocratic style of Mozart, in spite of all the similarity on the surface.

After four measures of Introduction, Schubert starts right in with a series of melodic phrases that his admirers might voice in this way:

The second theme arrives considerably later, in the key of F major (the dominant or fifth above the symphony's tonic, B-flat). Again it is thoroughly singable, and a natural tribute to the young composer (transposed an octave down).

The development uses snatches of the first theme and later chords which may have been based on the second. The reminder of the complete opening tune (recapitulation) is in a new key, which is unusual, but the subordinate theme goes conventionally into B-flat. Scales and chords are enough material for the modest *Coda,* which gives just a hint of the main theme near the finish, and then exits laughing up a zig-zag ladder of broken octaves to the closing harmonies, solidly settled on the key-note.

The slow movement of Schubert's fifth symphony begins with a beautiful melody, worthy of Mozart at his best. It is hard to believe that it is the creation of a boy of nineteen.

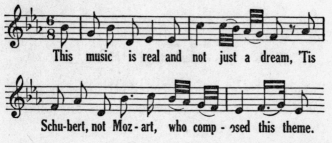

This music is real and not just a dream, 'Tis Schu-bert, not Moz-art, who comp-osed this theme.

There is a subordinate melody, but most of the movement is devoted to the main theme, in a miniature sonata or sonatine form.

Next comes a *Menuetto,* whose fast pace really makes it a *Scherzo.* It begins in G minor (the relative minor of B-flat major), with the full orchestra playing in octaves.

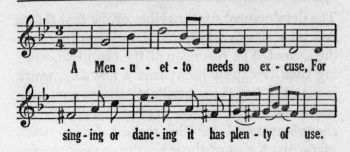

A Men - u - et - to needs no ex - cuse, For sing - ing or danc - ing it has plen - ty of use.

The *Trio* is in G major, with a contrasting bit of minor, and both sections follow the Minuet tradition in their extensions and repetitions.

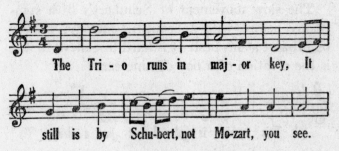

The Tri - o runs in maj - or key, It still is by Schu-bert, not Mo-zart, you see.

In the *Finale* young Schubert gives us a fast scale tune, which is as attractive as anything in the whole symphony.

Now up the scale and down again, Al - le - gro takes it fast, And Schubert has saved up his best un-til the last.

A second melody keeps up this lilting spirit of jovial song:

No wond-er that you like a Schu-bert piece, For he sings gail-y till you nev-er want him to cease.

The sonata form is followed, with a development that concentrates on the first theme, and both melodies coming back in recapitulation. There is no real *Coda,*—just a straightforward run home to the B-flat major chords that logically finish a symphony in that key.

SCHUBERT'S C MAJOR SYMPHONY

Franz Schubert died in Vienna in the fall of 1828. He had become a friend of Beethoven and visited that great master when he himself was on his death-bed a year earlier. That his reverence for Beethoven had finally influenced his own symphonic music is evident in Schubert's tenth symphony, in C major, which was completed as late as March, 1828, and only discovered by Schumann ten years later.

At that time it was called the seventh in Schubert's list, but when three more symphonies later came to light, its number was changed to ten, as it was obviously the last of the series. In many ways it is also the greatest, coming close to the highest standards that had been set by Beethoven himself.

There are actually details of notes, and certainly of the general spirit, that bind this final symphony by Schubert to its logical companion, the ninth and last of Beethoven. Schubert's Introduction is a broad, unaccompanied melody, of the type that Beethoven's choral *Finale* sought and found. It is voiced by the horns, softly and simply:

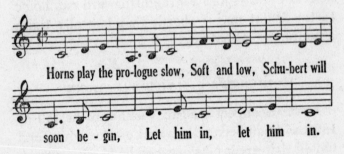

As with Beethoven's choral melody, harmonies are gradually added to this, until the full orchestra is proclaiming its majestic beauty.

The actual first theme is less distinctive, sounding more like a finish than a start, with the orchestra tearing away at octaves, establishing the key, leading to chords, first soft then loud.

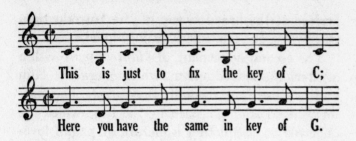

It is really an interlude between the calm breadth of the Introduction and the charming gaiety of what is to come.

It is this second tune that the average hearer will remember most easily and with the greatest enjoyment, introduced by the wood-wind:

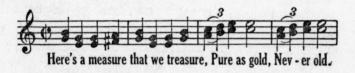

We now begin to realize what Schumann meant when he described this symphony as of "heavenly length." Schubert takes plenty of time in both the exposition and the development of his material, yet there is never any impression of padding or useless repetition. It is the second theme that properly gets most attention, and it remains in the memory even after the return of the earlier material, with a special welcome for its recapitulation in C minor. There is still some extension and repetition, with a long *Coda* which finally arrives at the broad sweep of the Introduction, with which the movement fittingly ends.

The second movement, *Andante,* opens with a mysterious Introduction, which suggests elfin spirits tip-toeing through the forest. The pastoral mood is emphasized by the tune which the oboe plays, completing a picture of pagan loveliness and charm.

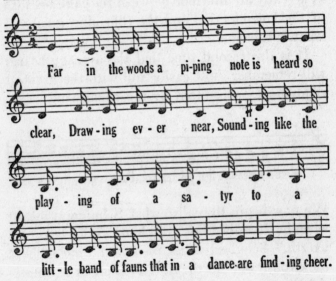

A repetition, with surprising changes of melody, leads into a little major tune that suggests the enthusiastic response of the fauns to the music:

This is followed by more vigorous phrases, with the satyr perhaps insisting on more action:

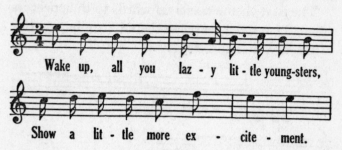

Wake up, all you laz - y lit - tle young-sters,

Show a lit - tle more ex - cite - ment.

In time they all tire of the dance, and the real second theme indicates a quiet gathering as twilight shadows begin to fall:

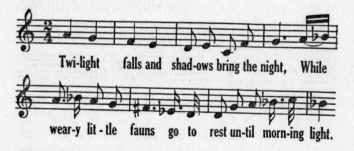

Twi-light falls and shad-ows bring the night, While

wear-y lit - tle fauns go to rest un-til morn-ing light.

All of this material is reviewed, of course, with many individual touches that only the mature Schubert would have thought of.

The third movement is a *Scherzo* which can almost stand beside the extraordinary *Scherzo* of Beethoven's ninth symphony, and shares with it the distinction of adding sonata form to such a movement, which occurs nowhere else in symphonic literature.

The first theme needs no words to interpret its spirit. If it must be remembered vocally, a series of tra-la-la's is sufficient:

If you think of this *Scherzo* as a gigantic round dance, it may be permissible to imagine its second tune as fitting an adaptation of the old nursery rhyme (sung an octave lower):

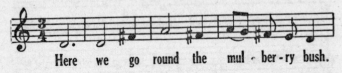

Here we go round the mul - ber - ry bush.

After this material has been carried through the regular processes of sonata form, the horns, clarinets and trombones play an interlude on one note, leading to a *Trio,* whose melody proved useful to Franz Liszt in his symphonic poem, *Les Preludes,* years later. It has the mood of a farewell, and actually appears again in a modern popular song of that type.*

*Good-night, Sweetheart, if you must know.

148

Good-night, —— good-night, sweet dreams till the morn-ing, Fare-well, fare-well, There's no more to tell.

The *Finale* opens with trumpet calls, full of portent:

Sound the horn! This is the end.

These few tones of the tonic major chord are enough to supply a large part of the movement, with triplets and other rhythmic decorations gradually added. The second tune is a fascinating one, sounding the same note four times in a row, an effect which may have been based on the successive notes at the start of the second movement. But here the mood is decidedly cheerful, as though the dancers were willing to go on forever:

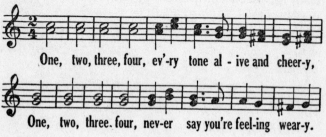

One, two, three, four, ev'ry tone al - ive and cheer-y,

One, two, three. four, nev-er say you're feel-ing wear-y.

The treatment of this theme gives some advance notice of what eventually becomes an independent melody in the development section, and this melody turns out to be a curious mixture of Schubert's own *Military March* and the choral theme of Beethoven's ninth symphony, of which this work seems so continuously aware. It can be remembered this way:

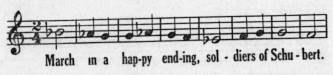

March in a hap-py end-ing, sol - diers of Schu - bert.

Both the recapitulation and the *Coda* keep reminding us of that important pattern of repeated tones, as well as the trumpet calls of the first *Finale* theme, and near the end the special march melody is echoed again. Rhythmically and from the standpoint of modulation the writing is completely engrossing to the very finish. The key of C major has once more asserted itself as a universal medium of human expression, and the symphonic bridge from Classicism to Romanticism has been completed by Franz Schubert.

SCHUMANN'S FOUR SYMPHONIES

ROBERT SCHUMANN (1810–1856) picked up
the torch of Romanticism where Schubert had
dropped it and became the leader of a movement
which fought against the artificialities of the classic formula and insisted that subject matter and
personal expression were far more important
than technical correctness. He was a splendid
musician, nevertheless, with a special gift of individual melody, a remarkable command of
rhythmic and harmonic devices, and outstanding
literary talent and critical insight as well. He admired Franz Schubert enormously, and person-
ally discovered some of his most important
works, including the great C major symphony,
ten years after Schubert's death. Schumann also
had a strong influence on the careers of Chopin
and Brahms, whose genius he recognized in their
earliest compositions.

He followed in the footsteps of Schubert as
an outstanding writer of songs, and also produced some of the world's greatest pianoforte

music, which was the more appreciated by reason of the interpretations of the great concert pianiste, Clara Wieck, who eventually became Schumann's wife. The latter part of Schumann's comparatively short life was clouded by insanity, and he died in an asylum after having attempted suicide.

Robert Schumann produced four symphonies, of which the first and last are still very popular on orchestral programs. The other two possess many points of interest, and even though all four are far removed from earlier models, it would be a mistake to call them formless, rambling or incoherent, as some critics have been inclined to do.

SCHUMANN'S SPRING SYMPHONY

Schumann's first symphony was written in 1841, when he was at the height of his creative powers, and happy in his marriage to the beloved Clara, who had inspired so many of his beautiful songs and piano compositions. It took him less than a month to write this symphony, and he himself gave it the title of *Spring,* which fits it perfectly.

Every movement and every melody in this romantic work seems to concentrate on celebrating that most romantic of all seasons. Trumpets and horns majestically announce the introductory theme, echoed by the full orchestra in chords, in the key of the symphony, B-flat.

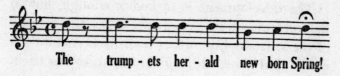

The trump - ets her - ald new born Spring!

It is some time before the real opening tune is heard, and it imitates, in a lighter fashion, the outlines of the Introduction:

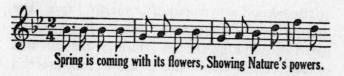

Spring is coming with its flowers, Showing Nature's powers.

This is soon followed by a second melody, full of ecstatic adoration, with a suggestion of whispering winds and running brooks in the background. It is a charmingly youthful message of welcome:

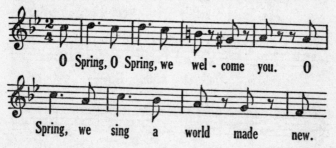

O Spring, O Spring, we wel - come you. O

Spring, we sing a world made new.

There ensues a passage which has led to the criticism that Schumann wrote for the orchestra too much as if it were a piano. This may be justified, but it is a defect which will hardly worry the average listener.

The development is orthodox enough, but in the recapitulation Schumann takes the melody of the Introduction rather than its fast imitation in the first tune, although this also comes back, considerably disguised. The lovely second theme likewise returns, in a new key (as commanded by the classics), and a long *Coda* pays its parting respects to snatches of the main melody.

The second movement, *Larghetto,* has a slow tune of great beauty, with one of those syncopated accompaniments of which Schumann was so fond. The spirit of pomp and circumstance is in it, and in spite of the slow tempo, it is full of suppressed gaiety.

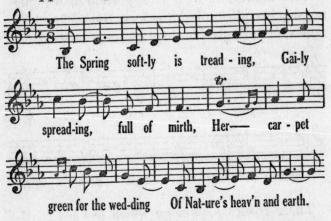

The Spring soft-ly is tread-ing, Gai-ly spread-ing, full of mirth, Her—— car - pet green for the wed-ding Of Nat-ure's heav'n and earth.

In form the movement is a slow *Rondo,* or round dance, with two subordinate themes alternating with the principal tune. This one melody stands out, however, and is enough to identify the movement as a whole. At the very end, an apparent echo of this melody assumes a new outline, which turns out to be that of the first *Scherzo* theme, into which the orchestra goes after only a momentary pause.

To Spring we shall sing, While we fling her— all the flow'rs we bring.

An answering melody, of smoother proportions, invites a further piling up of Spring rhymes:

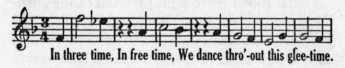

In three time, In free time, We dance thro'-out this glee-time.

This *Scherzo* is unusual in that it has two *Trios*. The first changes the time from three beats to two, an effect that is highly successful, and easily recognized at a first hearing:

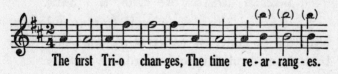

The first Tri-o chan-ges, The time re-ar-rang-es.

The second *Trio* returns to the triple beat, with
a melody that starts up the scale in the bass, very
similar to a passage in Schumann's *Papillons*
(*Butterflies*):

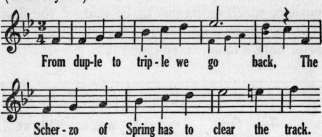

From dup-le to trip-le we go back, The

Scher-zo of Spring has to clear the track.

Both of the *Scherzo* melodies are heard again,
with slight changes, and, after a short pause, a
suggestion of the first *Trio* as well. Then a sudden trick of rhythm and harmony, typically
Schumannesque, brings the whole thing to an unexpected end.

In the *Finale* there is the first hint of the possibility that Spring may not always be lovely and
gracious, and that storms are perhaps lurking
on the horizon. A broad, syncopated scale serves
as an Introduction, to be remembered for its later
appearances:

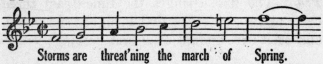

Storms are threat'ning the march of Spring.

Undaunted, the strings begin to play a dainty,
elfin dance tune, so captivating that one hesi-
tates to encumber it with words.

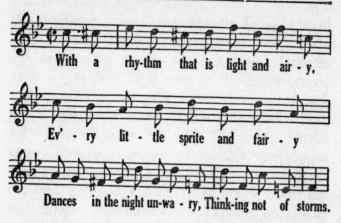

With a rhy-thm that is light and air - y,

Ev' - ry lit - tle sprite and fair - y

Dances in the night un-wa - ry, Think-ing not of storms.

A second tune, which might be a folk-song or a nursery rhyme, hints at a warning, to be rudely interrupted by the storm theme:

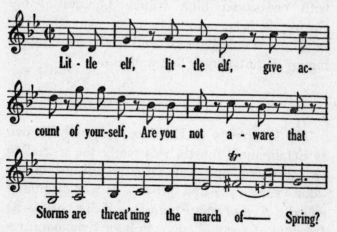

Lit - tle elf, lit - tle elf, give ac-

count of your-self, Are you not a - ware that

Storms are threat'ning the march of—— Spring?

This happens twice, and finally the storm scale turns miraculously into a heartily co-operative melody, which helps to bring the movement up to the point of the traditional development, where it continues as the leading feature. A slow interlude emphasizes a chord pattern in the horns, which Beethoven had used in his fifth symphony, and which Wagner was to perfect dramatically in years to come. The flute is permitted a long trill, plus a flowery *cadenza* (this being quite against the rules) and back comes the dainty elfin dance again. Once more we hear the faint warnings ("Little elf," etc.) and the blustering interruptions of the storm theme, but by this time everybody knows it is all in fun. The weather is given the run of the *Coda,* both bass and treble, and it turns out to be moderate, with occasional high winds. Unquestionably Spring is here, and Schumann can afford to settle down calmly at the end to the mere building of B-flat chords for a finish.

SCHUMANN'S FOURTH SYMPHONY

The symphony in D minor, generally known as Schumann's fourth, was really the second to be composed, and was actually finished in the same year as the first (1841). It was originally called a *Symphonic Fantasia,* which explains its freedom of form. Ten years later Schumann revised the orchestration and published it as the fourth and last of the series.

If the first could be called *Spring,* this sym-

phony in **D** minor may perhaps merit the title
of *Autumn*. Its themes are as melodious and
original as those of the first, but mellower, and
with a touch of the yearning that comes upon
men as they see another year fading away.

The opening theme is completely unvocal, and
suggests the sighing of the wind through trees
already turned to gorgeous colors by early frost.
The notes alone are sufficient:

But Schumann's lyric instinct will not allow
him to go long without a more definite melody
than this. It comes in the form of a second theme
that has all the color and vitality of Autumn,
capable of infinite changes of key and tonal
quality:

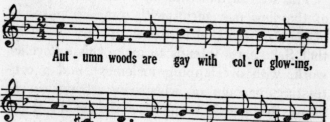

With these materials following the general
outlines of sonata form, there is no pause between movements, and a wonderful, plaintive

melody starts the melancholy *Romanze* (*Romance*). It is sung by the oboe, and its appeal becomes all the more impressive when you later find both Brahms and Cesar Franck imitating it.*

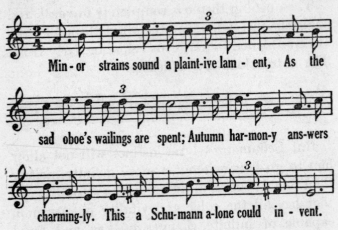

Min - or strains sound a plaint-ive lam - ent, As the

sad oboe's wailings are spent; Autumn har-mon-y ans-wers

charming-ly. This a Schu-mann a-lone could in - vent.

This well sustained theme is the chief material of the slow movement, with some reminiscence of the Introduction to the symphony (showing that Schumann intends to make this a "cyclic" work, with overlapping melodies) and a contrasting passage of whispering strings in D major that merely emphasizes the beauty of the minor melody, when it returns in a different key.

The *Scherzo*, also entering without a break, gives the first suggestion of a blustering, stormy Autumn, with a wind that howls down all oppo-

*See pp. 204, 219.

sition. There is an immense, boisterous robust-
ness in this movement which should appeal especially to masculine listeners.

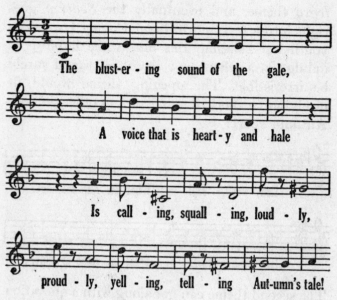

The blust-er - ing sound of the gale,

A voice that is heart - y and hale

Is call - ing, squall - ing, loud - ly,

proud - ly, yell - ing, tell - ing Aut-umn's tale!

A second melody implies a gentler mood,
logically induced by some of the practical bless-
ings of the season.

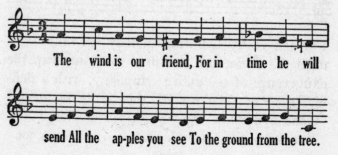

The wind is our friend, For in time he will

send All the ap-ples you see To the ground from the tree.

A flowing *Trio,* in B-flat, closely related to the whispering middle section of the *Romanze,* is followed by a slow version of the opening *Allegro* theme, and eventually the *Scherzo* goes right into a fast and brilliant *Finale.* If modern youth were singing this music, the impulse to indulge in a school or college yell would surely be irresistible. The opening theme would fit nicely into a football game, or any other outdoor Autumn sport:

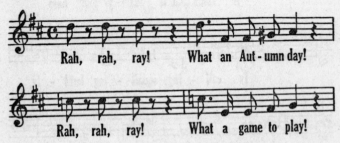

The second theme can get along with a quotation of its notes:

For the really haunting melody we must wait until the *Coda,* and this final tune sums up the exuberance of the entire symphony, with a definite note of "Au revoir" that is by no means "Good-bye":*

*Beethoven had a similar idea some years earlier. See p. 104.

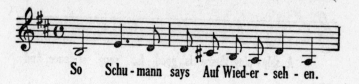

So   Schu - mann says Auf Wied-er - seh - en.

SCHUMANN'S C MAJOR SYMPHONY

Schumann's contribution to the symphonic literature in C major is generally called his second, although it was actually his third symphony, written in 1845–46. It is perhaps the least known of his four works in this form, yet it contains materials and treatment fully as interesting as in any of the others, although possibly less appealing from the purely melodic standpoint.

Like so many symphonies, this composition in C major opens with the introductory notes of a trumpet call, although this one is subdued rather than declamatory. (Compare the loud opening of Haydn's *London Symphony,* and Wagner's later motif in the *Flying Dutchman.*)

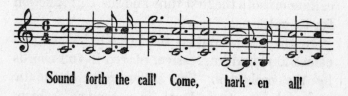

Sound forth the call! Come,   hark - en   all!

The real first theme introduces a far lighter touch, using a skipping rhythm which could be danced or sung at pleasure:

163

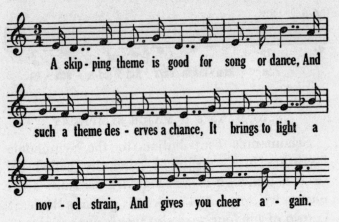

A subordinate theme consisting mostly of chromatic scales (with the notes half a tone apart) completes an unusually short exposition (statement of melodic material).

The development is distinctly more elaborate, calling on both the first tune and the Introduction for its patterns.

In the recapitulation the principal theme becomes loud and impressive, played in full chords by the orchestra. The subordinate chromatic scales change their level, in orthodox fashion, and the rather long *Coda* contents itself mostly with experiments on snatches of the skipping rhythm.

Schumann shows his independence of tradition by putting the *Scherzo* after the first movement, instead of saving it until a slow section has been heard. It begins with an exuberant, overflowing passage in the violins, something like the natural song of a wren, and therefore needing no words to make its meaning clear:

But the first of the two *Trios,* while still rapid in pace, is fairly singable, starting like this:

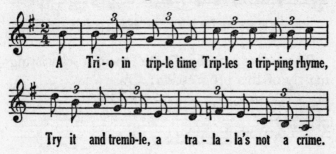

The second *Trio* definitely slows up the movement, using a rather broad theme in this fashion:

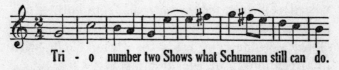

With the bubbling bird-song of the violins returning as often as permitted, this gay *Scherzo*

rushes to its conclusion, echoing the introductory trumpets briefly near the close.

The third is the slow movement, *Adagio,* with its principal melody indulging in the leisurely syncopations that occur so often in Schumann's music. Its mood might thus be interpreted verbally, transposed from C to A minor:

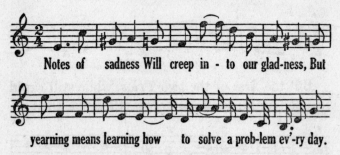

Notes of sadness Will creep in - to our glad-ness, But

yearning means learning how to solve a prob-lem ev'-ry day.

There is a subordinate theme, consisting mostly of this progression:

In place of the conventional development, Schumann introduces a short polyphonic (many-voiced) episode, using material from both of the themes, which are closely related. Recapitulation of the regular type leads to a brief *Coda,* with final reminders of the first melody.

The *Finale* is perhaps a bit rambling, but contains a wealth of melodic ideas which may excuse the composer for his occasional uncertainty of arrangement. A short and rapid Introduction leads quickly to a lively theme, somewhat similar to the opening of Mendelssohn's *Italian Symphony* (see p. 176). A practical wording might be as follows:

To - geth - er, to - geth - er we march a - long, To-
geth - er, to - geth - er we sing our song.

This melody is carried on in a series of episodes, in which some of the materials of the slow movement eventually appear. There is also a new treatment of the progression first heard in the *Finale's* Introduction, which finally becomes an independent melody of great beauty, definitely demanding words of the jubilant type:

Hal - le - lu - jah! Hal - le - lu - jah!

An echo of the introductory trumpets is heard again, and the triumphant spirit of the *Hallelujahs* is more and more evident, as the symphony marches confidently to its conclusion.

SCHUMANN'S RHENISH SYMPHONY

The last symphony written by Robert Schumann is in E-flat major, and dates from 1850, only six years before the composer's death. It is generally numbered three, because of the still later publication of the so-called fourth symphony (in D minor), which was actually second in the series.

This E-flat symphony of Schumann's is called *Rhenish,* because it was definitely influenced by the atmosphere of the Rhineland. Schumann succeeded Ferdinand Hiller as conductor at Duesseldorf in 1850, and was already by that time steeped in the legends and beauty of Germany's famous river. There is tragic irony in his attempt, only a few years later, to drown himself in this same river Rhine.

But the *Rhenish Symphony* shows no signs of depression or insanity. It is as serene and lovely as the Rhine country itself, with its woodlands, its vineyards and its historic castles and legendary rocks. Schumann is the ideal Romanticist in this symphony, with materials that lend themselves to highly individual expression, but also with the firm command of established musical technique that gives authority and permanence to such expression.

The vividly pulsating theme with which the *Rhenish Symphony* opens is a new note in absolute music, something that Richard Strauss himself must have been aware of when he composed the glorious opening of his *Don Juan*. This soaring melody is as exultant as Wagner's own inspirations, and as dramatic in character.

Rhine - land, love - ly Rhine - land, Su - per-
fine land, Full of beaut - y, song and
sto - ry, Land of le - gend, land of glo - ry!

A second theme also has the Wagnerian mood, though quieter in spirit, and its notes may have influenced the actual motif of the Rhinemaidens in the *Nibelungen Ring*. So why not give it similar words?

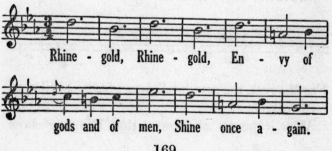

Rhine - gold, Rhine - gold, En - vy of
gods and of men, Shine once a - gain.

Little need be said about the structure of the first movement. Its melodies would be sufficient to overcome any technical defects, and actually it owes no apologies to any of the classic symphonies.

Again Schumann shows his originality by putting the *Scherzo* second instead of third in the order of movements. Its principal melody starts in the bass, whimsically accented, suggesting the spirit and song of the peasants who work in the Rhenish vineyards.

Up - on the vines aglow The Rhenish grapes they grow, And spreading ev' - ry - where The fra-grance fills the air.

(Actually this melody is based on an old German drinking-song.)

A second tune serves as a gay answer:

For the rest, the regular *Scherzo* form is followed faithfully enough.

Was it purely accidental that Wagner chose

the key of E-flat to represent the steady flow of the river Rhine, building up from that sustained key-note at the start of his *Rheingold* to a convincing drama of supermen? Schumann selected the same key for his *Rhenish Symphony,* although the third movement, which most clearly suggests the actual flow of the river, is in A-flat. The main theme of this slow movement might well be transposed into the Wagnerian key of E-flat, to make its range a little more practical vocally:

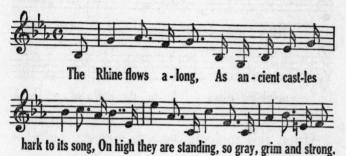

The Rhine flows a - long, As an - cient cast-les hark to its song, On high they are standing, so gray, grim and strong.

There is a second tune, in the manner of a tenderly appealing song:

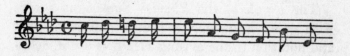

The two melodies combine to make an attractively sentimental interlude.

Another bit of Schumann independence turns

up when you suddenly discover that this *Rhenish Symphony* has five movements instead of four. There is an extra section, in moderately slow time, before the *Finale* is reached. The trombones play an important part in the chief theme of this additional movement, and they can be imagined as summoning the worshippers to the solemn interior of Cologne's great cathedral, which watches over one end of the Rhine.

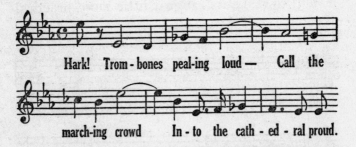

Hark! Trom-bones peal-ing loud — Call the march-ing crowd In-to the cath-ed-ral proud.

Upon this melodic basis Schumann builds a musical structure which has the lofty dignity of Gothic arches themselves. (The movement was actually inspired by a ceremony in the cathedral at Cologne.)

The *Finale* of the *Rhenish Symphony* begins with an exultant melody that is similar in spirit and notation to the closing *Hallelujahs* of Schumann's earlier work in C major. It maintains the religious tone, but in a lively and thoroughly human fashion, possibly representing a final song of praise to the river itself.

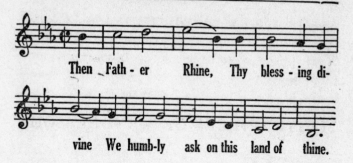

The second theme of the *Finale* is definitely in the farewell mood. But it is not a sad good-bye,—rather again a cheerful "Auf Wiedersehen" of the sort that sang through the closing measures of the *Autumn Symphony*. (See p. 163.) The music tells the story, not the words (with the second part down an octave):

MASTERPIECES OF MENDELSSOHN

FELIX MENDELSSOHN (BARTHOLDY), who lived a comparatively short life, from 1809 to 1847, contributed much to music, including the symphonic field. He was a rarity among musicians in having a comfortable existence, free from financial difficulties. His grandfather was the well known Jewish philosopher, Moses Mendelssohn, and his father, Abraham Mendelssohn (who later added Bartholdy to the family name), was a prosperous banker in Berlin.

Mendelssohn belongs among the precocious musicians (which includes most of the great composers), creating excellent pieces at the early age of ten. He was only seventeen when he wrote the great *Overture* to *A Midsummer Night's Dream,* which is justly ranked among the outstanding masterpieces of music. A fine pianist and violinist, Mendelssohn wrote many successful pieces for both those instruments, including the most popular of all violin concertos. Among his oratorios is the great *Elijah,*

174

a fitting successor to Handel's *Messiah*. His works included a number of symphonies, among which two are especially popular.

Mendelssohn belongs to the Romantic school of music, and was a close friend of Schumann and others of that progressive type. But at heart he was a classicist, worshipping the works of Bach, Mozart and Beethoven, and writing in a technically flawless style that suggested the earlier masters rather than his contemporaries. His melodic inspiration was remarkable, and he had a strong leaning toward lyric expression, writing many actual songs, as well as those popular piano pieces known as the *Songs without Words*. The two symphonies by Mendelssohn most often heard are known by the names of *Italian* and *Scotch*.

MENDELSSOHN'S ITALIAN SYMPHONY

The earlier of these two symphonies in point of composition (although numbered 90 among his works) is the *Italian*, in A major, written largely while Mendelssohn was in Italy, from 1830 to 1833. Except for a typical Italian dance (*Saltarello*) in the *Finale*, it does not particularly draw on that country for its inspiration. Yet its melodious character easily suggests the music of Italy, and it is not difficult to find words that fit the Italian atmosphere.

Almost immediately there is a lively, attractive tune, that might be summed up in this way, (using the second violin part for convenience):

It - al - ian, It - al - ian is Mend-els-sohn's

name For a symphony whose melody with light is a-flame.

This idea is treated at some length before another tune enters, shorter and more casual, in the new key of E major:

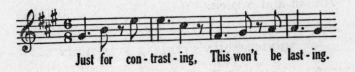

Just for con - trast - ing, This won't be last - ing.

These two tunes are developed in a polyphonic (many-voiced) style that is reminiscent of Bach rather than the symphonic composers. This reduces the length of the recapitulation (reminder), but the *Coda* is of good size, with many new and original touches.

The second movement might be a religious procession, with a dignified melody in minor key, first played by wood-wind and violas, accom-

panied by soft, *staccato* octaves that give a
realistic impression of actual walking:

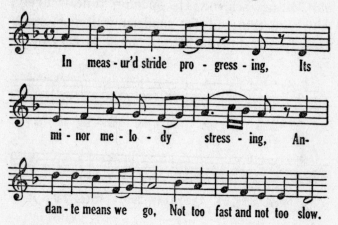

In meas-ur'd stride pro-gress-ing, Its
mi-nor me-lo-dy stress-ing, An-
dan-te means we go, Not too fast and not too slow.

There is a second tune in major key, with interesting effects of alternating voices:

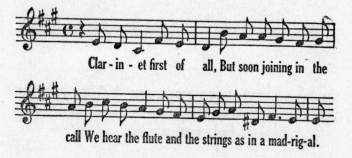

Clar-in-et first of all, But soon joining in the
call We hear the flute and the strings as in a mad-rig-al.

There is practically no development in this
movement, and both themes come back surprisingly soon, each in a new key (which is unusual
for the first theme).

The third movement could be called a *Scherzo,* but with a rhythm and formal outline that fit the old Minuet scheme. Its opening tune is lively, with something of the modern waltzing spirit, (transposed down a fifth, from A to **D**):

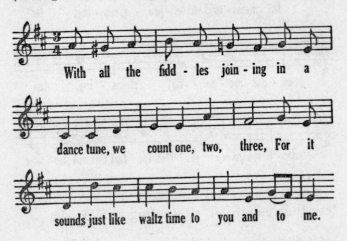

With all the fidd - les join - ing in a dance tune, we count one, two, three, For it sounds just like waltz time to you and to me.

The *Trio* begins with chords by the horns and bassoons:

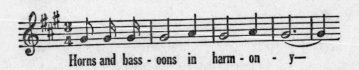

Horns and bass - oons in harm - on - y—

The whole movement is an interesting adaptation of the classic Minuet form.

The name of "Italian" is justified in the *Finale* of this symphony, whose principal tune is a

Saltarello, a dance somewhat like the *Tarantella,* musically. It is very fast and lively:

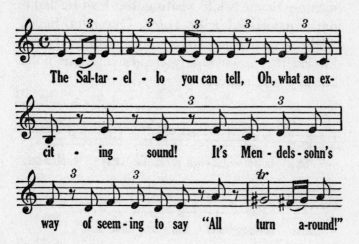

The Sal-tar - el - lo you can tell, Oh, what an ex-cit - ing sound! It's Men - dels - sohn's way of seem - ing to say "All turn a-round!"

(The original key is an octave higher.)

An imitation of this vivacious rhythm serves for a subordinate theme, and while there are sections that could be called development and *Coda* (but no real recapitulation) Mendelssohn's main idea seems to be a dramatically realistic reproduction of the popular Italian dance.

MENDELSSOHN'S SCOTCH SYMPHONY

The so-called "Scotch" symphony of Mendelssohn (both titles are his own) was composed in 1842, much later than the Italian, although it is listed ahead of it, because of the order of publication. Its name is justified by the use of the

Scotch five-tone scale in the second movement, as well as the fact that Mendelssohn created his opening theme while visiting the historic landmarks associated with Mary, Queen of Scots.

The *Scotch Symphony* begins with an Introduction that immediately strikes a serious note. The key is A minor.

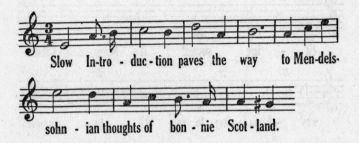

Slow In-tro - duc - tion paves the way to Men-dels-sohn - ian thoughts of bon - nie Scot - land.

The first theme is an adaptation of this Introduction, in a much faster time, which could be interpreted thus:

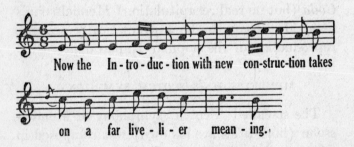

Now the In - tro - duc - tion with new con-struc-tion takes on a far live - li - er mean - ing.

There is a second theme, of somewhat different character:

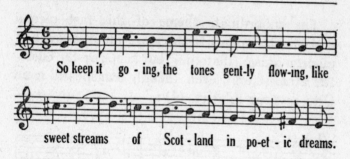

So keep it go - ing, the tones gent-ly flow-ing, like sweet streams of Scot - land in po-et - ic dreams.

The development is extensive, the recapitulation thorough, and the *Coda* quite elaborate, ending in a repetition of the slow Introduction, and going right into the *Scherzo,* without pause.

It is in the second movement that the Scotch character of this symphony is emphasized. Its main theme is built quite definitely on the five-tone pattern that is the foundation of so much of the folk-music of Scotland (and found also in many other countries).*

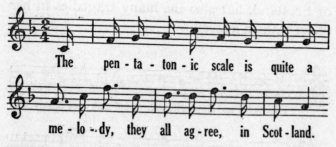

The pen - ta - ton - ic scale is quite a me - lo - dy, they all ag - ree, in Scot - land.

*It is interesting to note how the American Macdowell, of Scotch descent, made frequent use of this pentatonic (five-toned) scale, as in the *Song* in *Sea Pieces.*

The subordinate theme of this fast second movement changes to the more familiar scale of modern music (diatonic), but keeps up the cheerful atmosphere (even though transposed from C to its near relative, **G**):

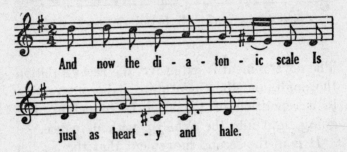

And now the di - a - ton - ic scale Is just as heart - y and hale.

Development, recapitulation and *Coda* follow in their regular order, and one realizes that Mendelssohn knows his classic form, even though he seems to be writing in the style of folk-song.

A sadder note creeps into the slow third movement, which brings to mind the natural beauties of Scotland, but also the many tragedies in her blood-stained history.

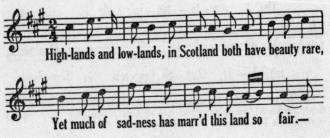

High-lands and low-lands, in Scotland both have beauty rare, Yet much of sad-ness has marr'd this land so fair.—

The second melody might have been one of the battle-hymns of those brave warriors who fought for their country.

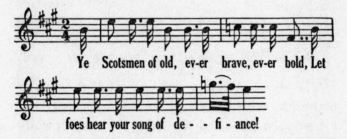

Ye Scotsmen of old, ev-er brave, ev-er bold, Let
foes hear your song of de - - fi - ance!

Little development is needed for this material, the whole movement having the quality of a sustained song.

In the *Finale,* Mendelssohn becomes cheerful again, making Scotland seem a gay and happy country after all. The first theme skips about with considerable abandon:

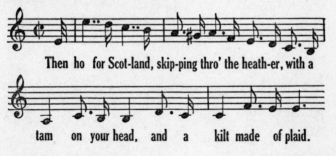

Then ho for Scot-land, skip-ping thro' the heath-er, with a
tam on your head, and a kilt made of plaid.

A second tune contains suggestions of the opening of the symphony, but in a much faster time:

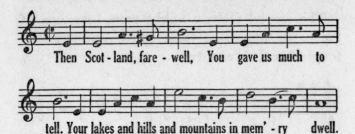

Then Scot-land, fare-well, You gave us much to tell. Your lakes and hills and mountains in mem' - ry dwell.

The regular sonata form is applied to these materials, with the *Coda* developing practically a new theme toward the close. It is a typically Mendelssohnian treatment of excellent melodies and leaves us with a real respect for this gifted musician.

BOWING TO BRAHMS

SO NOW we come to Johannes Brahms, one of the greatest of all composers. He lived from 1833 to 1897, which brings him right into our own time, or at least the time of our parents. There are many people living to-day who knew Brahms in Germany, and heard him play the piano and conduct orchestras in his own compositions.

He was short and square and solid, with a long white beard and a black cigar. But he wrote beautiful music, something like Beethoven's and Schumann's rolled into one. It was mostly "absolute" music, symphonies, concertos, sonatas, quartets, no operas, but many fine songs, and several big works for chorus.

There are four symphonies by Brahms, and they are all great, perhaps as great as any ever written. His first symphony, which he began at 29, but did not finish till many years later (1876), has been called "the tenth," because it was fine enough to have followed the nine symphonies of Beethoven, who might have been proud to write it.

The key of this symphony is C minor, the same as Beethoven's fifth, and its main idea is also similar. Beethoven described Fate knocking at the door, and showed how people can get the better of bad luck and shape their own lives by hard work and courage. (See pp. 91ff.)

Brahms does the same thing in a different way. His tunes are not as easy to follow as Beethoven's, and he uses them in a more original style. But that makes a Brahms symphony more and more interesting, the oftener you hear it. Once is never enough.

The first thing you will notice in the Introduction to this symphony is the regular beat of the kettle-drum, as the other instruments of the orchestra go soaring high up in the scale, as if ambitious to reach the sky. That beat of the drum is Fate again, knocking at the door. But this time the knocking is in regular groups of three (slow 6-8 time) and you can think of it in such syllables as these:

After quite a long introduction on this rhythmic pattern, which fills you with awe, and perhaps even fear, there is a sudden change. The other instruments seem to realize that there is a struggle coming, and they silence the drum with a wild, desperate song that starts like this, (transposed from C minor to G minor):

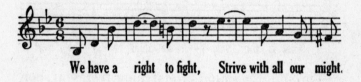

We have a right to fight, Strive with all our might.

The battle with Fate is now on, and you seem to hear the fighters shouting:

On - ward! On - ward!

The first wild theme is turned into a subordinate melody, expanding calmly and quietly. This first skirmish sounds like a victory over Fate, with the strings viciously snarling:

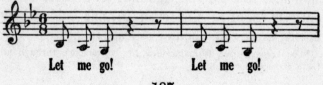

Let me go! Let me go!

like an animal that is cornered. But the orchestra picks up this vicious little snarl and turns it into a cheerful and courageous song:*

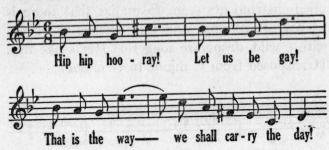

Hip hip hoo - ray! Let us be gay!

That is the way—— we shall car - ry the day!

Through the sound of marching feet, you soon hear a broader, more triumphant melody:

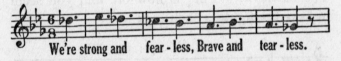

We're strong and fear - less, Brave and tear - less.

This appears in both major and minor moods, and as the movement develops, all the other tunes appear in various ways and keys. It is quite exciting trying to follow them, as if you were watching an army in battle, through field-glasses. At the end of the movement you feel pretty sure that Fate is conquered.

But now comes the second movement, which is slow and sad. Brahms reminds us that no life is entirely happy. Yet even in this melancholy music, there is a mood of courage:

*The transposition is maintained for convenience through all these themes.

Sor-row must come to all, Fate leaves us no es-

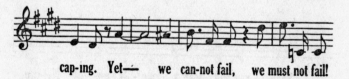

cap-ing. Yet— we can-not fail, we must not fail!

This is the main melody of the second movement
of this Brahms symphony, No. 1, but it flows on
like a great river, seemingly without any end.
After a while there is a ripple of slow syncopation (rag-time) in the strings, and suddenly the
oboe sings a tune that clearly indicates what is
coming in the cheerful third movement:*

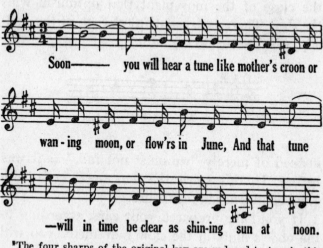

Soon———— you will hear a tune like mother's croon or

wan - ing moon, or flow'rs in June, And that tune

—will in time be clear as shin-ing sun at noon.

*The four sharps of the original key are reduced to two in this
transposition.

But the mood is still that of a moonlight night rather than a sunny day, even when the whole orchestra shows itself ready to play the new tune:

Soon   you will hear a   love - ly tune of Nat-ure.

(The original key is here actually D-flat, but transposed to G for convenience in singing.) The slow, sad melody insists on coming back, although the instruments surround it with all kinds of notes, some of which, like the plucking of the cellos, sound quite angry. It is only near the close of the movement that optimism wins the day. There is a beautiful change in the melody, which seems to say:

We   shall   not fail!

instead of merely "we must not fail," as it was before. In this spirit the movement ends with quiet confidence in the future.

If you have prepared your ears, according to the oboe's hints in the slow movement, you will immediately recognize the calm and lovely tune

which the two clarinets play at the start of the
third:*

This is one of those wonderful melodies that
sound as if they could not have been written in
any other way, yet Brahms himself shows how
it gradually developed in his mind until it
reached this perfect form. Even without words
it would tell us clearly that the world is a beautiful place to live in, and that there is no excuse
for bitterness and evil.

But the battle with Fate is not over yet. We

*The original key of A-flat is changed to F for vocal purposes.

hear the ominous knocking once more, very much as Beethoven had it in his fifth symphony:

Let me in!   Let me in!

This last challenge is immediately answered:

We can bat-tle with Fate and the brav-est will win!

And now Brahms gathers himself together for a supreme effort that will express the triumph of man over Fate. Starting his *Finale* with what seems a despairing wail, he gradually builds up to a stirring march, whose melody really becomes a song of praise for the composer himself. It may remind you a little of the final Ode to Joy in Beethoven's ninth symphony (see p. 128) especially in the second half, but that is in its favor, and Brahms may actually have had it in mind. In any case, here is the tune, to which you can march with Brahms right up to the gates of Heaven itself:*

*The original is of course C major, as in the *Finale* of Beethoven's *Fate Symphony,* but this would be a bit low for singing. G should be practical.

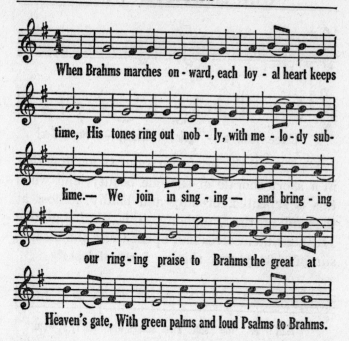

When Brahms marches on - ward, each loy - al heart keeps time, His tones ring out nob - ly, with me - lo - dy sub- lime.— We join in sing - ing — and bring - ing our ring - ing praise to Brahms the great at Heaven's gate, With green palms and loud Psalms to Brahms.

There are two more things that you ought to remember in this great symphony. One is a short melody played a number of times by the horns and other wind-instruments. Its notes are the same as those of the Westminster Chime, sounded by Big Ben, the huge clock in London, and also by many clock-towers and grandfather's clocks all over the world. Perhaps Brahms used this pattern on purpose, too, as a compliment to his English friends. Here is the original chime, and also the way you could sing the Brahms tune, as a reminder (both still in the key of G):

Chime forth a - gain! Chime, — Big Ben!

Finally all the brass instruments get together in a short chorale of sublime beauty, and when this is repeated, broadly and loudly, almost at the end of the symphony, it is as though the Heavens themselves had opened and the blazing sun of victory were shining forth at last:*

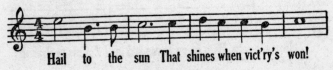

Hail to the sun That shines when vict'ry's won!

Only the triumphant finish remains. Nobody has to worry any more about the result of this musical battle. Fate is defeated, and Brahms is the master, and captain of our souls.

BRAHMS' SECOND SYMPHONY

Johannes Brahms was more like Beethoven than any other modern composer, both in his music and in some of his personal characteristics, such as rough humor and the hatred of insincerity or superficiality.

*The notes are moved down a fifth for singing.

194

Beethoven wrote his fifth and sixth symphonies in close succession, and Brahms completed his first and second on a similar "twin" schedule. If Brahms' first symphony can be given a background of Fate, like Beethoven's fifth, it is certainly fair to call his second a *Pastoral Symphony,* the same as Beethoven's sixth.

This second symphony, in D major, dated 1877, is in many ways the easiest of all the four Brahms masterpieces for the average listener, and might well be heard before the more complicated number one. In addition to a wealth of melody, which seems unrestrained by the conventions of symphonic writing, Brahms uses a basic motif of four notes, heard immediately at the start, and serving as a very short Introduction.

These four notes play an important part in the whole first movement, and you should keep your ears open for them, as they appear in all sorts of positions, sometimes most unexpectedly.

The principal theme of this movement starts quietly in the horns, using the simple tones of the major chord. Brahms had a similar effect, in the same key of D major, at the start of his great violin concerto and his popular song, *Sapphische*

Ode (*Sapphic Ode*). This theme comes to no definite ending, and can use words only part of the way:

It leads, with various reminders of the basic motif, into a more elaborate group of phrases, which are purely instrumental in character:

There is not a waste note or a weak moment in the music as the second theme is approached. This is a broad, beautiful melody in minor key, which was imitated in the modern popular tune, *Play, Fiddle, Play,* and actually suggests something of a gypsy spirit:*

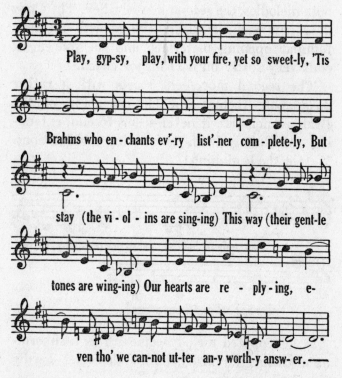

Play, gyp-sy, play, with your fire, yet so sweet-ly, 'Tis

Brahms who en - chants ev'-ry list'-ner com - plete-ly, But

stay (the vi - ol - ins are sing-ing) This way (their gent-le

tones are wing-ing) Our hearts are re - ply - ing, e-

ven tho' we can-not ut-ter an-y worth-y answ- er. ——

(Brahms was familiar with gypsy music, through his tour as accompanist to the violinist Remenyi,

*This melody, introduced by violas and cellos, is here given in B minor, as it appears in the recapitulation.

and he arranged and adapted many of these folk-tunes in his *Hungarian Dances, Zigeunerlieder,* and other small compositions of real charm.)

The development section emphasizes both the basic motif and the first theme, and there is a recapitulation in the classic style, bringing back both melodies, the second in a new key. The *Coda* does new and surprising things with the now familiar opening materials, and the movement ends very softly on a D major chord.

The second movement starts with a rather melancholy theme, and like so many of the Brahms melodies, it never seems to end, extending indefinitely with fascinating modulations. Here is the beginning:

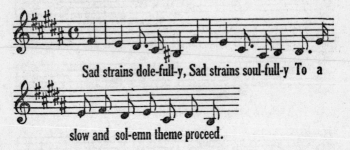

Sad strains dole-full-y, Sad strains soul-full-y To a

slow and sol-emn theme proceed.

A syncopated melody comes in as a subordinate theme, its instrumental character hardly permitting words:

There are variations on this material which do not disturb the steady flow of the music, ending in a *Coda* whose close is again a soft chord.

The third movement is a delightful dance piece, which might be called a *Scherzo,* although Brahms himself does not use that title. It starts with a gay tune in the wood-wind, with the cellos plucking out a fast accompaniment:

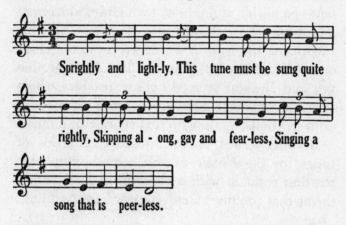

Sprightly and light-ly, This tune must be sung quite

rightly, Skipping al - ong, gay and fear-less, Singing a

song that is peer-less.

Just when you have become accustomed to this tune in triple time, Brahms gives you a surprise by putting it into a very rapid 2-4 measure.

This might be considered a *Trio,* in which case another *Trio* may be said to follow a restatement of the principal theme, with scales in triple time, including some interesting syncopations:

The final hearing of the main tune wavers between major and minor, with new and irresistible harmonies entering into the *Coda.* A final surprise is the leap of an octave near the close, one of those touches of genius that both Beethoven and Brahms seemed able to produce whenever they wished. The end is quite simple and unpretentious, again with soft chords for a finish.

Brahms writes another wonderful series of tunes for the *Finale* of this second symphony, starting right in with a cheerful and exuberant theme that promises an absolutely happy ending:

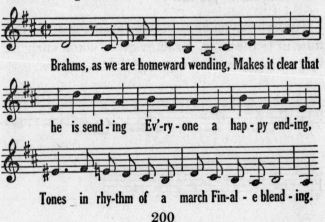

Brahms, as we are homeward wending, Makes it clear that

he is send-ing Ev'-ry-one a hap-py end-ing,

Tones in rhy-thm of a march Fin-al-e blend-ing.

There is a broader sweep to the second theme, which seems to express even more solid satisfaction:

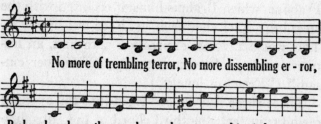

No more of trembling terror, No more dissembling er - ror,

Brahms has shown the way, has made us gay, and joy is here to stay.

The development deals mostly with the first tune, introducing some remarkable effects of harmony and rhythm as it nears the recapitulation, which is sturdily straightforward and rushes the symphony ahead to a brilliant and triumphant close in the opening key of D major.

BRAHMS' THIRD SYMPHONY

If the second symphony of Brahms can be called *Pastoral,* the third certainly deserves the title of *Eroica,* whose Beethoven model it suggests in many ways. It is not heard as often as the other three, but it may prove to be the one that can best stand indefinite repetition. Certainly it represents a sustained nobility of invention and as compact and perfect a technique as can be found in the entire symphonic literature. (The date is 1884, and the key F major.)

Like the second symphony of Brahms, this *Eroica* starts with a motto or basic motif, in this case three chords, topped by F, A-flat and the F above, which Brahms himself credited with the meaning "Frei aber froh" ("Free but happy"). This was a favorite expression with him, an improvement on Joachim's motto, "Frei aber einsam" ("Free but lonely").

These three chords lead right into the opening melody; in fact, the third chord of the Introduction is the first in the theme, which itself follows the chord tones downward, with nobly exultant effect:

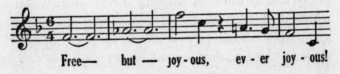

Free— but — joy-ous, ev - er joy - ous!

The second tune is in sharp contrast, having almost the atmosphere of a lullaby, a gentle duet between clarinet and bassoon, over a slow, syncopated accompaniment. It might be sung like this:

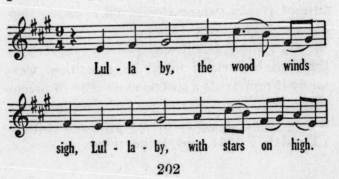

Lul - la - by, the wood winds

sigh, Lul - la - by, with stars on high.

Brahms uses this material in many interesting ways, particularly in the development section, where the second theme appears in a minor variant, throbbingly ʼuttered by cellos and bassoons. The *Coda* treats ʼhe first tune in even more novel fashion, finally bringing it right down the F major chord (the key of the symphony) with a tranquillity which would never have been suspected at the outset.

The second movement has a beautiful slow melody, of distinctly pastoral character, played first by the wood-wind, in the manner of actual shepherds. So we may be justified in imagining a nocturnal scene under the stars, with mildly pastoral meditation:

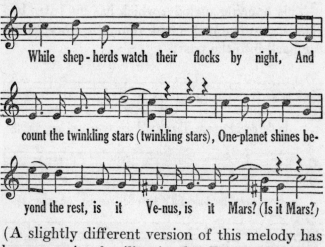

While shep-herds watch their flocks by night, And count the twinkling stars (twinkling stars), One-planet shines beyond the rest, is it Ve-nus, is it Mars? (Is it Mars?)

(A slightly different version of this melody has become quite familiar in the *Zampa Overture* of Herold.)

The slow movement really requires no more melodic material than this, with Brahms again showing his infinite command of musical detail by his continually interesting treatment.

The third movement should be a cheerful dance, conventionally. But, while it is in a faster time and a triple rhythm, its mood is one of yearning, almost melancholy. The appealing melody which the cellos sing, against a weaving design by the other strings, is definitely reminiscent of the *Romanze* of Schumann's fourth symphony (see p. 160), and the entire movement has much of the spirit of Schumann himself, who was a good friend to Brahms, encouraging and influencing him in many ways.

This opening melody, which has no Introduction, suggests a rather sad, romantic story, going far back into the past:

In the days long ago, They would sing sweet and low, And the moon heard the tune, till it soon Be-came an e - cho to fade far a - way, far a - way, — far a - way.

The second theme is also Schumannesque, and carries on the plaintive mood of the first, although a trifle more optimistically:

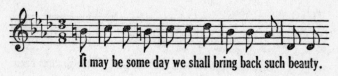

It may be some day we shall bring back such beauty.

This twice goes into a passage of indescribable beauty, played by the strings (here given in its second form):

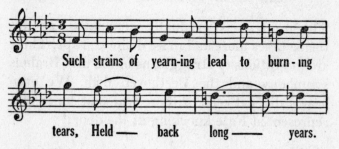

Such strains of yearn-ing lead to burn-ing

tears, Held —— back long —— years.

A fine piece of orchestration appears on the return of the first melody, when it is given to a solo horn, with the oboe supplying the decorations. Brahms has sometimes been accused of "muddy" instrumentation, but there is no evidence of it in his symphonies, so long as the players are able to carry out his intentions. And if anyone still thinks of Brahms as a rather dry, scholarly composer, let him listen with open heart to this intensely romantic, thoroughly melodious and universally appealing movement.

The *Finale* is in heroic vein. Its opening is portentous, full of suppressed excitement, a bit mysterious.

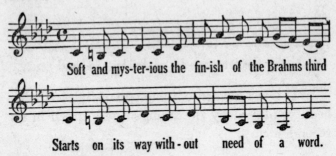

Soft and mys-ter-ious the fin-ish of the Brahms third

Starts on its way with-out need of a word.

The mystery is gradually eliminated, as this theme takes more and more definite shape. There are indications of struggle, as in the first Brahms symphony and the Beethoven fifth. We even hear a distinct echo of those fearsome tones that represented Fate knocking at the door:*

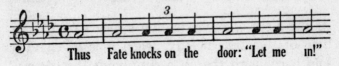

Thus Fate knocks on the door: "Let me in!"

The triumphant spirit of the symphony asserts itself before long, in a broad theme that the cellos play in a cross rhythm of three against two:

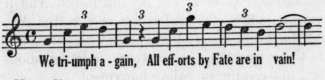

We tri-umph a-gain, All eff-orts by Fate are in vain!

*See p. 91.

This mood is intensified by an exultant series of phrases in the strings:

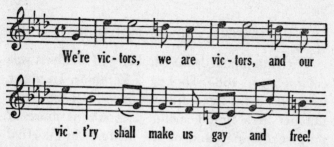

There is one dramatic climax after another, with Brahms seemingly inexhaustible in his musical resources and virile imagination. A surprising treatment of the introductory theme of the *Finale* is heard in the muted strings. But the closing page of the symphony is perhaps the most astonishing of all. With victory firmly established, an unmistakable triumph over unseen forces, the opening motif and theme of the entire symphony return for a final touch of unity, with the notes of the F major chord descending once more in tranquil satisfaction, as though the listener were looking at a beautiful sunset at the end of a strenuous day. It is a far more impressive close than the conventional slam bang of scales and chords that most composers consider necessary for the termination of their symphonies, and even though it may not show off the average conductor to his own satisfaction, it will inevitably create in the hearer the vast feeling of calm that Brahms himself must have experienced in the creation of such incomparable music.

The fourth and last symphony of Brahms was completed in 1885. Its key is E minor. In many ways this is the most difficult of the Brahms symphonies at a first hearing. It contains more of pure scholarship and of the austere, intellectual spirit than any of the others. Yet it is essentially a romantic work, full of human qualities, and with an adequate proportion of simple, appealing melody.

The opening is almost naïve in its childlike spirit, forming its tune from a succession of two-note patterns, each starting and finishing in a different way, as though a number of people were calling to each other, with voices of different pitch.

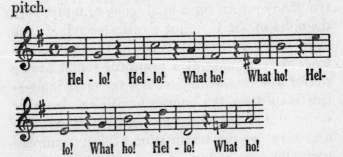

This childlike simplicity does not last long, however, and some complicated maneuvres lead

to a second theme which has two distinct melodies. The first is of a leaping, triumphant character:

The second is broader, with an argumentative
strain, as though Brahms were trying to work
things out logically, without resorting to the easy
expression of musical satisfaction that most composers would prefer. (The key here is that of its
recapitulation):

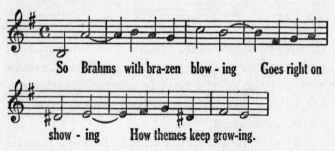

The development justifies this thought in its
continued mental and spiritual wrestling with
problems of harmony and rhythm, difficult to
follow, perhaps, but never dull or meaningless.

In his recapitulation, Brahms turns his opening theme into broadly sustained notes, creating
an entirely new effect, and then gets back to its
original spirit and movement with surprising
melodic changes. All through the movement

there are interesting derivative passages that give the impression of absolutely new melodies:

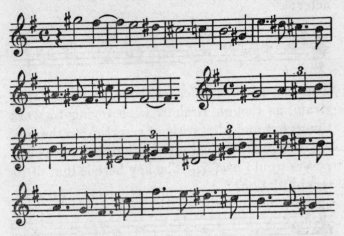

Finally the *Coda* adds still more of individuality, with one startling progression in which the two-tone pattern of the start is constantly alternating between treble chords and bass octaves, in melodic imitation.

The slow movement is one of the most beautiful inventions of Brahms or any other composer. Its main melody appears immediately as an Introduction in C major, with the horns joined by the wood-wind in octaves, until a surprising modulation changes the key suddenly to E major, in which the complete theme is played. This melody has the sunset calm and repose of the end of the third symphony, and is typical of Brahms in his tenderly romantic moods.

Sun-set, gold-en sun-set, In the dist-ance fleec-y cloud-let, Like a ha-lo, light and air-y, O'er the tress-es of a fair-y, Far ho-ri-zon soft-ly call-ing at calm close of day, Its voice seems to say "Come away, ah, come a-way."

This material appears in several ways, with thrilling variations of both harmony and melody, until a second theme is reached, a broad chorale, played by the cellos through a soft tracery of orchestral patterns. It might be expressed in hymn-like words in the key of recapitulation:

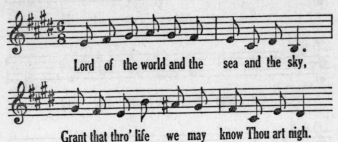

Lord of the world and the sea and the sky,

Grant that thro' life we may know Thou art nigh.

The repetitions and extensions are beautifully decorated with instrumental coloring, and at the close Brahms comes back momentarily to the C major key of the Introduction, only to show how easily he can modulate right out of it into E major once more, an astonishingly effective ending.

The third movement, *Allegro giocoso,* corresponding to a jocular *Scherzo,* gets off on the run, with an immensely spirited scale tune in the manner of folk-music. It is interrupted by a dismal chord, over rolling drums, but picks right up again, undaunted, and sets a pace that insists on cheerfulness regardless of handicaps.*

Shall we have some dancing? Shall we have some prancing? No?

*Tschaikowsky later used a similar idea for the *Scherzo* of his fourth symphony. See p. 230.

A graceful melody enters as a subordinate theme, with a suggestion of pretty girls dancing and singing on the village green.

In the development the interrupting chords are given more prominence, and a real argument is staged between the cheerful and the gloomy sides. The happy melody wins again, and makes a totally unexpected entrance in a new key and with a brand new instrumental garb, hastily put together by the wood-wind, with both charming and smugly comic effect. Another individual change turns part of the first theme into what is practically an independent melody, of great breadth and solidity.

In a final return to the key of C major, Brahms employs the utmost simplicity, emphasizing the descending scale of his first tune, and then dismissing the whole affair with a happy-go-lucky gesture.

It is just as well that this third movement was cheerful, for the *Finale* has a solemn, almost tragic note, and carries the hearer far beyond the simplicities of folk-music. The theme of this unique *Finale* is little more than a scale of E minor (the key of the symphony), whose struggling ascent might be worded thus:

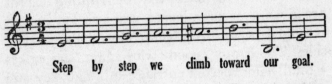

Step by step we climb toward our goal.

Brahms uses this scale melody as the foundation for a series of variations known among the classic composers as a *Chaconne* or *Passacaglia*. The outstanding characteristic of these old forms is that the melody appears in the bass rather than the treble. Technically perhaps this should be called a *Chaconne,* which permits the use of the melody above the accompaniment, and is not generally polyphonic (many-voiced) in structure. (Bach's famous *Chaconne* for the unaccompanied violin is a good example, whereas his great *Passacaglia* for the organ is really a polyphonic treatment of a bass theme.)

There are actually thirty-four variations on this E minor melody in the *Finale* to the fourth symphony of Brahms, a technical feat without parallel in symphonic music. Far more important, however, is the amazing way in which the composer has maintained human interest in this complicated movement, with a sustained sublimity of conception and a consistent dramatic power that should be ranked with the most impressive choral and instrumental effects of Beethoven and Bach.

CESAR FRANCK'S ONE SYMPHONY

AFTER all four of the Brahms symphonies had been written, performed and published, it seemed that the last word had been said in this musical form. But as late as 1889 one great work appeared, which not only deserves to rank with the masterpieces of Brahms, but which definitely bridges the gap between the classic symphony and modernism. This important composition is the symphony in D minor by Cesar Franck (1822–1890), the only one produced by that composer.

A Belgian by birth, Franck spent most of his life in Paris, where he was first a prize-winning pupil and eventually a Professor at the *Conservatoire,* meanwhile acting as choirmaster and organist at the church of Ste. Clotilde. His life was uneventful, with plenty of hard work. Among his pupils were such famous modernists as Debussy and d'Indy, and his compositions, in addition to this symphony, included five oratorios and other choral works, a number of smaller orchestral pieces, among them four *Symphonic Poems,* some important chamber music (particularly a quintet and a violin sonata), three operas, about twenty songs, and a large amount of organ and piano music.

Cesar Franck was like Brahms in his combination of classic and romantic tendencies, but he went even further in the direction of modern harmony and freedom of structure. His one symphony is not only an outstanding piece of musical originality, but has become one of the most popular numbers on modern orchestral programs.

The Franck symphony in D minor has only three movements, instead of the conventional four, and shows individuality also in carrying themes from one movement into another, far more than Beethoven, Schumann or Brahms had dared to do.

The opening theme is based largely on three notes, which might be considered a "motto." They appear in slow time at first (suggesting a similar passage in Liszt's *Les Preludes*) and might represent the muttering of a sleepy giant:

Let me sleep.   Let me sleep.

But these same notes soon take on a fast tempo, thus becoming a full-sized melody, with an entirely new significance. (They might now be fitted with the words "wide awake.")

There is a return to the sleepy mood of the start, in a new key, and also a new pitching of the faster version. But chromatic scale progressions have already indicated a leaning toward a different theme, and this finally enters in a subdued, almost plaintive fashion:

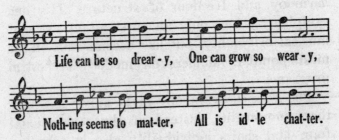

Life can be so drear-y, One can grow so wear-y,

Noth-ing seems to mat-ter, All is id-le chat-ter.

Chromatic intervals play an important part in its extension, and soon a new note is added, virile in its syncopated rhythm and sturdy in its melodic line:

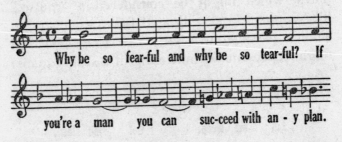

Why be so fear-ful and why be so tear-ful? If

you're a man you can suc-ceed with an-y plan.

This melody, however, is also in time given a plaintive atmosphere, as softly sung by horns and wood-wind, and this leads to a series of experiments (development) to which snatches of the first theme are soon added. The recapitulation of both themes is orthodox enough, although the whole melodic and harmonic scheme has a striking originality as compared with conventional symphonic writing.

A remarkable series of harmonies introduces the *Coda,* which indulges in further surprising modulations, until the three-note motto returns with tremendous volume at the close, finishing quite unexpectedly on an agitated D major chord.

The second movement starts like the song of an ancient minstrel, to the accompaniment of the harp, which is heard immediately in a long Introduction, whose harmonies actually suggest the sustained melody which the English horn soon introduces:

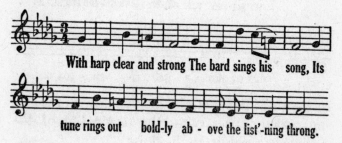

With harp clear and strong The bard sings his song, Its tune rings out bold-ly ab - ove the list'-ning throng.

There is a second broad singing melody, to which the strings play an accompaniment, giving a new effect, although the tones are similar:

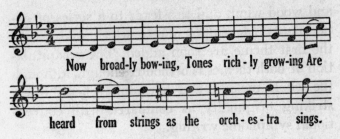

Now broad-ly bow-ing, Tones rich-ly grow-ing Are
heard from strings as the orch-es-tra sings.

This is extended and amplified in various ways, until the English horn picks up the original tune again. Then a soft whispering of strings leads to an entirely new and surprising treatment of the main melody.

Still another tune is heard in this astonishing movement, related to the rest, yet entirely distinctive. (This might be considered as a fragmentary *Scherzo,* introduced before the *Finale*):

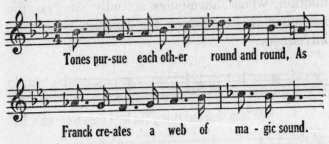

Tones pur-sue each oth-er round and round, As
Franck cre-ates a web of ma-gic sound.

In the *Coda* this material alternates with the second melody, preserving the originality of the movement right up to the finish.

The *Finale,* after a brief Introduction, goes into a zestful syncopated tune, first played in the bass, (here transposed from D to A):

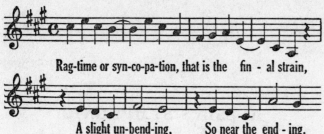

Rag-time or syn-co-pa-tion, that is the fin - al strain,

A slight un-bend-ing, So near the end - ing.

The second tune also hints at modern popular music, for it was literally borrowed for the song, *Mardigras:*

Gay like Mard - i - gras, brass choir, play loud-ly.

Instead of regular development, the main melody of the slow movement is heard, again with the whispering comments of the violins. It appears again still later, but with interruptions and decided rhythmic changes. Finally it starts the *Coda,* with full orchestral volume. Then there is a complete reminder of the syncopated theme of the first movement, in two different keys. The opening motto of the whole symphony is also heard here, completing a final unity which binds together all three movements. It is such workmanship, combined with distinctive melodic invention and close sympathy with the modern style of musical expression, that has made Cesar Franck's single symphony so deservedly popular.

RUSSIA'S SYMPHONIC
CONTRIBUTION

OUTSIDE of Germany and Austria, the country that has contributed most to symphonic literature is Russia. Most of the outstanding Russian composers wrote symphonies, in addition to other works, and the leading Russian composer of to-day, Rachmaninoff, is perhaps best known for his compositions in the symphonic style.

But the most popular of Russian composers is unquestionably Peter Ilyitch Tschaikowsky. (This spelling is the one most generally used, although you will see it also as Tchaikovsky. Remember that the *w* or *v* stands for the sound of *ff*. Pronounce the *ai* like the *y* in shy, making the whole name *Tshy-koff-ski,* with the accent on the second syllable. Never mind his middle name.)

Tschaikowsky lived from 1840 to 1893, mostly in Russia, but also for a time in Switzerland and Italy, besides touring various European cities (and even visiting New York in 1891) as conductor of his own compositions. His life was quiet, but he was inclined to melancholy, and his extremely sensitive, sentimental nature was easily affected by even trivial things about him. He taught at the Moscow Conservatory, and produced a large amount of interesting and effective music, often utilizing Russian folk-songs, although by no means nationalistic in his attitude. His output includes six symphonies, eleven operas, excellent concertos for the piano and the violin (among the most popular of their kind), songs, chamber music, and smaller orchestral works, among which his *Nutcracker Suite, Marche Slav, 1812 Overture* and *Romeo and Juliet Fantasy* stand high in the affections of concert-goers.

The first three symphonies of Tschaikowsky do not require detailed attention, as they are seldom heard in public. But the last three are all masterpieces of the romantic style, each with at least the suggestion of a "program," and all combining melodic beauty, spectacular orchestration, dramatically human appeal, and an impressive command of musical scholarship. Tschaikowsky was for a time almost too popular on the concert stage, and as a result his music is sometimes condemned as obvious and superficial. An examination of his three great symphonies proves the unfairness of such a criticism. About the worst that can be said of Tschaikowsky is that he knew music and life so well that he could make his compositions immediately successful with practically every listener, instead of waiting patiently for the appreciation that every piece of permanent music receives in time.

TSCHAIKOWSKY'S FOURTH SYMPHONY

The story of man's struggle against Fate, so popular with composers in general, and so wonderfully portrayed by both Beethoven and Brahms, must have appealed tremendously to the introspective, poetic soul of Tschaikowsky. Certainly it represents the basic idea of his fourth and sixth symphonies, and possibly the fifth as well. He himself has indicated this in letters regarding the fourth symphony, and it is fairly clear that in this case at least the composer takes the optimistic rather than the pessimistic point of view.

The fourth symphony (1877) opens with a trumpet call (horns and bassoons) which serves as a "motto" for the whole work, reappearing later and giving it a "cyclic" form. This Introduction is quite definitely a challenge to Fate, robust and courageous:

Hark! Ta - ta - ta - ra - ta,   Ta - ta - ta - ta - ra - ta,

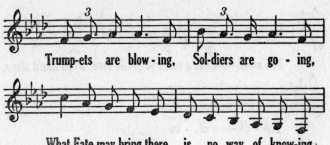

From the later notes of this motto, there is a logical easing into the first theme, which is a series of scale passages, fascinatingly syncopated, with a decidedly cheerful effect.

After much expansion of this material, a second tune enters, rather mocking in spirit, with apparently no serious aim beyond showing off the possibilities of the wood-wind in chromatic scales:

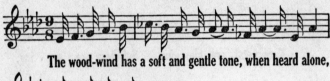

The wood-wind has a soft and gentle tone, when heard alone,

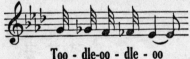

Too - dle-oo - dle - oo

Little interludes in thirds, over a ground bass, punctuated by the drums, alternate with snatches of the first theme:

Thirds in gent-le mot-ion, Like the waves of o - cean

There is also a touch of the major chord pattern, which Beethoven used for the triumphant *Finale* of his fifth symphony (see p. 98) but here coming down instead of going up, as he had it:

Fall in line, For this mus-ic is yours and mine.

Soon the motto is heard again, loudly played by the trumpets themselves, over a long drum roll. This begins the development, which progresses through rhythmic imitations of the first theme, with occasional echoes of the motto, until the melody itself returns, but greatly abbreviated, and in a new key, which is unusual. The chromatic theme of the wood-wind also comes back, conventionally enough, with eventual reminders of the interludes as well.

A tremendous blast on the notes of the motto introduces the *Coda*, which later turns this material into something entirely new, largely by rhythmic changes and a faster time:

From there to the end it is mostly a rush to get to the final F octaves. (The key of the symphony is F minor.)

The second movement starts right in with a plaintive slow melody, inevitably sung by the oboe, but with a second part in a far more encouraging mood. The two might combine like this:*

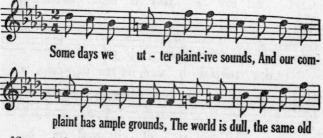

Some days we   ut - ter plaint-ive sounds, And our com-

plaint has ample grounds, The world is dull, the same old

*Some of the notes of the second part have been put down an octave for singing.

things are mak-ing their e-tern-al rounds. No won-der

ev'-ry-one is bored, They all com-plain with one ac-

cord, It seems as tho' there'd ne-ver be a real ex-

cit-ing thing to see, But just the dull rout-ine of

time, With-out a tune, with-out a rhyme.

But now a voice is heard, With Nat-ure's

clear and kind-ly word, We rush out-doors to

see What this ex-cit-ing sound can be.

After a highly decorated repetition of this material, you hear what sounds like an echo of the main tune of the first movement, but turns out to be an anticipation of the subordinate tune for the second. It is sturdy and courageous, square-cut and straightforward:

All to-geth-er, all to-geth-er, Nev-er mind the kind of weath-er, Step-ping for-ward, light-ly danc-ing, Don't you find this life en-tranc-ing?

When the principal theme of this slow movement returns, you get another surprise, for its decorations are unmistakable imitations of the wood-wind scale passages in the first movement, with the flute and clarinet alternating. The *Coda* combines the two parts of the main slow melody in an interesting way, allowing the courageous chords to interrupt the plaintive phrases. The bassoon then sings all of the first part, with a skip in the middle, almost as though it were an oversight, and then, with various instruments making false starts on the same familiar tune, insistent chords allow the whole movement to end very softly.

The third movement is perhaps the most surprising *Scherzo* in all music. It is marked *pizzicato ostinato,* meaning that the plucking of strings continues all the way through. This is not literally true; but the strings do not use the bow at all, and when the brass and wood-wind are heard, they are also *staccato,* as though the tones were actually plucked from their mouth-pieces.

Tschaikowsky himself described this movement as representing vague thoughts, dreams and visions of those people who are trying to forget the cares of life and enjoy themselves. Musically it is remarkable because the three choirs, strings, wood-wind and brass, are all used separately, practically never even overlapping. The main theme is introduced by the strings, playing a very fast *pizzicato:*

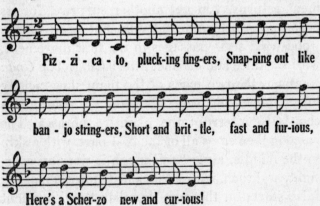

Piz - zi - ca - to, pluck-ing fing-ers, Snap-ping out like ban - jo string-ers, Short and brit - tle, fast and fur-ious, Here's a Scher-zo new and cur-ious!

The *Trio* is played by the wood-wind, still in a snappy, brittle style, although the bass notes are sustained, and here it is easy to imagine the composer's suggestion of gay folk-music:

Hear the sound of a peas-ant song, As the tune runs along.

The brass band interrupts all this with a slower version of the *pizzicato* theme, played in *staccato* chords:

Piz - zi - ca - to now be-

comes stac - ca - to.

The wood-wind passages soon begin to cut into this brazen display, eventually reminding us of the *pizzicato* theme itself, which rouses the strings once more, until, after some false starts, they get together and repeat the whole of the *pizzicato* section.

There is a whimsical *Coda,* in which all three choirs compete, each insisting on its own specialty of tone color. It is a toss-up almost to the end, when the strings softly slip past the other instruments, to win by a neck. (Wind instruments have throats, but no necks.)

The *Finale* has a noisy opening, using the identical notes that start the familiar hymn tune, *Joy to the World,* which Handel composed. Actually they are nothing more than four descending tones of the scale, and if you look back you will be surprised to find that every movement of this fourth symphony of Tschaikowsky's has started with such a descending scale tune. This *Finale* carries it right on down to the bottom, but with a whirl of strings camouflaging the middle:

Joy   to   the world!

The horns begin to play "Hail, hail" (you can hardly keep from adding "the gang's all here") and then the real tune starts. This is an actual Russian folk-song, known as *The Birch Tree,* so why not use words that convey its original meaning?

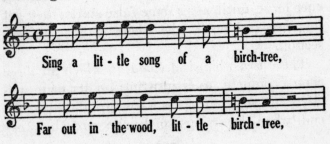

Sing a   lit - tle song   of   a   birch-tree,

Far out in the wood, lit - tle   birch - tree,

Ai lu lu li lu li lu li,

Ai lu lu li, lit - tle birch - tree.

This melody becomes more and more elaborately decorated as the movement proceeds, with the whirling scale passages a favorite form of musical fireworks. It serves as a subordinate as well as principal theme, and gives way only to a recapitulation of the "Joy to the World" opening with new variations. Its own reminder introduces new touches of melody and harmony, and the *Coda* finally shouts it in the bass, while the strings are playing it four times as fast above, in snatches.

The unity of the symphony is established when the motto rings out suddenly, loud and confident, in the brass choir. This is further emphasized by an echo of the phrase that produced so much of the melody of the first movement, and then a variant of "Joy to the World," briefly heard before, becomes a really important tune in its own right:

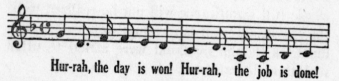

Hur-rah, the day is won! Hur-rah, the job is done!

From there to the end of the symphony everything becomes more and more triumphant, with Fate definitely put in its place and humanity rampant on a field of scales and chords, finishing solidly on the key-note of F major. It is unquestionably a happy ending, and therefore a real achievement for its pessimistic composer.

TSCHAIKOWSKY'S FIFTH SYMPHONY

The date of the fifth Tschaikowsky symphony is 1888, making it a fairly modern work. It has the unusual key of E minor, which up to that time had appeared prominently only in the fourth symphony of Brahms.

It would be easy to interpret this fifth symphony of Tschaikowsky as also a struggle against Fate. But in view of man's recent struggles against himself, which seem far more vitally significant, it may be possible to give it a spiritual meaning, with possible ideals of peace on earth, good will to men. Certainly this interpretation is justified by the religious character of the opening and close of this symphony.

Its Introduction could again be called a motto, whose full significance will not be realized until the *Finale*. Here it is in minor key, rather subdued, as though mankind were afraid to utter such thoughts aloud:

Glor - y to God in the high - est,

Glor - y to God in His Heav - en, And

peace on earth to men, Good will must reign a-

gain. Peace! Peace!

The first real melody is lively with syncopation, a rallying theme to bring people together:

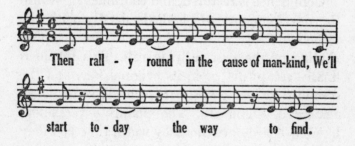

Then rall - y round in the cause of man-kind, We'll

start to - day the way to find.

This is expanded at some length, leading eventually to a confident theme, that seems to fear no opposition:

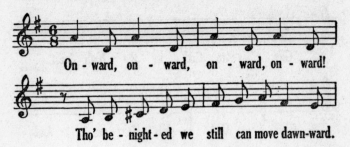

But there are complaints, nevertheless, voiced
in a rather sad and yearning strain, which turns
part of the preceding theme upside down:

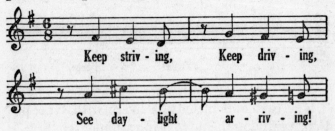

Confidence is restored, and continues right into
the development, which deals mostly with the
second melody, with reminders of the skipping
rhythm of the first rallying call. This theme is
finally recapitulated in its original key, and the
second tune also comes back, with the customary
change of signature. The plaintive version is
likewise heard once more, by which time you may
realize that its accompaniment is taken from a
part of the earlier melody, which has been reversed above. There is plenty of *Coda,* and it all
ends very softly in a low, dying *tremolo.*

The slow movement begins with a minor scale, played in chords, something like the basis of the Brahms *Chaconne* in the *Finale* of his fourth symphony. (See p. 214.) But this is a mere Introduction to a lovely melody sung by the solo horn. This tune was used some years ago as incidental music to the play, *The Song of Songs,* with sentimental words. It would seem to fit the modern situation better thus:

Tell ev'-ry na-tion, All of cre-a-tion, That it is time we should end—— all war-fare. Ut-ter it loud-ly, Ut-ter it proud-ly, "Ye who are wise, ye can bring — your powers to bear." No more in-cit-ing madmen to fight-ing, All of the world, wise and calm, — pro-

gress-ing — ev-er stead-i-ly toward the star gleaming, Goal of man's dreaming, Follow its light thro' the night.

A second strain contains a distinct note of optimism:

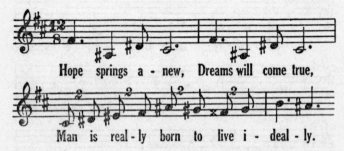

Hope springs a-new, Dreams will come true, Man is real-ly born to live i-deal-ly.

There is some subordinate melodic material, but these two passages stand out and really create the movement as a whole. An echo of the opening motto is heard just before the *Coda,* but this is ignored for the time being, and a long, soft chord finishes one of Tschaikowsky's most popular lyric inventions.

The composer's independence asserts itself again in the third movement, which is a waltz, and a very attractive one. After all, why not a waltz, just as well as a Minuet? It is the same type of dance, adapted to different periods of history. Tschaikowsky may wish to emphasize the fact that he is dealing with ordinary, everyday people, and therefore lets his *Scherzo* take this popular form. In any case, it is not a bad idea at all, and musically it works out very well.

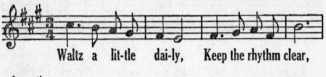

Waltz a lit-tle dai-ly, Keep the rhythm clear,

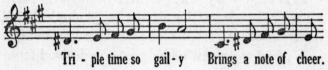

Tri - ple time so gail - y Brings a note of cheer.

There are many variations on this theme, with some contrasting material as well. At the very end the foreboding tones of the introductory motto are heard again, and this time Tschaikowsky is ready to show us what he intends to do with them.

The start of the *Finale* gives it away. The motto has been changed from minor to major key, and you suddenly realize that it has the making of a fine, stirring tune. It is not long before this actually appears, in a triumphant march time, with the strings playing a steady accompaniment of octaves in triplets.

Glo - ry to God in the high - est,

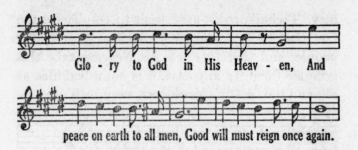

Glo - ry to God in His Heav - en, And peace on earth to all men, Good will must reign once again.

It is fair to say that nowhere in music is there a better demonstration of the psychological difference between the major and the minor moods.

A practically new melody is soon derived from fragments of the preceding, carrying on the spirit of triumph:

When this degenerates into a mere bass rhythm, another tune emerges, even more exultant than what has gone before:

These materials are developed and finally recapitulated in an amazing display of musicianship, with continuous melodic interest and fascinating experiments in orchestration. The original motto interrupts again, in its minor key of long ago, but the orchestra leaves no doubt as to its choice for a finish. It supplies an elaborate accompaniment in E major, just to show what it can do, and after only two measures of this sample, the majestic march begins for the last time, with everybody joining in to make it unanimous.

A *Presto* version of what was already a fast tune seems to hurry us toward the exits, but before we leave we are astonished to hear a great blaring major version of the first theme of the first movement trumpeted by the brass, and it is through this that we reach the final E major chords, a most unexpected close to an extraordinary symphony.

TSCHAIKOWSKY'S PATHÉTIQUE SYMPHONY

For his sixth and last symphony Tschaikowsky supplied the title of *Pathétique* (*Pathetic*), and this is all that is needed to make its program quite clear. It is by far the most pessimistic of the three, and practically unique in symphonic literature in the despairing melancholy of its final movement. Yet it has been easily the most popular of the Tschaikowsky symphonies, and will probably retain this position indefinitely, with increasing recognition of its many masterly strokes and of the true greatness of its conception. It is full of melody, and by no means completely "pathetic," even though pathos and tragedy unquestionably supply its basic mood. The symphony was written in 1893, shortly before the composer's death, which gives its title an added significance.

A soft, mournful Introduction opens the *Pathétique Symphony* with what seems once more a motto, in minor key. (The key of the symphony as a whole is B minor.) But this four-note figure turns out to be the start of the first theme, which is far livelier in tempo and mood.

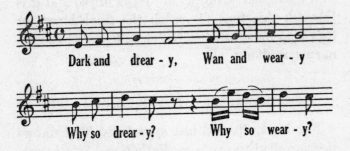

Dark and drear - y,   Wan and wear - y

Why so drear - y?   Why so wear - y?

A great deal of orchestral excitement accompanies the expansion of this theme, with much emphasis on the decorative four notes of its second phrase, until the cellos begin to repeat them monotonously, as if to force the acceptance of a second melody. There seems to be agreement on the part of the other strings, and a beautiful tune enters quietly, with much more of optimism, though still touched with pathos. (The key of the recapitulation is used, as closest to a vocal range.)

This mus-ic has a less path-e - tic strain, It sounds more sane and not so full of pain. Sor - row is end-ed, Grief may be mended, It seems Tschaikowsky will be calm a - gain!

An additional strain follows immediately, with a triple rhythm running through the treble, against pairs of beats in the bass, and then reversing the process in alternating imitation.

The exposition ends very softly, and is interrupted by a sudden and startling crash, which sends the development off at top speed, mostly on snatches from the first theme. Both melodies

are heard again, complete, and at the end a new
and solemn theme rises from the brass, over a repeated downward scale of B major, acting as a
ground bass.

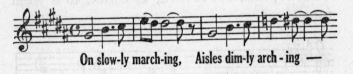

On slow-ly march-ing,   Aisles dim-ly arch - ing —

This *Coda* serves to bring the movement to an
impressive close.

The second movement is one of the few examples of sustained 5-4 time in symphonic music,
full of charm and originality. Actually such a
beat is merely an alternation of twos and threes,
yet it requires the inspiration of genius to keep
such a rhythmic pattern moving consistently, as
Tschaikowsky does. Here is a way to remember
it:

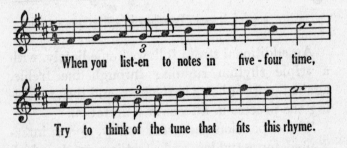

When you   list-en   to notes in   five - four   time,

Try   to   think of   the tune   that   fits   this rhyme.

After several variations of this tune, the composer seems to settle into melancholy once more,

and the subordinate theme is completely pessimistic:

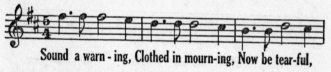

Sound a warn - ing, Clothed in mourn-ing, Now be tear-ful,

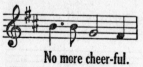

No more cheer-ful.

Even the repetition of the more cheerful melody cannot dispel this mood entirely, and the
movement ends with sorrow predominating.

Now comes one of Tschaikowsky's most original creations. He upsets precedent first of all by
saving his slow movement for the last, and making his third movement practically a *Scherzo*
(*Allegro, molto vivace*); and he also arrives at
his principal theme by the individual method of
building it gradually from short snatches, instead
of conventionally stating it first and breaking it
up later, as most composers would have done.

At the start one hears nothing but galloping
triplets in the strings, softly at first, and gradually becoming louder. Then from various instruments short phrases are heard, easily distinguished by their rhythmic pattern, ending in a
decided syncopation, and these phrases become

steadily more prominent. One *staccato* sequence tries to straighten it out thus:

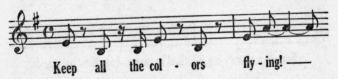

Keep all the col - ors fly - ing! ——

Another works it out in this form, still *staccato*:

Keep all the col - ors

fly - ing, for we'll fight.

But Tschaikowsky refuses to accept any of these suggestions until he has reached the point that would ordinarily demand a subordinate theme. Then suddenly, and at first softly, the whole melody is disclosed, of which there have been only hints thus far, but which has actually been the basis of the entire movement. It will become a triumphant march of victory before long, so its words should have that significance:

Keep all the col - ors fly - ing, For we'll

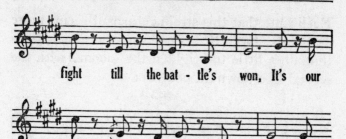

fight   till   the bat - tle's   won,   It's   our

work,   and   it must   be   done.

The rest of the movement is mostly divided between the enjoyment and the anticipation of this melody, for it is never entirely out of sight. Now that we know the trick, it is all the more interesting to follow its tonal course. This is all confidence, joy, optimism, high spirits. If the symphony had ended here, or if this movement had been placed last among the four, Tschaikowsky might have shared popular honors with Beethoven's own courageous *Fate Symphony*. But he deliberately refused the happy ending that most audiences demand, and gave way in his *Finale* to the very depths of hopeless melancholy, with scarcely a redeeming note.

The start of this final movement (*Adagio lamentoso*) is a terrific wail of human disappointment and self-pity:

Why   do   I   feel   so   mourn - ful?

Each time that this strain returns it seems more desperate. Even the second and more melodious tune does little to brighten the gloom (with the second line down an octave):

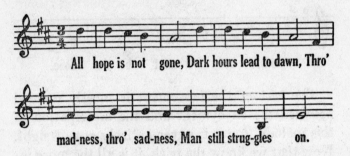

All hope is not gone, Dark hours lead to dawn, Thro'

mad-ness, thro' sad-ness, Man still strug-gles on.

Symphonic conventions of development, recapitulation and *Coda* are forgotten in the sustained gloom of this *Finale*. It is the second theme that holds out to the end, but with emphasis on its most pathetic, wailing measures, and in the minor key of melancholy. Muttering syncopations in the bass hold out no hope. It is all completely tragic, the most thorough expression of introspective misery in the whole literature of music.

RIMSKY-KORSAKOFF'S SCHEHERAZADE

While there are many other Russian symphonies of interest and merit, public approval has concentrated on a work which is really a suite, yet of symphonic proportions, and frequently found in place of a regular symphony on concert programs. This is the *Scheherazade* of Nikolai Rimsky-Korsakoff (1844–1908). (Pronounce each syllable as spelled.)

Since the suite, which was originally a mere succession of disconnected dance movements, actually developed into the symphony as we know it to-day, it is perhaps legitimate to include here the most universally popular example of that form in its larger dimensions. The temptation is the greater because *Scheherazade* is distinctly a piece of program music, representing a series of pictures and stories which the composer himself made quite clear in his published comments.

Rimsky-Korsakoff was one of the group of Russian composers who devoted themselves to restoring the folk elements in the music of their country and making it more truly nationalistic. He was particularly close to Moussorgsky, the outstanding genius of them all, and was to a great extent responsible for the opera, *Boris Godounoff,* as we know it to-day.

An amateur in spirit, and by vocation a naval officer, Rimsky-Korsakoff showed perhaps a greater adaptability than any of his colleagues, and was particularly successful in catching the spirit and melodic outlines of the Oriental music, which is so closely allied to the Russian. His own operas included the fantastic *Coq d'Or* and

Sadko, the latter containing the familiar *Song of India,* which has reached even the fox-trot stage. He wrote symphonies and symphonic poems, as well as smaller orchestral works, but *Scheherazade,* generally called a "symphonic suite," is recognized as his masterpiece, and well deserves inclusion here.

The literary materials of *Scheherazade* are taken from the famous *Arabian Nights.* The name is that of a favorite Sultana, who succeeded in saving her own life and those of her companions by telling the Sultan each night a new story, so that eventually he could not bear to kill her, which had been his habit with wives in general. Thus the stories are literally the *Thousand and One Nights,* and this name appears in the composer's sub-title to his symphonic suite.

Rimsky-Korsakoff made it clear that he did not want this background to be taken too literally. Each movement, to be sure, represents a definite story and a different set of characters, all bound together by the recurrent theme of the solo violin which represents Scheherazade herself, saying "Once upon a time." But the composer says expressly "I meant these hints to direct but slightly the hearer's fancy toward the path which my own fancy had followed, and to leave more detailed and particular conceptions to the will and mood of each listener."

So we are permitted to use our own interpretations throughout, merely following the general outlines of Rimsky's program. In some cases the same theme does duty in several ways, suggesting different characters and episodes. There is much that can be considered merely technical musicianship, with no thought of story or picture. Yet *Scheherazade* is essentially program music of the highest type, bringing us not only a musical account of exciting adventures and fascinating characters, but making vividly real the whole atmosphere of Orientalism by an almost unique command of melodic materials and subtleties of instrumentation.

The suite opens with a brutally domineering theme, played in unison by trombone, tuba, horns, wood-wind and low strings, clearly representing the Sultan Schariar himself, demanding that his bloodthirsty orders be obeyed.

Scha-riar   calls   for his   fair —   Sul - tan - a.

Soft chords answer timidly, and then we hear the voice of Scheherazade herself, beautifully suggested by the solo violin, soaring in florid passages high up on the E string, and definitely announcing the plan which is to keep the cruel Sultan interested and eventually save her life.

Hark! — Sche-her - a - za - de is go-ing to
tell you a wond-er - ful tale! —

The first story is that of Sinbad the Sailor, and
the rocking tones of the cellos immediately create
an illusion of the sea itself in motion. The Sultan's theme now becomes a description of Sin-
bad's ship, as it ploughs through the waves:

Through the sea Sin-bad's ship is plung-ing.

(The trill near the finish may have been originally the Sultan's voice shaking with rage, but
now represents equally well the trembling of the
ship as it battles against the waters.) There is a
real ocean in this music, real sails, real winds
and a real tropical sky, even a bit of a storm and
ensuing calm. The story does not matter. You
can read it in the *Arabian Nights* if you wish.
This music is descriptive rather than narrative at
the moment.

A second melody, calmer and smoother than
the first, might be interpreted thus:

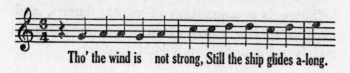

Tho' the wind is not strong, Still the ship glides a-long.

That is all the thematic material Rimsky needs for his first picture. At the end the Sultan is heard again, but the voice of Scheherazade answers bravely, and we have the assurance that at least one more story will be heard.

The second movement is called "The Tale of the Prince Kalendar," and again it is impossible to tell exactly what the story may have been. The voice of Scheherazade is heard again, accompanied by the harp, as before, but with a little more confidence, and closing with a brilliant *cadenza* of musical ornamentation. Then the bassoon begins the story, which evidently deals with a rather grotesque character. (The Kalendars were a species of wandering fakirs, among whom a prince would in any case have some comic significance.)

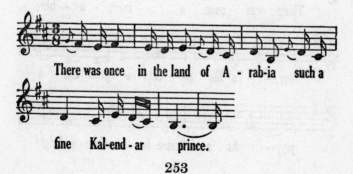

There was once in the land of A - rab-ia such a fine Kal-end-ar prince.

There is a suggestion of exotic dances, and eventually the apparent calm of the scene is rudely interrupted by a loud fanfare:

Hark-en all!— A men-a-cing trum-pet call!

What happens then is enigmatic, but excitement is plentiful. Trumpets answer each other in defiant tones, and there is conflict in the air.

In the third movement the mood becomes quieter again. This musical story has the title "The Young Prince and the Young Princess." According to the original, these two were brother and sister, and known as "children of the Moon." The charming melody at the start immediately suggests the Prince, still in his boyhood:

There was once a re-mark-a-ble

boy,— To his par-ents a pride and a

joy,— As a Prince he was hon-or'd right

254

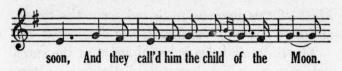

soon, And they call'd him the child of the Moon.

The theme of the Princess enters a little later, more lively in its rhythm, and suggesting an actual Oriental dance:

And a Princ-ess too,— like the

morn-ing dew, Of a beaut-y rare, Quite be-

yond comp-are, In the rhyth-mic beat of her

ti-ny feet There was mu-sic utt-er-ly sweet.

Again the voice of Scheherazade is heard at the close, and it is now apparent that her trick has worked, and that she can go on telling stories to the Sultan indefinitely.

The *Finale* has a compound title: "Festival at Bagdad. The Sea. The Vessel is Wrecked upon a Rock Surmounted by a Bronze Warrior."

Most of this may be gathered from the music, although some of the details are obscure.

The Sultan's voice is heard again at the start, but once more Scheherazade distracts his attention, and the musical description of the Bagdad Festival assures us that he will be occupied for some time to come. This theme is lively and picturesque:

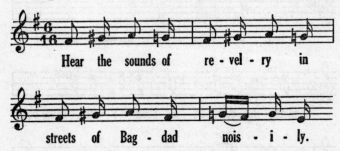

Hear the sounds of re - vel - ry in
streets of Bag - dad nois - i - ly.

There is a second festive melody, derived from earlier materials, but with novel rhythms:

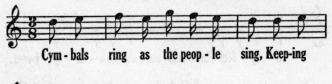

Cym - bals ring as the peop - le sing, Keep-ing

time to a sim - ple rhyme.

We hear echoes of the Princess theme, from the preceding movement. The excitement rises again and again. We are back on the sea once more and this time the storm-winds are unmistakable. The magnetic rock looms up, with the bronze warrior on top. The ship crashes, and all is over. The wood-wind reminds us of the calm after the storm, and Scheherazade utters her story-telling theme once more, through the voice of the solo violin. The Sultan seems by this time persuaded that his wife is worth keeping alive; and the violin soars to exquisite harmonics, as the chords in the orchestra indicate a happy ending.

DVORÁK'S NEW WORLD SYMPHONY

It is fitting that this book should close with an American symphony, even though it was written by a visiting Bohemian. Anton Dvorák (1841–1904) came to New York in 1892, as Director of the National Conservatory, and lived in this country until 1895. (Pronounce his name as if it had an *sh* in the middle of it: Dvoreshock.) Much of the work on his American symphony was done at Spillville, Iowa, where there was a colony of Bohemians, with whom he felt more at home than he did in New York.

Dvorák composed seven symphonies altogether, of which two were published after his death, eight operas, three concertos, two oratorios and other choral works, much chamber music, piano pieces and songs, and some fine orchestral compositions of the smaller type. He taught at the Conservatory in Prague, and had a strong influence on European as well as American musicians. Brahms openly selected him as his own successor in the field of composition, and Liszt also greatly admired his work.

The symphony *From the New World* is number five in Dvorák's list, and by far his best work in that form. Whether it is predominantly American or Bohemian has been much discussed, and really makes little difference. He composed an American string quartet, which contains negro themes, and it is logical to suppose that he was at least influenced to some extent by our negro music, with which he must have been familiar.

The important point is that Dvorák was able to express himself in an individual fashion, under new conditions, producing something that pleased his American listeners (and still does), certainly suggesting enough of the negro idiom to give it a native touch, and yet sacrificing nothing of the instinct for melody that he had inherited abroad, or of the excellent musicianship that characterized all his work. Actually the *New World Symphony* is far more American in spirit than many a composition written by an American born musician, enslaved by European traditions and too timid to try to express what the average hearer will recognize as belonging to the United States.

The *New World Symphony,* completed in 1893, is in E minor. There is a substantial Introduction, mostly for the creation of atmosphere, and then the opening theme sounds in E minor, with an immediate touch of rag-time (syncopation) that appeals to every American:

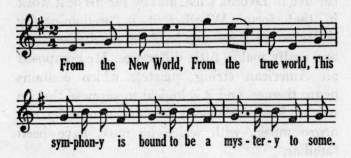

This proceeds in a straightforward fashion until a second melody is heard, perhaps more Bohemian than American:

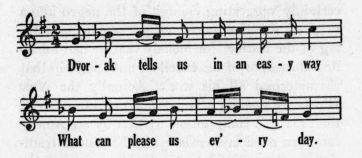

It is the third melody of this first movement that carries the conviction of a negro background. Nobody could overlook its close relationship with the tune of *Swing Low, Sweet Chariot.* (There is an old slave song which is even closer to

Dvorák's theme, but he may not have been aware of this.) A suggestion of the spiritual words is sufficient:

Swing, sweet char-iot, come to take me home;

All the peo-ple wor-ship, ne-ver a-way they will roam.

The development is comparatively simple, dealing entirely with the first melody, which reappears in the recapitulation, along with its melodic successors. The *Coda* contents itself with further treatment of the first theme, leading to E minor chords at the finish.

Now comes the famous *Largo,* the slow movement, which William Arms Fisher has made familiar to a new public by his words, "Goin' Home," accepted by many as an authentic spiritual, but actually a white man's text to a white European's music. You will find it quite easy and satisfactory to sing "Goin' Home" to this melody (it has since been borrowed again for the popular tune of *Wagon Wheels*), and it adds to the negro atmosphere of the symphony, although this can hardly be called basically a negro theme.

The main melody of this slow movement, after

an Introduction of solemn chords, is sung by the English horn, and these words may be a reminder of that fact, and of its plaintive, simple spirit:

English horn, all for-lorn, pipe your plaintive lay,

Dreaming slow, soft and low, What does Dvorak say?

Nothing loud, nothing proud, naught of pomp or pow'r,

Sim-ple song, not too long, shy as hidden flow'r.

Once a - gain, sad re-frain, hear it rise and fall,

Ten-der, true, ev-er new, human heart-throbs' call.

A more agitated theme enters later, with a questioning voice:

Whither a-way? No answer? Whither away? No answer?

Seeming to say "Let the music play, Let's call it a day".

Before the slow, plaintive tune returns, there have been echoes of both the first and the last melodies of the opening movement, giving the symphony a cyclic significance, in the modern style, as used by Cesar Franck and Tschaikowsky. The *Coda* repeats the solemn chords of the Introduction to this movement.

The third movement is a brilliant *Scherzo*, a bit reminiscent of that of Beethoven's ninth symphony in its Introduction, and also of Tschaikowsky's (and Beethoven's) method of building a theme from snatches of melody. The actual tune is brief and self-perpetuating:

Mer-ri - ly   pip-ing,   pip-ing   mer-ri - ly

A *Trio* soon arrives, with a change to the major key and something of the spirit of peasants dancing (again more Bohemian than American) :

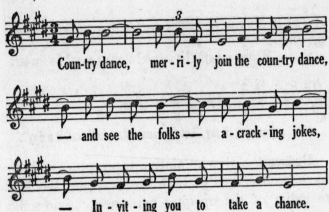

Coun-try dance, mer-ri-ly join the coun-try dance,

— and see the folks — a-crack-ing jokes,

— In-vit-ing you to take a chance.

A loud repetition of the first tune is followed by softer snatches, with interlarded echoes of the opening theme of the whole symphony. Then comes a second *Trio,* melodically rather commonplace, built mostly on the tones of the major chord.

It is a relief to get back to the first sprightly notes and the lively honesty of the first *Trio.* The *Coda* reminds us of the symphony's opening theme once more, whispers snatches of the *Scherzo* tune, and swings from the floor for a final *fortissimo* chord in E minor.

The Introduction to the *Finale* starts with octaves and chords which may have been derived from the chord progression at the beginning and end of the slow movement. But their function is merely to bring on another big E minor theme, which supplies most of the melody for this last movement. It has an almost prophetic sound:

From the New World at last Great songs will be heard, Rebuilt from a glorious past, Toward future achievement spurr'd.

There is an unrestrainedly joyous reaction to this, which expresses itself in a fast, skipping tune, only faintly related to what has gone before, and hardly admitting of words:

A subordinate theme of the *Au revoir* type cuts in soon, with hints of postilion horn-calls in the accompaniment:

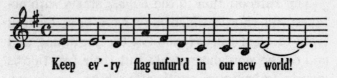

Keep ev'-ry flag unfurl'd in our new world!

After some passages that sound strangely like *Three Blind Mice,* the development alternates the broad and the skipping parts of the earlier melody, and soon arrives at an effect which, whether accidentally or deliberately, is quite obviously American. The broad theme, which has been changed from minor to major key, suddenly has its notes doubled into a rhythmic pattern that strongly suggests *Yankee Doodle,* with some melodic resemblance as well. Try it and see if you agree:

The same effect, with elaborations, appears several times, which makes it seem intentional. The recapitulation of both melodies, however, eliminates further theorizing. There is a long, elaborate *Coda,* starting with a reminder of that syncopated opening theme of the symphony which has been so prominent all the way through, then splitting the first theme of the *Finale* again, with another snatch of the opening, and finally bringing back even bits of the slow movement and the *Scherzo,* a thematic summary such as no symphony had ever made before. It is the syncopated opening that hangs on at the finish, and its octaves eventually form the bass to the E major chords with which the *New World Symphony* inevitably ends.

CONCLUSION

No APOLOGIES are made for restricting the body of this book to thirty-six symphonic works. They are the ones that, on the whole, are most likely to be heard over the radio or on the concert stage, and if anyone has a clear idea of the principles that underly all their individual designs, it will not be difficult to grasp, perhaps even at a first hearing, the significance of some of the compositions that could not be included here.

Emphasis has purposely been laid on the *tunes* of these symphonies, for "by their tunes ye shall know them." If you can recognize one or more themes from each movement of a great symphony, you are in possession of the points of contact which create familiarity. The tunes are the characters in these dramas of absolute music. Their development and treatment constitute plots, conflicts and suspense, just as surely as those factors appear in a play or a novel.

Eventually you will be able to follow all such details of plot, and take the same interest in the

welfare of melodic *dramatis personae* as in the
adventures of any hero or heroine of fiction. Remember always that the human equation is essential to good art. A mere command of formulas
and technique will not make a symphonic composer, any more than the ability to write words
on paper makes a novelist or a playwright. There
must be human interest in the basic materials
as well as in the manner in which they are used.

It has been impossible to avoid the use of some
technical terms, and if the text does not make
these clear at the time, they can be looked up immediately in the Glossary at the back of the book.
Biographical information can also be found
there, both on the composers discussed and on
many others who had to be omitted from the body
of the book. The list of phonograph records
should also be helpful, and it is strongly recom-
mended that they be used whenever possible, so
that the ear can grasp what the eye alone might
not comprehend.

There are many lovely things in the great symphonies which cannot be described in print, or
followed by note, but which a listener of even
limited experience will quickly learn to appreciate. Some of these things have been only briefly
indicated, and some had to be passed by altogether, for fear of burdening the reader with a
mere technical vocabulary. It does not matter if
you are not always aware of what a composer is

doing with his materials. Keep track of them as far as possible, and leave the rest to your instinctive enjoyment of beauty.

If you try to sing the words to some of the tunes, don't worry about the correctness of tempo or key. The main thing is to make it as easy as possible for you to remember these basic materials, for through them alone can you become really familiar with any symphony as a whole. You can easily find out, through records and public performances, how these themes really sound in the orchestra. Please do not under any circumstances sing the words into the ear of a neighbor at a concert.

It may have been gathered by this time that the author of this book is distinctly fond of symphonic music. You are right in that guess, and you can have the same pleasure yourself by simply listening when you have the chance, grasping the more obvious beauties first, and gradually branching out into more and more detail, as though you were coming back again and again to a cathedral, to find something beyond the first impressions of arches and stained glass. A symphony is truly a cathedral in the architecture of music, a climax of absolute and abstract yet human and practical beauty, on which centuries of loving workmanship have been spent to bring it to an aesthetic and spiritual perfection.

QUESTIONS

(For class-room use, or checking up in general)

Pages 1–9

What is the meaning of the word "symphony"? What composer is called "the father of the symphony"? What nickname was applied to him? What are the general characteristics of Haydn's music? How did the *Surprise Symphony* get its title? Sing the first tune in this symphony (after the Introduction). How does the second tune of the first movement go? Sing the melody of the second movement, and clap hands or stamp on the surprise chord. How does the *Menuetto* start? What is the tune of the *Trio?* Sing the main tune of the *Finale* of the *Surprise Symphony.*

Pages 9–17

How did Haydn come to write his "London" symphonies? How many were there altogether? What is the key and date of the symphony specifically called *London?* Describe and sing the opening notes. What is the first real tune? What can you remember of the second tune? How does the *Menuetto* start? Sing or whistle the start of the *Trio.* How does the *Finale* begin? Sing the countermelody. What other tune do you know in this *Finale?*

Pages 17–22

How does the word "clock" apply to Haydn's symphony of that name? Sing the first melody. What is the second tune? What is the rhythmic significance of the second movement? Sing the first tune of this movement. Sing the start of the *Menuetto.* Can you whistle the tune of the *Trio?* What sort of accompaniment has it? Give the two melodies of the *Finale* of the *Clock Symphony.*

Pages 22–29

How did Haydn's *Oxford Symphony* come to be written? Sing the melody of the Introduction and the two other tunes of the first movement. Describe the form of such a movement. Why is it called sonata form? What is the difference between a symphony and a sonata? What is a concerto? Sing the melody of the *Adagio* of the *Oxford Symphony*. What is the Minuet melody? Describe the regular form of a Minuet. How did the *Trio* get its name? Describe the *Trio* in this Minuet. Give the main tune of the *Finale* of the *Oxford Symphony*.

Pages 29–36

Tell what you know about Haydn's *Military Symphony*. Why was it so called? What is the melody of the Introduction? Sing the first and second themes. What is the tune of the second movement of the *Military Symphony*? Sing or whistle the opening of the third movement and the tune of the *Trio*. Sing the main theme of the *Finale* of the *Military Symphony* of Haydn. Which of the Haydn symphonies do you prefer, and why?

Pages 37–47

Give a brief account of the life of Mozart. What were his three outstanding symphonies? How does Mozart's symphony in G minor differ immediately from those of Haydn? What is its opening tune? Give two more melodies in its first movement. Describe the opening of the *Andante* and sing its first theme. What other tune do you know in this movement? Give the tunes of the Minuet and its *Trio*. What are the two tunes of the *Finale* of Mozart's symphony in G minor?

Pages 47–53

How does Mozart's symphony in E-flat differ from the other two? What are the important notes of the Introduction? Sing the themes of the first movement. What is the main melody of the *Andante*? Can you sing a second tune from this movement? Identify the opening melody of the Minuet, singing it if possible. How does the *Trio* go? Sing or whistle the start of the *Finale*.

Pages 53–60

When was Mozart's *Jupiter Symphony* written and what is its key? Can you explain its name? What melodies of the first movement can you remember? How does the slow movement start? What is the chief Minuet melody, and of what does it remind you? What parts of the *Finale* can you sing? How is the *Coda* remarkable? Which of the Mozart symphonies do you prefer, and why?

QUESTIONS

Pages 61-70

Tell what you know about Beethoven and compare him with Haydn and Mozart. What was his method of composing? What are the melodies in the opening movement of Beethoven's first symphony? Sing the tunes of the second movement. What does the word *Scherzo* imply, and how does it relate to Beethoven? Sing the tunes of the Minuet and its *Trio* in Beethoven's first symphony. Describe the start of the *Finale* and sing its two melodies.

Pages 70-76

What was the date of Beethoven's second symphony? How does it differ from the first? What is its key? Give the melodic themes of its first movement. How has the chief slow melody of this symphony become familiar? Can you sing it? What other melodies can you remember in the slow movement? What is a novel feature of the third movement? Give its main melody and that of the *Trio*. What themes of the *Finale* can you sing?

Pages 77-85

What is the name of Beethoven's third symphony and why? Give its date and key, and tell what you know of its history. What tunes can you sing from its first movement? What is the character of the second movement? Can you sing its three melodies? What is the first tune of the *Scherzo?* What does the *Trio* represent, and how does it go? How many tunes can you remember in the *Finale?*

Pages 85-91

Compare Beethoven's fourth symphony with the *Eroica*. What is its date and key? Sing the melody of the Introduction. What other melodies of the first movement do you know? What hymn does the start of the slow movement suggest? Can you sing Beethoven's melody? What are the melodies of the *Menuetto* and its *Trio?* Can you whistle the first tune of the *Finale* and sing the second? (Not at the same time.) What is the form of the *Finale* of the fourth symphony?

Pages 91-101

How many symphonies did Beethoven write? How do you explain the popularity of the fifth? What is its key and date? What do the opening notes represent, and how would you sing

them? How much of the first theme can you remember? What is
the second theme of the first movement? What other melodies
do you recall in this movement? Sing both parts of the slow
melody of the fifth symphony. How is this material treated in
the second movement? With what earlier music could the opening of the third movement be compared? Describe the *Trio* and
whistle some of it if possible. Sing as many tunes of the *Finale*
as you know.

Pages 101–107

What is the name of Beethoven's sixth symphony? How is it
related to the fifth? What are its individual characteristics?
Give Beethoven's explanation of the first movement. Sing the
opening theme. Can you remember any other melodies in this
movement? What did Beethoven call the second movement?
How much of it can you remember? What bird-calls are imitated
in this movement? What is the atmosphere of the third movement, and what did Beethoven call it? What is its main melody?
What natural phenomenon is described next? How did Beethoven
explain his *Finale?* What does the Introduction represent? Sing
the main melody of the *Finale* of the *Pastoral Symphony.*

Pages 107–114

What is the date and key of the seventh symphony? How is it
usually interpreted? What are the two outstanding melodies of
the first movement? Sing the main theme of the second movement
and its countermelody. Can you remember another tune in this
movement? What are the two chief tunes of the third movement
(*Presto*)? Sing or whistle the first tune of the *Finale.* Can you
remember any further melody in this movement?

Pages 114–121

How is Beethoven's eighth symphony related to the seventh?
What is its character and how do they differ? Sing its opening
melody and whistle the second if possible. What is the significance of the second movement? Sing both of its tunes. Sing the
Minuet melody and its *Trio.* Try to sing or whistle the two
melodies of the *Finale* of the eighth symphony.

Pages 121–132

How does Beethoven's ninth symphony differ from all the
others? How long after the eighth was it finished? How early
had he begun to work on it? How much of the first movement

can you remember? (Sing or whistle.) Describe the *Scherzo.*
How many of its tunes can you sing? Sing the opening melody
of the slow movement (*Adagio*). What other themes can you recall in this movement? What is the significance of the opening
of the *Finale?* Describe the steps leading to the announcement
of the choral melody. What poem did Beethoven use to put
words to this melody? Sing it. Describe the various treatments
of this theme. How does the baritone solo introduce it? What
surprising variation on the main theme is given by the orchestra?
What was this type of instrumentation called in Beethoven's
time? What counter-theme is sung by the solo tenor? What new
theme is introduced by the male voices? Describe its treatment.
How does it finally sound in fast time? Which of the Beethoven
symphonies do you prefer, and why?

Pages 133–138

Tell what you know of the life of Franz Schubert. What are
the important points in connection with his *Unfinished Symphony?* What is its key and date? How does the Introduction
go? What is the first theme? Sing the second melody. What modern tune was borrowed from it, and why? Sing the first melody
of the slow movement. What instrument plays the second melody,
and how does it go?

Pages 139–143

When did Schubert write his fifth symphony in B-flat? How
old was he at the time? What earlier composer does its style
suggest? Sing the two melodies of the first movement of this
symphony. What is the main theme of the slow movement? What
is the key of the *Menuetto,* and how does its main tune go? What
change of key does the *Trio* present? How does it go? What are
the two tunes of the *Finale* of Schubert's B-flat symphony?

Pages 143–150

What is the key of Schubert's tenth symphony? When was it
completed, and how close was this date to the death of the composer? Who discovered the symphony and when? By what other
number is it known, and why? What are its general characteristics and with what earlier symphony can it be compared?
What is the melody of the Introduction? Describe or sing the
actual first theme. How does the second tune go? What is the
mood of the opening of the second movement? What instrument
plays the first melody, and how does it go? What other tunes

QUESTIONS

can you remember in this slow movement? How does the *Scherzo* resemble that of Beethoven's ninth symphony? Can you sing its opening theme? What is the second tune? Sing the main melody of the *Trio*? How does the *Finale* open? What is its second tune? What melody appears in the development section, and with what others can it be compared?

Pages 151–158

Tell what you know of the life of Robert Schumann. When was his *Spring Symphony* written and how is its name justified? What instruments play the introductory theme? How does it go? What is the real first melody? Sing the second tune and describe its mood. What is the spirit of the slow movement and how does its opening tune go? What is the form of this movement? What individual device is used in going into the *Scherzo?* What is its opening theme and answer? Name another unusual feature of this *Scherzo.* How do the two *Trios* differ in time? What are their melodies? What new thought appears in the *Finale?* Sing the Introduction. What is the first tune, and how can it be interpreted? Sing the second tune. What part does the introductory theme now play? What other details can you remember in the rest of this symphony?

Pages 158–163

Why is Schumann's fourth symphony incorrectly numbered? What was it originally called? How can it be compared with the *Spring Symphony?* Describe the opening theme, and whistle it if possible. Sing the second tune. What instrument plays the opening of the *Romanze?* What composers later imitated this effect? Sing the melody. How is this slow movement continued by Schumann? What is the spirit of the *Scherzo?* Sing the opening melody. What is the second tune, and how does it change the mood? What are the characteristics of the opening of the *Finale,* and how could it be sung? Can you whistle the second theme of the *Finale?* What memorable tune occurs in the *Coda?* Describe and sing it.

Pages 163–167

How is Schumann's symphony in C major numbered? What is its date? Describe the opening and compare it with other similar effects. Sing it. What is the first real theme? Describe the subordinate theme. In what ways is the second movement original? Describe its opening theme, and whistle it if possible. How does the first *Trio* go? Sing the melody of the second *Trio*. Sing the main melody of the slow movement (*Adagio*). What do you know of the subordinate theme in this third movement? How does the main melody of the *Finale* go? What is the spirit of the finish?

Pages 168–173

What is the date of Schumann's *Rhenish Symphony,* and where does it stand in his life? What number is it generally given, and why? What is the significance of its title? Describe the symphony in general. Sing the opening theme of Schumann's *Rhenish Symphony*. How does the second theme suggest Wagner, and how does it go? What individuality is shown by the *Scherzo?* Sing its chief tune. What is the key of this symphony, and what other Wagnerian relationship does it suggest? What is the main theme of the slow movement? In what way does Schumann upset the conventions of the symphony after the slow movement? How can you characterize this additional movement? Sing its chief theme. In what spirit does the *Finale* open? Sing its first melody. Describe and sing the second theme of this *Finale*. Which of Schumann's four symphonies do you like best, and why?

Pages 174–179

What do you know of Mendelssohn's life? What are his two most popular symphonies? Which was written first, and when? Explain the name of the *Italian Symphony*. Sing its opening theme. What is the second melody? How is this material developed? What is the character of the second movement? Sing its first theme. What is the second tune? How does the form of this movement differ from the conventional? What is the opening tune of the third movement? Its spirit? How does the *Trio* begin, and what instruments are used? How does the *Finale* justify the name of the symphony? Sing or whistle its main tune.

Pages 179–184

What was the date of Mendelssohn's *Scotch Symphony?* How did it get its name? What is its key? Sing the Introduction. How does the first theme go? Sing the second theme. What is the Scotch characteristic appearing in the second movement? Sing or whistle the main theme. What is the second theme, and how does it differ in scale from the first? How does the mood change

In the third movement? Sing both its melodies. What is the mood of the *Finale?* Sing its chief melody. Which of these two symphonies of Mendelssohn do you prefer, and why?

Pages 185–194

Give a brief summary of the life and personality of Brahms. With what earlier composers can he be compared? Give the date and key of his first symphony. What program does it suggest, paralleled by what earlier symphony? What is the significance of the Introduction? Sing the first theme. Describe the first movement and sing as much of it as you can. What is the mood of the second movement? Sing its opening melody. What is the significance of the oboe melody that follows? Sing it. How does the orchestra take up this melody? What important change occurs in the opening theme? How could it be sung? How does the third movement start? What is the instrumentation of the melody? What other suggestions of the Beethoven fifth symphony do you find? Sing the answer to the challenge of Fate. Sing the chief theme of the *Finale.* How does Brahms suggest the Westminster Chime? Sing this brief theme. What is the final theme introduced by the brass?

Pages 194–201

How does the second Brahms symphony suggest a new parallel with Beethoven? What is its key and date? What novel feature appears at the start? What is the pattern of the opening theme, and where else did he use similar effects in the same key? Sing the opening melody as far as possible. Can you whistle any of the phrases that follow this? What is the spirit of the second tune, and how does it go? How did Brahms become familiar with gypsy music? Sing the opening theme of the second movement. Can you whistle its subordinate theme? How does the third movement start, and what is the instrumentation? How does Brahms change this tune? How does he handle the *Trio?* What is the character and tune of the first theme of the *Finale?* Sing the second melody. Describe the rest of the symphony.

Pages 201–208

Which of Beethoven's titles might be applied to the third symphony of Brahms? What is its date and key? How did Brahms interpret the opening notes? Can you sing this motto? What is the first theme? Sing the second theme. How is the first theme changed at the close of the first movement? What is the character of the second movement? What is the instrumentation at the start? Sing the main melody. What earlier melody, by another composer, is suggested by the start of the third movement? What is its instrumentation here? Can you sing the Brahms theme? Give the second theme of the third movement. What solo instrument appears in a reminder of the first theme? What is the opening of the *Finale* of the third symphony of Brahms? What other details and melodies can you remember in this movement? How is the ending of the symphony individual?

Pages 208–215

Give the date and key of Brahms' fourth symphony. Describe and sing its opening theme. What are the two melodies of its second theme? What individual touches are found in the recapitulation? Describe the opening of the slow movement. Sing the main melody. What is the second theme, and by what instruments is it introduced? What is the character and melody of the opening theme of the third movement? Describe and sing the subordinate theme. What new melodic idea is introduced before the close of the movement? Describe the character and structure of the *Finale*. Sing the basic theme. What do you know about the *Chaconne* and *Passacaglia* forms? Which title could best be applied to this movement, and why? How many variations on the basic theme does this movement contain? Try and follow these variations in an actual hearing of the *Finale*. Which of the four Brahms symphonies do you like best, and why?

Pages 216–221

Tell what you know of the life of Cesar Franck. How is his one symphony significant? What is its date and key? How does it differ from most other symphonies? What is its introductory motto, and how can it be interpreted? Sing it. How do these notes sound in faster time, as in the first theme? What other melodies in the first movement can you remember? What does the start of the second movement suggest? What two instruments are prominent, and which is heard first? Sing the main melody. What is the second theme? Can you remember a third? What is the syncopated tune of the *Finale?* Sing the second tune. What earlier melody is first brought back in the *Finale,* and how is it used? What other earlier parts of the symphony are heard in the *Finale?* What term is applied to such reminders of earlier material?

QUESTIONS

Pages 222–234

What significance has Russia in the symphonic field? Who is the most popular Russian composer? Give a summary of his life. How many symphonies did Tschaikowsky write? Which ones are outstanding? What basic idea is common to these symphonies? What is the motto of Tschaikowsky's fourth symphony, and how can it be interpreted? Sing the opening theme. What instruments are featured in the second tune? How could it be sung? What other melodic materials of the first movement can you remember? How does the first tune appear in the *Coda?* What is the key of this symphony? Sing both parts of the opening melody of the second movement. What instrument first carries the tune? How does the second tune go? What are some of the devices used by Tschaikowsky in the rest of this movement? What are the individual characteristics of the *Scherzo?* How did the composer describe it? Can you sing or whistle the main theme? How does the *Trio* go? What is the brass version of the *pizzicato* theme? Describe the *Coda.* How does the *Finale* open? What hymn does it suggest? What was the main melody originally, and how is it introduced? Sing it. How is it treated later in the movement? In what way does Tschaikowsky achieve a final unity? What variant of the opening tune is heard? What is the spirit of the finish?

Pages 234–241

Give the date and key of Tschaikowsky's fifth symphony. How can it be interpreted as a whole? What is the motto? Sing the first theme. How could it be interpreted? What rhythmic characteristic has it? Sing the second theme. How is this theme partially inverted? Which melody is most prominent in the development section? How does the slow movement begin, and of what does this remind you? What is the chief melody, and what instrument has it first? Give the second strain of this melody. What modern dance form appears in the third movement? Sing the main theme. How is the motto used at the start of the *Finale?* Sing the major theme that results from this change. What other tunes can you remember in the *Finale?* What earlier material is introduced at the close?

Pages 241–248

What can you tell about Tschaikowsky's sixth symphony? Give its date, key and special name. Sing the introductory notes.

QUESTIONS

How are they related to the first theme? What is the second theme? What additional melody appears near the close of the first movement? What rhythmic individuality appears in the second movement? How could the main theme be sung? What is the subordinate theme, and what is its mood? What original ideas does the *Scherzo* contain? What can you remember of the preliminary snatches of the main theme? How does the theme itself go? How does the last movement differ from the conventional *Finale*? What is its opening theme? Can you sing the second melody? What is the final effect of the *Pathétique Symphony* of Tschaikowsky? Which of these three symphonies by Tschaikowsky do you prefer, and why?

Pages 248–257

What do you know about Rimsky-Korsakoff? Why is his *Scheherazade* included among symphonies? On what famous collection of stories is it based? What does its title mean? Would you call this absolute (pure) or program music? How can the opening theme be interpreted and sung? What is Scheherazade's personal theme and what does it represent? What is its first instrumentation? Can you sing it? What is the first story and how is it suggested by the music? How is its main theme related to earlier material in the suite? Sing it in its new form. What is the second theme? How does the movement end? What is the title of the second movement? How does it open? What is the main theme? What other melodic material can you remember? What is the title of the third movement, and what story is its basis? Sing both of the melodies. How does this movement end? What subjects are treated in the *Finale*? How does it open? Sing the Bagdad Festival theme. What second melody can you remember? What materials return in the remainder of the movement? How is the close worked out, and what is its significance?

Pages 258–270

Give some biographical details concerning Dvořák. When and where was his symphony *From the New World* written? What is its significance in relation to the United States? What is its key? Sing the opening theme. What is its outstanding rhythmic characteristic? How does the second theme go? Can you sing the third melody? What negro spiritual does it suggest? By what words is the *Largo* best known? What solo instrument is heard near the start? Sing the melody. What is the agitated

QUESTIONS

theme that follows? What earlier melodies are echoed in this movement? What is the main theme of the *Scherzo?* How does the *Trio* go? Can you remember the second *Trio?* What is the main theme of the *Finale?* What other melodies can you remember in this movement? What American tune is suggested in the development? What earlier material appears before the close? Which of all the symphonies in this book are your favorites? What final comments can you make on symphonies in general?

GLOSSARY OF SYMPHONIC TERMS

A. The first letter of the musical alphabet, representing the sixth tone in the perfect scale of C major. The tone to which the whole orchestra tunes; the second highest string of the violin. Also an Italian and French preposition, meaning to, at, by, in, etc. *A tempo:* literally "in time", i.e. returning to the tempo used earlier; *a cappella:* in the manner of a choir, referring to unaccompanied vocal music; *a capriccio:* at pleasure, in a free style; *alla breve:* common time (4–4) with two instead of four beats to a measure, indicated by a vertical line through the signature (C), and usually making the tempo twice as fast as otherwise; *alla marcia:* in march style; *alla moderna:* in modern style; *alla turca:* in Turkish style (with cymbals, triangle, etc.); *alla zingara:* in gypsy style.

Absolute music. Pure music, without aid of words, descriptive title, or a "program" of any kind. See Program Music. Most symphonies are absolute music, depending for their appeal on the tonal patterns of rhythm, melody, harmony, tone color and form, instead of a musical story or picture.

Accelerando. Italian term meaning "growing faster".

Accent. Emphasis on a particular note, either through playing it louder than the rest, or through its length, or its position at the start of a measure (where it automatically receives the strongest beat of the time).

Accidental. A sharp, flat or natural sign (and the resulting tone) occurring irregularly, not part of the general key-signature of a composition.

Accompaniment. The music that accompanies a melody.

Acoustics. The science of musical tones caused by regular vibrations of the air (as distinguished from noises, caused by irregular vibrations). The acoustics of an auditorium are considered good or bad according to the effectiveness of a musical performance or spoken words from the stage.

Adagio. Slow time, hence a slow movement in a symphony. *Adagietto:* slightly faster than *Adagio;* also a shorter *Adagio* movement.

Adaptation. An arrangement of music, differing from its original form.

GLOSSARY OF SYMPHONIC TERMS

Ad libitum. At pleasure, in free style. Generally shortened to *ad lib.*

Agitato. Italian word meaning "agitated". Commonly used of *tremolo* chords or single notes rapidly repeated, but also of an agitated style.

Air. Melody, tune.

Al, alla. To the, in the, in the style of, etc. See under *A* above.

Allargando. Italian for "growing slower".

Allegro. Literally "happy, cheerful", hence, lively, in rapid time. Frequently applied to the first movement of a symphony, particularly after a slow introduction. *Allegretto:* not as fast as *Allegro.*

Allemande. A German dance, appearing as one of the movements of the classic suite.

Alto. The deeper female voice, singing the second part in a mixed quartet, also known as contralto. Often applied to the second part in any harmony, and to instruments playing such a part (especially horns). There is also an alto-clef, infrequently used.

Amateur. Literally one who does a thing for the love of it, hence a non-professional in music. An amateur may be an excellent performer, and the term should be considered a compliment rather than an insult.

Andante. Italian for "going, moving, walking"; hence a moderately slow pace in music, faster than *Adagio,* but slower than *Allegretto.* Frequently applied to the slow movement of a symphony.

Andantino. Literally, a little slower than *Andante,* but often used to mean a little faster. Also a short *Andante* movement.

Animato. Italian for "animated", lively.

Answer. The second statement of the subject of a fugue, at a different pitch from the first. Also used of an answering phrase or theme in general.

Appassionato-a. Italian (masculine or feminine) for "passionate", impassioned.

Appoggiatura. Italian for "grace-note", a small note attached to another, as an introduction (known in modern popular music as a "blue note").

Arco. Italian for the bow of a stringed instrument, like the violin. The word appears in symphonic music when bowing is to be resumed after a *pizzicato* (plucked) passage. See *pizzicato.*

Aria. An air, tune or melody, usually for a single voice or instrument.

Arpeggio. Literally "in the manner of a harp", applied to broken chords.

Arrangement. Adaptation of a composition for other instruments than those for which it was originally written.

Assai. Italian for "sufficiently", hence "very". (Not so strong an expression as the Italian "molto"). It may be added to any indication of tempo.

Attacca. Attack. Used to indicate that the following music should be played without any intervening pause (as when one movement of a symphony leads directly into the next).

Attack. The agreement of voices or instruments at the start of a phrase or passage.

GLOSSARY OF SYMPHONIC TERMS

Augment. To increase in value. An augmented interval has an additional half-tone. Augmentation of a theme means an increase in the length of the notes, thus slowing up the time (as in substituting half-notes for quarter-notes).

Auxiliary note. A note not essential to the melody or harmony. A grace-note.

B. The second letter of the musical alphabet, and the seventh tone in the perfect scale of C major. (The Germans use the letter B for the tone of B-flat and give the tone generally known as B the letter H.)

Bag-pipe. Ancient wind instrument, providing the monotonous tone known as a "drone-bass".

Band. A company of musicians. Now applied specifically to a brass band, as differentiated from an orchestra, or to a jazz or dance band. Also used of one section of a symphony orchestra, such as the wood-wind or brass.

Bar. The vertical line that divides one measure from another. Loosely used as a name for the measure itself, as in "counting bars".

Baritone. The male voice between bass and tenor. Also an instrument in that range.

Bass. The lowest tone in a chord; also the lowest part in a harmony. The lowest male voice. Also an abbreviation of double-bass, meaning the bass viol. Bass clef: the sign used to establish the notation for the lower parts of a harmony or accompaniment, or for bass instruments or voices. In piano music it is regularly used for the lower line (in contrast to the treble clef above) and in an orchestral score it appears most frequently in the music of the cellos, bass viols, bassoons, trombones, tuba, etc.

Basset-horn. A tenor clarinet.

Basso. Italian word for bass. *Basso continuo:* a figured bass, the figures indicating the chords to be played above the bass notes. *Basso ostinato:* a sustained bass, or ground-bass, using the same pattern over and over.

Bassoon. The bass instrument of the wood-wind choir in a symphony orchestra. There are usually at least two, and often a double-bassoon or contra-bassoon as well, with a still lower range. The bassoon has a long, wooden tube, extending above the player's head, and is played through a curved mouthpiece entering at the side. Part of the tube is doubled over, which gives the bassoon its German name of *Fagott,* Italian *Fagotto,* meaning a faggot, or bundle of sticks. The tone is created by a double reed, as in the oboe, and has a mellow quality, capable also of humorous implications.

Baton. The stick with which a conductor beats time and makes other motions, some of which are quite unnecessary.

Beat. The movement of the conductor's hand or stick, to indicate the time. Also the fraction of a measure representing a unit of time. 4–4 or "common" time has four beats to the measure, 2–4 has two, 3–4 has three, etc. In conducting, the "down-beat" comes on accented notes, and the "up-beat" on unaccented. Strictly speaking, the first note of every measure should be indicated by a down-beat.

Bel. Italian word for "beautiful". *Bel canto:* beautiful song, i.e. the

Italian style of smooth, melodious singing, as contrasted with the declamatory type.

Bell. A metal instrument of percussion, often without definite pitch. Also the bell-shaped opening of such an instrument as the French horn.

Ben. Abbreviation of the Italian *bene,* meaning "well". *Ben marcato:* well marked; *ben sostenuto,* well sustained (of a melody).

Berceuse. Cradle-song, lullaby (French).

Binary. Two-part. *Binary form:* having two principal themes.

Body. The main part of an instrument.

Bourrée. A French dance, appearing in the classic suite.

Bow. The stick strung with horse-hair which sets a string in vibration, as on a violin. The horse-hair is rubbed with rosin to make it bite into the string. See *Arco.* A tone can be sustained as long as the bow is passing across a string, and it can also be moved rapidly back and forth to produce a *tremolo* or *agitato* effect. Pressure of the bow determines the loudness or softness of the resulting tone. The skill of a violinist is determined largely by the bowing, which is done by the right hand, while the left controls the pitch of the tones. In a well trained orchestra the bowing of each section of string players is uniform, all moving up or down at the same time.

Brass. The adjective applied in general to all wind instruments made of metal (except the silver flute, which is included among the wood-wind, as it was originally made of wood). The brass choir or section of a symphony orchestra includes trumpets, trombones and bass tuba, as well as French horns, although these are generally seated with the wood-wind. A brass band uses mostly metal instruments, including cornets, alto horns, etc. For popular music, the saxophone is added to the brass instruments.

Bratsche. German for viola.

Bravura. Italian for boldness, dash, brilliancy.

Bridge. That part of a stringed instrument which holds the stretched strings above the body or sound-box, communicating their vibrations to the resonance chamber. The bridge of a violin is made of thin wood, arched and cut in decorative scrolls, with feet that fit the curve of the body.

Brillante. Italian for brilliant, showy.

Brio. Italian for fire. *Con brio:* in fiery style.

Broken chord. A chord whose tones are sounded in succession instead of simultaneously. See *Arpeggio.*

Bugle. A familiar wind instrument of metal, with limited range of tones, on the pattern of the major chord. These tones have a military sound, by association.

Burden. A refrain. Also a drone-bass, as from a bag-pipe.

C. The third letter of the musical alphabet, and keynote of the perfect scale of C major, which has no sharps or flats.

Cadence. The close of a movement, or of a theme, section or phrase. Perfect cadence: the tonic chord, preceded by the dominant; also called full, whole and authentic cadence. Half or imperfect cadence: the dominant chord, preceded by the tonic (therefore not a complete stop). Plagal cadence: the tonic chord preceded by the subdominant (as in the familiar Amen). The word "cadence" is also used for *cadenza* (see below) and sometimes to indicate rhythm.

Cadenza. Italian for an elaborate interlude, technically brilliant, to show off a soloist. It has the effect of improvisation, and is usually unaccompanied, based on themes that have already been heard. Soloists often write their own *cadenzas* for concertos. *Cadenzas* are frequent in vocal music of the coloratura style.

Calando. Italian for growing softer, and sometimes slower.

Calmato. Italian for calmly.

Camera. Italian for chamber, small room. *Alla camera:* in the manner of chamber music.

Campanello-a. Italian for a small bell (masculine or feminine).

Cancel. To eliminate a sharp or flat in the signature (or within a measure) by the sign of the natural.

Canon. A melody harmonizing with itself, by overlapping or identical imitation in another key. When the imitation is in the same key (strict canon), the effect is the same as a round, like *Three Blind Mice.*

Cantabile. Italian for a singing style. (Accent the second syllable.)

Cantata. A type of vocal music, often sacred, using soloists and chorus, with instrumental accompaniment. (Originally any vocal piece).

Cantilena. Italian for a little song, hence a melodic passage or style.

Canto. Italian for song, hence melody. See *Bel canto.*

Cantus firmus. Latin for a given melody or "plain song"; the main melody in a passage of counterpoint (other melodies harmonizing with it).

Canzone. Italian for a song, particularly a folk-song or part-song.

Canzonet-ta. A short song or melody of the vocal type.

Capo. Italian for head, hence beginning, start. *Da capo:* repeat from the beginning. *Da capo al segno:* repeat from the beginning to a certain sign.

Cappella. Italian for chapel, hence choir, chorus, sometimes an orchestra or both combined. Note the spelling. See *a cappella.*

Capriccio. Italian for caprice, hence a whimsical piece. *A capriccio:* at pleasure.

Carillon. (French). A set of bells (see *Glockenspiel*), or the music for such an instrument; also a bell-tower.

Castanets. Percussion instruments (clappers) of wood or ivory, generally used in Spanish rhythms.

Catgut. The material from which violin strings are made, according to general assumption. Actually the gut comes from sheep.

Cavatina. Italian for a broadly melodic song or aria.

Celesta. A tinkling instrument like a small piano, often appearing in modern orchestration.

Cello. Abbreviation of violoncello (which see).

Cembalo. Italian name for the old-fashioned harpsichord or early pianoforte.

GLOSSARY OF SYMPHONIC TERMS

Chaconne. (French). Originally a Spanish dance. Technically a series of variations on a bass melody, as in the *Finale* of Brahms' fourth symphony.

Chamber music. Music that can be played in a small room, such as string quartets, sonatas, etc., as compared with orchestral or choral music or opera.

Change. Modulation, moving from one key to another.

Chant. A sacred song, or a melody in that style, usually with choral effect.

Chapel. The band of musicians employed by a musical patron (representing the early forms of orchestras and choirs). See *Cappella, Kapellmeister.*

Characters. Musical signs.

Chef d'orchestre. French for orchestral conductor.

Chime. A set of bells, usually metal tubes suspended from a frame, and struck with a hammer; also of the keyboard type, or *carillon.*

Chin-rest. A piece of hard rubber or ebony attached to the violin to support the chin of the player.

Choir. A group of singers, a chorus, particularly in church. In a symphony orchestra the word is applied to the various groups of instruments (strings, wood-wind, brass).

Choral. Pertaining to a chorus or choir; applied to instrumental music that has the effect of choral voices. As a noun, also spelled *Chorale,* a sacred melody or hymn-tune of the German Protestant type, such as Bach arranged.

Chord. A harmony of tones, usually three or more, sounding simultaneously.

Chorus. A group of singers, or choir. Also the refrain in vocal music.

Chromatic. Literally, colorful; relating to tones not a regular part of the diatonic scale (indicated by sharps and flats). The chromatic scale includes all the half-tones (black and white keys) and has twelve different tones in an octave.

Clarinet. An important member of the wood-wind family, played by a single reed, with a range of three octaves. Its tone is mellower than that of the oboe, which it resembles in shape, and it is often given important solos in symphonic music. There are always at least two clarinets in a symphony orchestra. In a brass band the clarinets take the place of the violins of the orchestra. The clarinet is a transposing instrument, generally tuned in B-flat or A. Sometimes spelled clarionet, *clarinetto.*

Clarion. A small, shrill trumpet.

Clavichord. A forerunner of the pianoforte, using metal wedges or "tangents" instead of hammers.

Clavier. Literally a key-board; also used for clavichord and pianoforte. See *Klavier.*

Clef. Literally key. A character or sign set at the start of a piece of music to indicate the pitch of all the following notes. Each line and space on the staff represents a different note, according to the clef at the start. The commonest clefs are the treble and bass, appearing regularly in piano-music.

Close. A cadence (which see).

Coda. Italian for tail; hence the closing section of a movement. In sonata form the *Coda* became increasingly important, as illustrated by the symphonies of Beethoven and Brahms. It may present entirely new material, or merely state some of the preceding material in a different way.

Codetta. A short *Coda;* often applied (as by Goetschius) to themes of minor importance in a symphonic movement.

Color. Tone quality or *timbre,* created by overtones.

Coloratura. Literally colorful, referring to the brilliant technical feats of a singer with a flexible voice. Also applied to instrumental music.

Come. Italian for "as, like". *Come prima:* as before. (See *a tempo*).

Common chord. A triad (three-tone chord). Common time: four beats to a measure.

Comodo. Italian for easily, at a leisurely pace.

Compass. The range of an instrument or voice.

Con. Italian for "with", frequently used to indicate musical expression. *Con moto:* with animated movement.

Concert. A musical performance. (Originally a band of players).

Concert-grand. The large pianoforte generally used on the concert stage.

Concert-master. The leader of the first violins in a symphony orchestra. He is responsible for their correct bowing, and often plays solo passages.

Concerto. A sonata for a solo instrument with orchestral accompaniment.

Concord. Harmony, consonance.

Conduct. To lead an orchestra.

Conductor. The leader of an orchestra.

Consonance. A harmonious combination of two or more tones, a concord.

Consonant. Containing no dissonant intervals.

Continued bass. Bass notes with figures to indicate the chords to be played above them. Also called *basso continuo,* figured bass.

Contra. Latin and Italian prefix meaning literally "against"; used to indicate a lower range in instruments. *Contrabass:* double bass, or bass viol. *Contrabassoon:* double bassoon (an octave below the regular instrument).

Contralto. See *Alto.*

Contrapuntal. Pertaining to counterpoint, or written in that style.

Cor. French for horn. *Cor anglais:* the English horn, or alto-oboe, an important instrument of the wood-wind, often used for solos, as in the *Largo* of Dvořák's *New World Symphony,* and the slow movement of the Cesar Franck symphony.

Corda. Italian for string.

Cornet. A brass instrument similar to a trumpet, but easier to play. Common in brass bands, but not generally found in orchestras.

Corno. Italian for horn.

Count. A beat or accent in a measure. Also as a verb, to keep time by counting.

Counter. Prefix meaning "against". Counterpoint: music written "point against point", i.e. note against note, polyphonically, one melody harmonizing with another. ("Horizontal music".) Countermelody: a melody harmonizing with another.

Country dance. A peasant dance, usually in lively rhythm.

Courante. An old French dance, sometimes appearing in suites.

Crescendo. Italian for increasing in volume.

Crook. A short tube which can be fitted into a horn to change its pitch.

Cyclical. Referring to compositions having a set or cycle of movements, like a symphony. Now used to indicate that the material of earlier movements reappears later, as in Cesar Franck's symphony.

Cymbals. Percussion instruments of brass or bronze, making a clashing noise.

D. The fourth letter of the musical alphabet and the second tone in the perfect scale of C major. Its key-signature is two sharps.

Da. Italian preposition meaning "from, by, of". See *capo. Dal segno:* from the sign.

Damper. A device for checking vibrations, a mute.

Deciso. Italian for "decided", energetic.

Declamando. In a declamatory style.

Decrescendo. Opposite of the Italian *crescendo,* meaning a gradual softening in volume.

Degree. A step, as in the scale. Degrees are counted upward from the key-note.

Del-la,-lo. Italian preposition and article, meaning "of the", etc.

Delicatamente. Delicately (Italian).

Descant. See *Discant.*

Development. The middle or contrasting section in sonata form, used in the first movement of a symphony, sonata, concerto, etc. elaborating thematic materials. Also known as "free fantasia". Any treatment, evolution or working out of a theme may also be called development in a general sense.

Di. Italian preposition, meaning "of, from, by".

Diapason. The interval of the octave. Also the foundation-stop in an organ.

Diatonic. Literally "by tones", referring to the standard major or minor scale.

Diminish. To lower an interval by half a tone (if it is already perfect or minor). Diminished chord: a chord whose top and bottom form a diminished interval.

Diminuendo. Italian for "decreasing in volume". (Similar to *decrescendo*).

Diminution. Repeating or imitating a theme in shorter notes, hence faster time.

GLOSSARY OF SYMPHONIC TERMS

Direct. To lead or conduct, or to have charge of a performance.

Discant (Descant). An early form of polyphony; also a melody harmonizing with the "cantus firmus". Also the highest part in vocal harmony.

Discord. Dissonance, cacophony.

Dissonance. Two or more tones not in consonance, requiring resolution.

Divisi. Italian for "divided", meaning that individual instruments in the same section play different parts (mostly used of the violins).

Do. The Italian name for C; still used in the Sol-fa system of reading music, for the first note of the scale.

Dolce. Italian for "sweet", hence soft, gentle.

Dominant. The fifth tone in a major or minor scale. Dominant chord: a chord built on the dominant. Dominant key: the key of the fifth above the tonic, often used for the second theme in the first movement of a symphony.

Doppio. Italian for "double". *Doppio movimento:* twice as fast.

Dot. A period set after a note, increasing its length by one-half its original time-value. Thus a dotted half-note becomes three quarters. Dots are also used above notes to indicate *staccato* (short) playing.

Double. An octave lower, as in double bass, double bassoon, etc. (See *contra.*) Also used of adding an octave to a note, above or below. Also in popular music, to play more than one instrument.

Double sharp. The sharp of a sharp, indicated by a cross. (A double flat is written as two flats, close together. These signs occur frequently.)

Double stop. Stopping two strings at once, and thus producing two tones simultaneously (as on a violin).

Double tongue. A way of getting rapid, *staccato* effects from wind instruments.

Down-beat. The downward motion of the conductor's hand or stick, representing the accented beat. Also the accent itself, or the first beat of a measure.

Down-bow. The action of drawing the bow downward over the string, or from the bottom to the top of the bow.

Drone. A monotonous tone, as in a drone-bass, which repeats the same tone continually. (See *bag-pipe, musette.*)

Drum. The commonest instrument of percussion, played with sticks on a head of skin stretched over a hollow body. The bass drum and side-drum (snare-drum) have no definite pitch. But kettle-drums (see *tympani*) are tuned to individual notes, generally the tonic and dominant of the key in which a composition is written. They can also be tuned during performance. There is a Chinese drum, of wood, popular in dance-bands. The tambourine is also a form of drum.

Duet. A composition or passage for two voices or instruments.

Dulcimer. A forerunner of the pianoforte, played with hammers on strings.

Duo. Duet.

GLOSSARY OF SYMPHONIC TERMS

Duple. Literally double. Duple time: a time-beat running in multiples of two (2–4, 4–4, etc.).

Dur. German for "major". (See *Moll.*)

E. The fifth letter in the musical alphabet, and the third tone in the perfect scale of C major. The signature of the scale of E major is four sharps. E is the top string of the violin, a fifth above A, by which it is tuned. The letter e is also the Italian word for "and" (changed to ed when followed by a vowel) and this appears frequently in musical directions.

Echo. The repetition of a strain or pas.. ge, generally more softly. Used also of a special stop and set of pipes in an organ.

Eighth. The interval of the octave, the eighth step above the key-note. Also used to mean an eighth note, one eighth as long as a whole note of four beats.

Embellishment. A decoration, like a grace-note.

English horn. Literal translation of *cor anglais,* the alto oboe.

Espressivo. Italian for expressively. Same as *con espressione.*

Essential. A sharp or flat belonging to the key-signature.

Étude. A study or exercise, or a composition written in that manner.

Execution. Style, technical ability, command of detail in interpreting music.

Exercise. A composition written chiefly for technical study and practice.

Exposition. The statement of themes in sonata form, appearing usually in the first movement of a symphony. It introduces the chief melodic material, and is generally repeated before the development begins.

Expression-mark. A sign, word or phrase, giving directions for the interpretation of a piece of music.

Extension. Carrying on a theme beyond its logical close, by repeating or slightly varying part of it.

F. The sixth letter in the musical alphabet, and the fourth interval in the perfect scale of C major. The scale of F major has a signature of one flat. Also used as an abbreviation of the Italian *forte,* loud. *Fortissimo,* very loud, is represented by a double f. There can also be a triple f, for the loudest effects. The holes on top of a violin are called f-holes, because of their shape.

Fa. The fourth step in the diatonic scale, according to the Sol-fa system. Also Italian for the note F.

Fagott. German for bassoon. Italian, *fagotto.*

False. Wrong in pitch, harmony, etc.

Falsetto. An artificial soprano quality assumed by voices in a high range.

Fanfare. Flourish of trumpets, or trumpet call.

Fantaisie, Fantasie, Fantasia. Literally improvisation. Used as a title for music in a free style. Free fantasia: the development section in sonata form.

F-clef. The bass clef (written like a C facing to the left).

292

Fermata. A sign, sometimes called a bird's-eye (a dot under a semi-circle), to indicate holding a note beyond its value.

Fermo. Italian for fixed, firm, unchanged. *Canto fermo:* see *cantus firmus.*

Fiddle. Informal name for violin.

Fife. A small flute, with shrill, high tones, used mostly in military music.

Fifth. The fifth step in the diatonic scale, also called the dominant. The term also applies to the interval of the fifth above the key-note.

Figuration. Decoration by rapid passages (figures).

Figure. A group of notes, a motif or motto (which see). A numeral. Figured bass: a harmony indicated by figures above the bass notes, representing chords.

Finale. The closing movement in a symphony, sonata, concerto, etc. The final part.

Fine. Italian for end. Often written at the close of a composition, like *Finis.*

Fingering. Applying the fingers to strings, keys, etc. Also the numerical markings to indicate which fingers are to be used.

Fioritura. Italian for a flowery passage, decoration, etc., in the coloratura style. Embellishment, flourish, not essential to the melody.

First. The unison, or first note of the scale. Also used of the principal or leading instrument in a group, or its player. Also the top part in harmony, as in first tenor, first violins, etc.

First movement. The opening movement of a symphony. Sometimes applied to sonata form.

Flageolet. A type of flute.

Flat. A musical character which lowers the pitch of a note by half a tone. A double flat lowers it by a full tone. Used as a verb and adjective, referring to playing or singing below pitch (out of tune).

Flauto. Italian for flute. Flautist: a flute-player.

Florid. Flowery; embellished with musical ornaments, trills, etc.

Flute. The soprano voice in the wood-wind choir. Originally made of wood, now often of metal, the flute (with its half-size relative, the *piccolo*) supplies the top tones among the wind instruments. Its lower tones are mellow, but it becomes shrill in the upper range, with the effect of whistling.

Folk-music, Folk-song. Music of the people, without scholarly technique. Natural, unstudied melody, generally handed down by word of mouth.

Form. The organizing factor in music which creates a composition as a whole, arranging the materials of melody, rhythm, harmony and tone color into a balanced and satisfying unity.

Forte. Italian for loud, strong. *Fortissimo:* very loud. (See the letter f.)

Forza. Italian for force. *Con forza:* with force, hence loudly.

Fourth. The fourth step in the diatonic scale. Also the interval of four steps above the key-note. The subdominant.

Free. Not bound by rules or traditions, allowing for individuality and imagination.

Free fantasia or *fantasy*. The development section in sonata form.

Frei. German for free. (See the Brahms motto, "Frei aber froh".)

French horn. The regular horn (originally hunting-horn, German *Waldhorn*, forest horn), of which there are generally four in a symphony orchestra, seated near the wood-wind. The instrument is of metal, with a long tube, twisted in a circle, ending in a wide bell, which can be stopped by the fist of the player. The tone is rich and mellow. The original horn could utter only a few notes (hence the limited parts in early orchestral music), but the modern valve horn has a wide range and considerable flexibility.

Fret. A ridge on the finger-board of a stringed instrument (banjo, guitar, etc.), indicating where the finger is to stop the string to produce a certain note.

Fugato. In the manner of a fugue (which see below).

Fugue. An elaborate form of polyphonic music, in which one or more themes pursue each other in a literal "flight". It is the highest development of counterpoint (one melody harmonizing with another). The chief theme is called the Subject. The Answer is the same theme in a different key (in real fugue). There is generally also a countersubject, a Stretto, representing a quickening of the pace by bringing the melodic materials close together, various Episodes, representing changes of key, an Organ-point, holding one note in the bass while the other parts modulate until the original key is reached, and a *Coda,* or tail-piece, similar to that of a symphony. Fugal passages are common in symphonic music, but a complete fugue is a rarity. The greatest fugues are those written by Bach for the organ and clavichord.

Fundamental. The real tone which gives the pitch to a note, to which are added various overtones (which see) producing color or quality of tone. Also the root or bass-note of a chord.

Funebre. French and Italian for funereal.

Fuoco. Italian for fire. *Con fuoco:* with fire, spirit.

G. The seventh letter in the musical alphabet, and the fifth step in the perfect scale of C major. The scale of G major has one sharp.

Gamut. The scale. Sometimes the musical staff.

Gavotte. Old French dance (Italian *Gavotta*), in duple time, starting on an up-beat.

G-clef. The treble clef, fixing the note G on the second line of the staff.

Giga. Italian for jig. French *Gigue*.

Giusto. Italian for "just, strict, reasonable." *Allegro giusto:* moderately fast.

Glissando. A gliding or sliding effect secured on stringed or keyed instruments by literally sliding the finger over a number of tones.

Glocke. German for bell. *Glockenspiel:* A carillon (which see). A set of bells, played with a hammer, hanging from a frame or resting on legs.

Grace-note. An extra note, decorating a melody, but not essential to it.

Grand. Adjective applied to the larger type of piano. See concert-grand.

Grande. Italian for large, grand, complete.

GLOSSARY OF SYMPHONIC TERMS

Grandioso. Italian adjective: with grandeur.

Grave. Low in pitch.

Grazia. Italian for grace. *Con grazia:* gracefully. Also *grazioso.*

Grosso. Italian for great, grand, full. *Concerto grosso:* great concerto.

Ground-bass. A repeated phrase in the bass; a *basso ostinato* (which see).

Group. A series of notes. A group of instruments.

Guitar. A stringed instrument, related to the lute, plucked by the fingers. It has six strings, and is used mostly for accompaniments.

H. German letter for the note B. Also abbreviation of Horn.

Half cadence. Incomplete cadence or close.

Half-note. A note half as long as a whole note, which has four beats.

Half-tone. A half step in the scale.

Hallelujah. Literally (Hebrew) "Praise the Lord". A triumphant form of sacred music.

Harmonic. Pertaining to chords and to harmony in general. Also a partial tone, sounding in harmony with the fundamental. A flageolet tone on a violin, etc.

Harmony. The organizing factor in music which produces pleasing effects from the simultaneous sounding of two or more tones. A chord. The accompaniment to a melody. The technical study of these phenomena.

Harp. An important stringed instrument, of ancient origin, plucked by the fingers. A symphony orchestra always includes one and perhaps two harps.

Harpsichord. A forerunner of the piano, using quills instead of hammers.

Hautbois. French for oboe.

Head. The playing surface of a drum.

Hold. The sign of a pause, or extension of a tone beyond its time value. (See *fermata*).

Homophonic. Having a single melody, accompanied by chords, etc. Opposite of polyphonic.

Horn. General term for any wind instrument, also the bell shaped opening of such an instrument. Specifically the French horn (which see).

Hymn. A sacred song.

Imitation. Repetition of a phrase or theme, generally in another key, possibly with distinct changes, yet remaining recognizable. It is an important element in counterpoint and polyphonic music in general.

Imperfect. Incomplete, of cadences, etc.

Impromptu. An improvisation, or a composition in that manner.

Improvisation. Extempore musical composition.

Instrument. The physical medium for producing music.

Instrumentation. The assigning of parts to various instruments.

Interlude. A connecting passage, not necessarily related to the preceding or following music.

GLOSSARY OF SYMPHONIC TERMS

Intermezzo. An elaborate form of interlude.

Interval. The difference in pitch between two tones, measured from the lower to the higher.

Intonation. Production of tone. Hence, correctness of pitch.

Inversion. Transposition of the notes of a chord. Also turning a melody upside down, by moving in the opposite direction from the original.

Jig. A country dance. Italian *Giga;* French *Gigue.*

Kammermusik. German for chamber music (which see).

Kapelle. German for a band, choir, orchestra (literally chapel).

Kapellmeister. German for conductor.

Kettledrum. A drum having distinctive pitch, looking like a copper kettle. Also known as *tympani.* There are at least two in every symphony orchestra.

Key. The melodic and harmonic basis of a scale or composition. Key-note: the tonic. The key of a piece is indicated by the signature (showing the number of sharps or flats). Also the ivory or ebony lever by which the finger of a pianist sets in motion a hammer to strike the strings. Also the padded disc by which a hole in a wind instrument is stopped.

Keyboard. The manual of a piano or organ.

Klavier. German for piano. Also a keyboard, a clavier, a clavichord.

Konzert. German for concerto. Also concert.

Konzertmeister. Concertmaster; the leader of the first violins in an orchestra.

La. The sixth step in the diatonic scale, according to the Sol-fa system.

Laendler. A German dance, ancestor of the waltz.

Lamento. Italian for lament. *Lamentoso:* mournfully.

Langsam. German for slow, slowly.

Largamente. Italian for broadly. *Largando:* growing broader.

Larghetto. Somewhat faster than a *Largo.* (See below.)

Largo. Literally large, broad; hence, slow in time, stately.

Lead. The leading part. The first statement of a theme. Leader: conductor.

Leading tone or note. The seventh step in the diatonic scale.

Legato. Italian for bound, tied together, hence smoothly, opposite of *staccato.*

Leger-line. A short line used for notes above or below the staff.

Leggeramente. Italian for lightly.

Legno. Italian for wood, stick. *Col legno:* with the stick of the bow (instead of the hair).

Lento. Italian for slow. (Slower than *andante* or *adagio;* not as slow as *largo*).

Lied. German for song. Now applied to the special type of art-song developed in Germany.

296

Lunga. Italian for long. Used to indicate a long pause.

Lyre. The ancient form of harp.

Ma. Italian for but. *Ma non troppo:* but not too much so.

Maestoso. Italian for majestic.

Maestro. Italian for master; usually applied to the conductor of an orchestra.

Major. Literally "greater", as opposed to minor, "lesser". Technically a major interval is half a tone higher than a minor. A minor scale substitutes minor for major intervals. Actually the difference between major and minor is one of mood, the former often connoting cheerfulness as contrasted with melancholy.

Marcato. Italian for well marked, with emphasis.

March. A piece in 4–4, 2–4 or 6–8 time, to which it is easy to keep step. French *marche;* Italian *marcia;* German *Marsch.*

Measure. The unit of written music, comprising the notes and rests between two bars. It contains a definite number of beats, indicated by a time signature.

Mediant. The third step in the diatonic scale.

Melody. Tune, air; the leading part, as compared with harmony. A logical progression of tones, pleasing to the human ear.

Menuet (French), *Menuett* (German), *Menuetto* (Italian). Minuet (see below). The term *Menuetto* implies a faster time than a regular Minuet.

Meter, metre. The grouping of musical rhythms; the measure of music.

Metronome. Maelzel's invention for keeping time mechanically.

Mi. The third step in the diatonic scale, according to the Sol-fa system. French and Italian for the note E.

Minor. Lesser, smaller. Less than major by a half-tone. See Major.

Minuet (also *Minuetto, Menuetto, Menuet, Menuett*). An old French dance, in triple time, long used for the third movement of a symphony. There are two sections, each repeated, followed by a *Trio,* also repeated, generally also in two parts. Each section of the Minuet has a final repetition at the close. In Beethoven's symphonies the Minuet developed into a *Scherzo,* at a faster tempo.

Mixed. Combining male and female voices, as in a chorus or quartet.

Mode. Originally a scale, covering an octave. Now applied mostly to the major and minor scales, collectively, and representing mood rather than key.

Moderato. Italian for moderate; at a moderate speed.

Modulate. To pass from one key or mode to another.

Modulation. A technical treatment of melody and harmony resulting in a change of key or mode.

Moll. German for minor. See *dur.*

Molto. Italian for much, very.

Monodic music. Having a definite melody and accompaniment. Opposite of polyphonic. See homophonic.

GLOSSARY OF SYMPHONIC TERMS

Monotone. An unchanging tone.

Mordent. A turn or fragmentary trill, introducing a grace-note, and returning to the note which is part of the melody.

Morendo. Italian for dying away.

Mosso. Italian for "moved", hence, having motion, rapid. *Piu mosso:* faster.

Motif. Motive. A short phrase or motto, containing basic melodic material, yet not a complete tune.

Motion. The progression of a melody or of a part in harmony, up or down.

Moto. Italian for motion, hence speed. *Con moto:* at a fast moving tempo.

Motto. A motif or short group of tones, used as a basic pattern.

Mouthpiece. The part of a wind instrument into which the player blows.

Movement. One of the four sections of a symphony. Also used of tempo.

Musette. A bag-pipe; a small oboe. Also a composition imitating such music. A drone-bass.

Music. The organization of sound toward beauty.

Mute. A device for subduing the tone of a string or wind instrument, besides changing its quality. See *sordino.* The mute of a violin, etc., fits over the bridge, damping the vibrations and deadening the sound. A wind instrument (particularly a horn, trumpet, etc.) is muted by inserting a pad, cone or cylinder in the bell. Muting with a derby hat is a development of modern jazz.

Natural. A sign which cancels a sharp or a flat. Used also of the white keys of the piano, and of any tone that is not sharped or flatted.

Ninth. An octave plus a whole or half tone.

Note. A character in musical writing or printing, indicating the duration of a tone and, by its position, the pitch. Notation: The writing of notes; also used of the printed score, as it appears to the eye.

Nuance. Expression, shading, details of tone color, tempo and volume in music.

Number. A piece of music. See *Opus.* Symphonies are usually numbered in the order of their creation.

O. A small circle is used over a note to indicate the open string of a violin; also a harmonic or flageolet tone.

Obbligato. Italian for obligatory, indispensable; hence literally an essential part, or melody, added to a composition. Note the spelling. The term is loosely used of a countermelody, or additional solo part (such as a violin with a singer), not necessary to the performance, but its real meaning is the exact opposite.

Oboe. An important instrument of the wood-wind choir, played by a double reed, held in the performer's mouth. The tone is nasal and often piercing, but well adapted to solos, especially of a melancholy nature. The oboe is non-transposing (playing the notes as written), and the entire orchestra tunes to its A, since it is difficult to alter the pitch.

GLOSSARY OF SYMPHONIC TERMS

Octave. The eighth step in the diatonic scale. The interval between the first and the eighth tone. A series of eight tones in the diatonic scale. (The octave sounds the same as the key-note, on a higher or lower level of pitch.)

Octet. (*Octette, Octuor*). A composition for eight instruments.

Opera. Drama set to music, with the words sung instead of spoken.

Opus. Latin for work. Often abbreviated to Op. The term applies to the works of a composer (sometimes to a group of works of the same type), each *opus* being given a number, according to the time of composition or publication. Low *opus* numbers usually indicate early works.

Orchestra (French *Orchestre,* German *Orchester*). The group of musicians, playing on various instruments, under the guidance of a conductor, interpreting orchestral music. Sometimes applied to the seats in an auditorium nearest to the actual orchestra, i.e. on the main floor.

Orchestration. The combination of parts to be played by the instruments in an orchestra; instrumentation; the art of writing such parts.

Organ. A wind instrument, with one or more key-boards (manuals), chiefly associated with religious music, but sometimes playing with a symphony orchestra.

Organ-point. A sustained tone, usually in the bass, over which other parts harmonize. Also a part of a fugue, using this device. See Pedal-point.

Ornament. A musical decoration or embellishment, like a grace-note.

Ossia. Italian for "or". Used to indicate an alternative reading in music, or the possible substitution of one tone for another.

Ostinato. Literally obstinate (Italian). Hence continuous, incessant. *Basso ostinato:* a ground bass or continuous bass, consisting of a single figure, constantly repeated, with varying harmonies and melodies above it.

Ottava. Italian for octave. *All' ottava:* an octave higher. *Coll' ottava:* with the octave added to the melody. (Playing in octaves).

Overtone. A practically inaudible tone harmonizing with the fundamental tone, and giving it color or quality. Every tone, as heard by the human ear, consists of a fundamental (fixing its pitch) and an indefinite number of overtones. The more obvious the overtones, the richer is the tone as a whole. (Compare the almost colorless whistle with a cello or bassoon tone.)

Overture. The instrumental introduction to an opera (or a play); sometimes an independent composition in sonata form. (French *Ouverture;* German *Ouvertuere*).

P. The letter indicating softness (for *piano*); *pp, pianissimo:* very soft. Also a sign for the pedal in piano music.

Paraphrase. Transcription or arrangement of a composition for other instruments, often with elaboration or variations.

Parlando. Italian for speaking; hence, music in the manner of speech.

Part. The music written for any one instrument in the orchestra. Also a division or section in any movement or composition.

Partial tone. An overtone or harmonic tone.

Partita. Another name for the old-fashioned suite.

Partitur. German for a musical score. Partition. (The complete orchestral parts.)

Part-music. Music written for several parts, in harmony (particularly vocal).

Part-singing. The singing of part-music.

Passacaglia. Old Italian dance in triple time, written on a ground-bass. (See *Chaconne*).

Passage. Any logical succession of notes in a piece of music. A repeated figure or pattern, generally in rapid time.

Pastoral. Having to do with shepherds or the rural life. Used as a title for such music. (Also spelled *Pastorale*).

Pathétique. French for pathetic. Italian *patetico.*

Pausa. A rest or pause. Also a *fermata* or hold.

Pedal. A foot-lever on a piano or harp. Also a large organ-key, played by the foot. Pedal-point: an organ-point, or sustained bass note.

Pentatonic scale. The old five-toned scale (omitting the fourth and seventh), prominent in folk-music, particularly in Scotland.

Percussion. The act or effect of striking. Instruments of percussion are those which are struck instead of blown or bowed or plucked, such as drums, cymbals, tambourine, castanets, bells, triangle, xylophone, piano.

Perdendosi. Italian for dying away.

Perfect. Applied to intervals that have no variation from major to minor. The perfect intervals are the fourth, fifth and octave. Also used of complete cadences.

Period. A complete musical theme, thought, or subject, from eight to twelve or sixteen measures in length, ending in a cadence or close.

Phrase. A short melodic pattern or figure, complete in itself, but possibly only part of a theme. Generally four measures, or half of a period.

Phrasing. The art of playing or singing phrases correctly, as in speaking. Also the signs to indicate how the composer wishes his music phrased. This is an important detail of interpretation. To "break a phrase" is always open to criticism.

Piacere. Italian for pleasure. *A piacere:* at pleasure, as you wish.

Piano. Italian for soft (originally flat, low). (From the Latin *planus*, as in plane). *Pianoforte:* generally shortened to piano. The familiar keyboard instrument, successor to the harpsichord and clavichord, invented by Cristofori. (Literally, "playing soft and loud"). Pianist, one who plays the piano, should be accented on the second syllable, since the Italian i is originally a Latin l, and therefore not a real vowel, but a consonant, which cannot be accented.

Piccolo. Italian for little, applied to a small flute, half as long as the regular flute, and playing an octave higher, with rather shrill tone.

Pick. A plectrum. Also to pluck or twang a stringed instrument.

Piece. A musical composition. Also an instrument. (A band or orchestra is said to have so many "pieces", meaning the number of players.)

Pipe. The basic wind instrument from which the flute, oboe, clarinet, etc.

were developed. Also the part of an organ from which the tone is produced.

Piston. A type of valve, used for increasing the range of wind instruments.

Pitch. The level of a tone in the musical scale. Absolute pitch represents a fixed position, depending on the number of vibrations per second. Relative pitch refers to the comparison between one tone and another. (Higher or lower). Standard pitch is based on the A above middle C at 440 vibrations per second. Concert pitch is a higher pitch. Most pianos are tuned to Standard Pitch. Pitch-pipe: A small pipe from which a definite pitch can be derived. (See Tuning-fork).

Piu. Italian for more. *Piu mosso:* more motion, hence faster.

Pizzicato. Literally "pinched" (Italian), hence, plucked with the fingers, instead of using the bow, as with violins, etc. Abbreviated *pizz.* (See *arco*).

Plectrum. A pick, such as is used for playing a mandolin.

Plus. French for more. (Italian *piu*).

Poco. Italian for little, sometimes abbreviated to *po'.* *Poco a poco:* little by little. (Applying generally to tempo).

Polyphonic. Having several independent melodies or voices which harmonize with each other; contrapuntal; many-voiced. Polyphonic music is sometimes called "horizontal", as compared with the "vertical" music, which consists of a single melody accompanied by chords. (See Homophonic, Monodic).

Polyphony. The harmonizing of independent melodies.

Pomposo. Italian for pompous, dignified, majestic.

Ponticello. Italian for bridge (of a violin, etc.).

Portamento. Gliding from one tone to another (Italian), (literally, carrying the finger or voice.)

Posaune. German for trombone.

Position. The way in which the left hand is placed on the fingerboard of a violin, etc., to stop the strings. It changes position for the higher notes. Also the arrangement of notes in a chord.

Prelude. A musical introduction.

Presto. (Italian). Fast, rapid. *Prestissimo:* very fast. (This represents the extreme of fast tempo).

Prima-o. Italian for first. Used of the leading part, or top voice; also of a previous portion of the music.

Primary accent. The down-beat or main accent in a measure.

Prime. The first note in the scale.

Principal. The leading player in any group, to whom solos are assigned.

Program music. Music that tells a story, paints a picture, or otherwise suggests a definite "program", something more than a mere pattern of tones. The opposite of "absolute music" or "pure music".

Progression. Musical advance from one tone or chord to another. (The first is called melodic, the second harmonic). Also a series of tones or chords.

GLOSSARY OF SYMPHONIC TERMS

Pulse. A beat or accent.

Punta. Italian for the point or top of the violin bow.

Quality. Tone color, created by overtones, distinguishing one instrument or voice from another.

Quarter-note. The unit of time in music, representing one beat in 4-4, 2-4 or 3-4 time.

Quartet- (*te*). A group of four instruments or voices, or the music for it.

Quasi. Italian for "as if, in the manner of, close to."

Quint. The interval of a fifth.

Quintet- (*te*). A group of five instruments or voices (French *Quintour*) or the music for it.

Quintuple time or *rhythm.* Five beats to a measure.

Rallentando. Italian for growing slower. Abbreviated *rall.*

Re. The second step in the diatonic scale, according to the Sol-fa system. French and Italian for D.

Recapitulation. The third section in sonata form, bringing back the themes of the exposition.

Recitative. Declamatory singing, in the manner of speech. Italian *recitativo.*

Reed. A thin strip of cane, wood or metal whose vibrations create vibrations of the air in a tube or pipe, resulting in musical tones. Wood-wind instruments are fitted with single or double reeds, on which the quality of tone largely depends.

Refrain. A short chorus or burden, repeated after each stanza of a song.

Register. Part of the range of a voice or instrument. Also a set of pipes in an organ.

Relative key. The key most closely related to another. The relative minor of a major key is always a minor third below its key-note. The keys of the dominant (fifth) and subdominant (fourth) are also considered as closely related to the tonic.

Remote key. An unrelated key.

Repeat. A sign (dots on the spaces of the staff) indicating that a portion of the music is to be repeated. Also applied to the repeated section.

Reprise. A repeat.

Resolution. The changing of a dissonance into a consonance.

Rest. A pause or interval of silence, or the character indicating such a pause.

Rhythm. The organizing factor in music which regulates and measures the time beats or accents. Often used as meaning time in general, but actually a broader aspect of the measure of music, having to do with groups of tones, phrases, etc., rather than individual notes.

Ritardando. Italian for growing slower. Abbreviated *rit.* The same abbreviation is used for *ritenuto,* having a similar meaning, literally "held back".

Roll. A tremolo or trill on the drum.

GLOSSARY OF SYMPHONIC TERMS

Romance. (German *Romanze*). A romantic piece of music.

Rondo. Originally a round dance; now an instrumental form of music in which the main theme alternates with others, ending in a *Coda.* Often used in symphonic and sonata movements.

Root. The lowest note of a chord in its fundamental position.

Rubato. Italian for "robbed", meaning that lesser tones are robbed of their full value to permit lingering on the more important ones. A familiar way of adding expression to a melody, often abused.

Run. A rapid passage, generally following the scale.

S. Abbreviation for *Segno,* sign.

Saltarello. An Italian dance, used by Mendelssohn in the *Finale* of his *Italian Symphony.*

Saltato. Italian for leaping, referring to a jumping bow.

Sarabande. A Spanish dance, appearing in the classic suites.

Saxophone. A brass clarinet, with curved body, resembling a Dutchman's pipe.

Scale. A regular progression of tones in major or minor key (diatonic). If all the half-tones are included, the scale is called chromatic.

Scherzo. Literally a joke or jest. (Italian). Applied by Beethoven and later composers to the fast movement of a symphony, formerly called *Menuetto.* Also used of independent compositions in that mood. *Scherzando:* in playful mood.

Score. The complete notation of a piece of music. Also an individual part. (The conductor's score contains all the parts.)

Scoring. Instrumentation, orchestration.

Second. The step above the key-note in the scale, or the interval formed by that step with the key-note. Also a lower part in harmony, or a subordinate voice, instrument, or group of instruments or voices.

Section. A short portion of a composition. Also applied to half of a phrase.

Secular music. The opposite of sacred music, i.e. not intended for the church.

Segno. Italian for sign. *Al segno:* play to the sign. *Dal segno:* play from the sign.

Segue. Italian for "follows", indicating what music is to come immediately.

Semitone. A half-tone, one step in the chromatic scale.

Sempre. Italian for always, continually.

Sentence. A logical sequence of eight to sixteen measures, usually ending in a complete cadence, and therefore having the same effect as its parallel in spoken or written language. (Cf. Phrase, Period, etc.)

Senza. Italian for "without".

Sept. The interval of the seventh.

Septet- (te). A group of seven voices or instruments, or a composition for such a combination.

Serenade. Literally an evening song, hence a composition in that style.

Seventh. The "leading tone", a half-tone below the octave, or eighth. Seventh chord: A chord containing a minor seventh (commonly added to the dominant, with its third and fifth). (Also the familiar "blue chord" of modern jazz.)

Sextet- (te). A group of six voices or instruments, or a composition for such a group.

Sforzando, Sforzato. An Italian direction indicating that a certain tone or chord is to be played with special emphasis or force. Abbreviated sfz, sf.

Shading. Expression, nuance.

Shake. A trill, playing two adjoining notes in rapid alternation.

Sharp. The sign that raises the pitch of a note by half a tone. Also used of any note so marked.

Si. The seventh note of the scale, according to the Sol-fa system. Also known as ti.

Signature. The group of characters engraved at the start of a composition, right after the clef-sign. The key-signature shows the number of sharps or flats appearing throughout (thus placing the key of the composition, or that part of it). The time-signature shows by a fraction how many beats there are to a measure (upper figure) and what is the length of the basic beat, usually a quarter-note (lower figure). 4–4 time is often indicated by a C, which stands for Common Time.

Simile. Italian for similarly.

Sinfonia. Italian for symphony. German *Sinfonie.*

Sixteenth note. A note one-sixteenth the length of a whole note, indicated by two tails.

Sixth. The sixth step in the diatonic scale, or the interval formed by adding this note to the tonic or key-note.

Slide. The movable part of a trombone, etc. Also to slide the finger over a string or keys. See *glissando.*

Slur. A curved line, binding two or more notes together, to show that they are to be played with a smooth continuity (*legato*). Also used to tie two identical tones together, creating a mere continuation of the tone.

Smorzando, Smorzato. Italian for dying away, fading.

Snare-drum. The small side-drum, played with two sticks.

Sol. The fifth step in the diatonic scale, according to the Sol-fa system.

Sol-fa. Solmisation. A system of singing syllables (do, re, mi, fa, sol, la, si, do) instead of the letters of the musical alphabet.

Solfeggio. A vocal exercise, using vowels or the Sol-fa syllables.

Solmisation. The Sol-fa system of reading music, using a different syllable for each note of the scale.

Solo. Italian for alone. Hence a part or passage played by one instrument, or sung by one voice, or an entire composition of this type.

Solo quartet. A quartet of soloists, as distinguished from a chorus (as in Beethoven's ninth symphony).

GLOSSARY OF SYMPHONIC TERMS

Sonata. Originally an instrumental piece, as contrasted with a *cantata,* to be sung. Later, a solo (mostly for piano or violin) in three movements, of which the first had a definite form, as described below.

Sonata Form. The form generally used in the first movement of a sonata, symphony, concerto, string quartet, etc. It consists of three parts, known as Exposition, Development, and Recapitulation, with the usual addition of a *Coda,* or tail-piece, at the end. The Exposition states at least two themes, of contrasting character, generally in different keys. The Development or Free Fantasia elaborates this material, applying musical scholarship in an interesting and often exciting fashion. The Recapitulation brings back the outstanding melodies, generally with a change of key for the second. The *Coda* gives a new twist to some of this material, for a finish. The entire principle of Sonata Form may be summed up as Statement, Contrast and Reminder, as in the simple Song Form, but with far more elaboration.

Sonatina, Sonatine. A small sonata.

Song. A poem set to music. Song Form: the form generally taken by a simple song, with two contrasting sections, A and B, ending in a repetition of A. (The A section is generally repeated also before B.)

Soprano. The highest voice in a mixed quartet or chorus. Also applied to instruments playing such parts.

Sordino. Italian for a mute (which see). *Con sordino:* with the mute.

Sostenuto. Italian for sustained, broad.

Sotto. Italian for under, below. *Sotto voce:* in an undertone.

Sound. A noise, not necessarily a musical tone, although often used with that meaning.

Sound-board, Sounding-board. The wooden surface used in stringed instruments to give resonance to the tone.

Space. In the musical staff, the white space between the lines.

Spirito. Italian for spirit. *Con spirito:* with spirit.

Springing bow. The jumping bow. Italian *spiccato, saltato.*

Staccato. Opposite of *legato;* playing short, sharply accented notes, in a brittle fashion. A *staccato* mark is a dot over the note.

Staff. The five lines and four spaces on which music is written.

Stem. The line attached to a note, running up or down.

Step. A degree in the scale. In the chromatic scale each step is a halftone. In the diatonic scale there are five whole tones and two half-tones to each octave.

Stop. Part of an organ. Also used as a verb to signify the stopping of a string to produce a certain tone. See Double Stop.

Strain. A melody, tune, air. Also used of a definite section of a composition.

Stretto. Part of a fugue, in which the themes are brought as close together as possible.

String. A cord which produces musical tones. Stringed instruments: those having strings. (Often called "the strings", including violins, cellos, etc. and their players.)

GLOSSARY OF SYMPHONIC TERMS

Stringendo. Italian for suddenly accelerating the time.

String quartet. The regular quartet of stringed instruments, consisting of two violins, viola and violoncello. This is the basis of the string section of a symphony orchestra, with each instrument duplicated many times, and bass-viols added.

Subdominant. The tone below the dominant, the fourth step in the diatonic scale.

Subito. Italian for suddenly.

Subordinate theme. The second theme in sonata form.

Suite. A set of dances or other forms of composition loosely strung together; forerunner of the symphony.

Sul. Italian for "on the". *Sul ponticello:* close to the bridge.

Sustain. To hold a tone for its full value.

Swell. To grow louder. Also part of an organ.

Symphonic. In the manner or style of a symphony.

Symphony. Literally "sounding together". The most important form of absolute music: an orchestral composition, generally in four movements, of which the first is almost always in sonata form. The second is usually a slow movement, the third a *Menuetto* or *Scherzo,* and the *Finale* in fast time, sometimes a *Rondo.* The key of the symphony is fixed by the first movement.

Symphony orchestra. An orchestra capable of playing a symphony (requiring generally at least sixty to eighty-five players).

Syncopation. The anticipation or delaying of the natural beat so as to produce an artificial accent, a common distortion of rhythm.

Tace, Tacit. Italian and Latin indication that an instrument keeps silent.

Tail. The extra line added to the stem of a note cutting its time value in half. Also the *Coda* in a movement.

Tambourine. A small drum, played by the hand, with jingling metals in the rim.

Tanto. Italian for as much, too much. *Ma non tanto:* but not too much.

Tarantella, Tarantelle. An Italian dance, in fast 6–8 time.

Technique, Technic. The mechanical skill in music, scholarship, technical excellence.

Tempo. Italian for time. Used for the rate of speed, not time in general.

Tenor. The high male voice, hence the corresponding part in a quartet or chorus.

Tessitura. Italian for the range of a part, generally vocal.

Text. The words of a song, opera, etc.

Theme. A tune, a melody, a subject for development or elaboration in music.

Third. The tone two full steps above the key-note, or the interval formed by that tone and the key-note.

Thirty-second note. A note having one thirty-second of the time value of a whole note. Written with three tails added to the stem.

Tie. A curved line joining two notes together, to make a continuous tone.

Timbre. Tone color or quality. (French).

Time. The measure of music, indicated by the grouping of beats. Duple time runs in multiples of two, triple time in multiples of three.

Timpani. See Tympani.

Tonality. The art and science of key relationship in music.

Tone. A musical sound, caused by regular vibrations of the air. In the scale, a half-tone is the smallest interval occurring in civilized music, the unit of the chromatic scale. A whole tone consists of two half-tones.

Tone color. Timbre, quality of tone, created by overtones.

Tonguing. Producing rapid effects on a wind instrument by use of the tongue.

Tonic. The key-note of a scale or composition.

Tranquillo. Italian for tranquil, tranquilly.

Transcription. Arrangement of music for a different instrument than that for which it was originally written.

Transpose. To change the key of a composition.

Transposing instrument. An instrument (such as a clarinet) whose natural scale is written as C major, although actually in a different key, requiring transposition if played on the piano or some other non-transposing instrument.

Tre. Italian for three.

Tremolo. A trembling or tremulous tone. Also the *agitato* effect produced by moving the bow rapidly back and forth.

Triad. A chord of three tones, the root or tonic, third and fifth.

Triangle. An instrument of percussion, made of a bent rod of steel, giving out a tinkling tone.

Trill. The rapid alternation of two adjoining notes. See Shake.

Trio. A composition for three instruments, or a group of three players or singers. The Trio of a Minuet or March has been so called because it was originally played by three instruments. It is actually the second section, contrasting with the main theme, which is later repeated.

Triple time. Time whose beats are grouped in multiples of three. (See Time).

Triplet. A group of three notes of equal time value.

Trombone. A bass instrument in the brass section, played with a slide.

Troppo. Italian for too much. *Allegro ma non troppo:* Fast but not too fast.

Trumpet. The soprano of the brass choir.

Tune. A melody or theme. As a verb, to put an instrument in tune.

Tuning fork. A small instrument which correctly vibrates to give a definite pitch.

Turn. An embellishment consisting of several grace notes.

Tutto-a. Italian for "all". *Tutti:* all the instruments, hence full orchestra.

Tympani. The kettledrums. Also spelled timpani.

Un. French or Italian for "one, a, an."

Unison. A tone corresponding in pitch with another; the first interval of the diatonic scale.

Up-beat. The unaccented beat in a measure. Also the motion of a conductor to indicate such a beat.

Up-bow. The upward motion of a bow (from top to bottom).

Ut. French for C. The original name of the first note of the absolute scale, changed to Do in the Sol-fa system (Solmisation).

Valse. French for waltz.

Value. The duration of a note in time.

Valve. A device for changing the pitch of a brass instrument.

Variation. Decoration or changing of a theme, for variety. (Often appearing in the slow movement of a symphony).

Variazioni. Italian for Variations. *Tema con Variazioni:* Theme with Variations.

Verse. A stanza in a song or poem.

Vibrato. The effect of a vibrating tone, practically the same as *tremolo;* produced on stringed instruments by shaking the finger that stops the string.

Viol. The family name for bowed instruments. Bass viol: the double bass.

Viola. The tenor of the viol family, lower in tone than a violin. (Its top string is A, a fifth below the violin.)

Violin. The soprano of the orchestra, with its four strings tuned G, D, A, E, and a range considerably higher. A symphony orchestra usually contains from twelve to twenty or more first violins, and nearly as many second violins.

Violon. French for violin. German *Violine* or *Geige.*

Violoncello. The bass of the string quartet, played upright, between the knees. It is tuned an octave lower than the viola, C, G, D, A.

Virtuoso. A highly skilled instrumental soloist.

Vivace. Italian for lively, vivacious, rapid.

Voice. Often used for an instrumental part. Actually the human voice in singing. French *Voix.* Italian *Voce.*

Waldhorn. German for the French horn; literally, forest horn, hence hunting-horn.

Waltz. The familiar dance in triple time. German *Walzer.* French *Valse.*

Whole Note. The longest note in common time, having four beats.

Whole Tone. A full step in the diatonic scale, consisting of two half-tones.

Wind. Instruments played by blowing. See Wood-wind, Brass.

Wood-wind. The wooden wind instruments of an orchestra (including the flute). Also those who play them.

Xylophone. An instrument of percussion, played with hammers on slabs of wood or metal.

LIST OF PHONOGRAPH RECORDS OF SYMPHONIES

THE best way to become familiar with symphonies or any other kind of music is by listening to phonograph records. Most of the great symphonies have been recorded, often several times, by various orchestras, under the best conductors. Some of them are available in sets or albums, and individual discs can always be purchased at a reasonable price.

The following list is based on the monumental Encyclopedia of Recorded Music compiled by R. D. Darrell, and published recently by the Gramophone Shop, 18 East 48th St., New York City. Composers are presented in alphabetical order, and each recorded symphony or movement is given with the name of the orchestra, the conductor, the number of sides (of discs) covered by the music, and the list number of the record. In listing these numbers, the following abbreviations are used, representing American and foreign recording companies:

B, Brunswick; C, Columbia; CM, Columbia Masterworks; D, Decca; G, Gramophone-His Master's Voice; GM, Gramophone Album; O, Odeon; P, Parlophone; PAT, Pathé; PD, Polydor; T, Telefunken; V, Victor; VM, Victor Musical Masterpiece.

Symphony	Orchestra	Conductor	No. of Sides	List Number
Composer: K. P. E. Bach (1714–1788)				
No. 1, D-Major (*Presto*)	Chamber	H. Benda	1	G–B8119
Composer: Ludwig van Beethoven (1770–1827)				
No. 1, C Major, Op. 21	Berlin Philharmonic	Hans Pfitzner	6	B–90204–6
" " " "	Casals Symphony	Pablo Casals	6	G–D1729–31
" " " "	N. Y. Philharmonic	Mengelberg	8	VM–73 (Album)
" " " "	Royal Philharmonic	Henschel	8	CM–57 (Album)
" " " " (*Finale*)	Symphony	Toscanini	2	G–DB417

LIST OF PHONOGRAPH RECORDS OF SYMPHONIES (Continued)

Symphony	Orchestra	Conductor	No. of Sides	List Number
No. 2, D Major, Op. 36	Vienna Philharmonic	C. Krauss	8	VM-181 (Album)
" " " " "	Berlin State Opera	E. Kleiber	8	B-90140-3
" " " " "	London Symphony	Beecham	8	CM-45 (Album)
No. 3, E-flat Major, Op. 55 (Eroica)	London Philharmonic	Koussevitzky	12	VM-263 (Album)
" " " " "	Berlin Philharmonic	Pfitzner	12	B-90060-5
" " " " "	Symphony	Max von Schillings	12	CM-138 (Album)
No. 4, B-flat Major, Op. 60	N. Y. Philharmonic-Symphony	Mengelberg	14	VM-115 (Alb.)
" " " " "	London Philharmonic	Weingartner	7	CM-197 (Alb.)
" " " " "	Minneapolis Symphony	Ormandy	10	VM-274 (Alb.)
" " " " "	Berlin State Opera	Pfitzner	10	B-90371-5
No. 5, C Minor, Op. 67	Hallè Orchestra	Hamilton Harty	10	CM-47 (Alb.)
" " " " "	London Philharmonic	Koussevitzky	9	VM-245 (Alb.)
" " " " "	Symphony	Weingartner	8	CM-178 (Alb.)
" " " " "	Queen's Hall	Henry Wood	8	D-K757-60
" " " " "	Berlin State Opera	Richard Strauss	8	B-90172-5
" " " " "	Vienna Philharmonic	F. Schalk	8	GM-112 (Alb.)
No. 6, F Major, Op. 68 (Pastoral)	Royal Albert Hall	Landon Ronald	8	VM-5 (Alb.)
" " " " "	Boston Symphony	Koussevitzky	10	VM-50 (Alb.)
" " " " "	Colonne	Paul Paray	9	CM-201 (Alb.)
No. 7, A Major, Op. 92	Vienna Philharmonic	F. Schalk	10	GM-66 (Alb.)
" " " " "	Berlin State Opera	Pfitzner	11	B-90189-94
" " " " "	Philadelphia	Stokowski	10	VM-17 (Alb.)
" " " " "	N. Y. Philharmonic	Toscanini	10	V-14101 (Alb.)
" " " " "	Royal Philharmonic	Weingartner	10	CM-63 (Alb.)

No. 8, F Major, Op. 93	Boston Symphony	Koussevitzky		(in preparation, Victor)
"　" "	B. B. C. Symphony	Adrian Boult	6	VM-181 (Alb.)
"　" "	Berlin Philharmonic	Pfitzner	6	B-90252-4
"　" "	Vienna Philharmonic	F. Schalk	6	V-9342;V-9640-1
"　" "	Royal Philharmonic	Weingartner	6	CM-64 (Album)
No. 9, D Minor, Op. 125 (*Choral*)	Vienna Philharmonic	Weingartner	16	CM-227 (Alb.)
"　" "	Berlin State Opera	Oskar Fried	14	B-90179-85
"　" "	Philadelphia	Stokowski	17	VM-236 (Alb.)
Battle Symphony, Op. 91	Berlin State Opera	F. Weissmann	4	P-E10555-6

Composer: Hector Berlioz (1803-1869)

Harold in Italy, Op. 16 (*Marche des Pelerins*)	Victor Orchestra		2	V-24755
Romeo and Juliet, Op. 17 (*Excerpts*)	London Philharmonic	Harty	4	C-DB1230-1
"　" "	Colonne	Gabriel Pierné	4	O-123526-7
"　" "　(*Queen Mab Scherzo*)	Paris Conservatoire	P. Coppola	2	G-DB4827
"　" "	Hallé Orchestra	Harty	2	C-67422D
Fantastic Symphony, Op. 14	Paris Symphony	Pierre Monteux	12	VM-111 (Alb.)
"　" "	Paris Symphony	S. Meyrowitz	12	PAT-PDT-10-5
"　" "	London Symphony	Weingartner	12	CM-34 (Alb.)

Composer: Alexander Borodine (1834-1887)

No. 2, B Minor	London Symphony	Albert Coates	6	VM-113 (Alb.)

Composer: Johannes Brahms (1833-1897)

No. 1, C Minor, Op. 68	Philadelphia	Stokowski	10	VM-301 (Alb.)
"　" "	Royal Philharmonic	Weingartner	10	CM-103 (Alb.)
"　" "	Berlin State Opera	Klemperer	12	P-E10807-12
No. 2, D Major, Op. 73	Philadelphia	Stokowski	12	VM-82 (Alb.)
"　" "	Berlin Philharmonic	Max Fiedler	11	B-90217-31
No. 3, F Major, Op. 90	Amsterdam Concertgebouw	Mengelberg	8	CM-181 (Alb.)
"　" "	Vienna Philharmonic	C. Krauss	8	GM-118 (Alb.)
"　" "	Philadelphia	Stokowski	10	VM-42 (Alb.)

LIST OF PHONOGRAPH RECORDS OF SYMPHONIES (*Continued*)

Symphony	Orchestra	Conductor	No. of Sides	List Number
Composer: Anton Bruckner (1824–1896)				
No. 4, E Minor, Op. 98	B. B. C. Symphony	Bruno Walter	10	VM-242 (Alb.)
" " " "	Berlin Philharmonic	M. Fiedler	11	B-90114-9
" " " "	Philadelphia	Stokowski	10	VM-185 (Alb.)
No. 1 & No. 2 C Minor (*Scherzo*)	Berlin State Opera	Fritz Zaun	2	G-C2635
No. 3, D Minor (*Scherzo*)	Vienna Symphony	Anton Konrath	1	V-11723
(On same disc, Jugend Symphony, *Scherzo*)				
No. 4, E-flat Major (*Scherzo*)	Vienna Philharmonic	Krauss	2	G-C1789
No. 5, B-flat Major (*Scherzo*)	Dol Dauber Salon Orchestra		2	G-AN189
No. 7, E Major	Minneapolis Symphony	Ormandy	15	VM-276 (Alb.)
" " " "	Berlin Philharmonic	Horenstein	14	B-90305-11
Composer: Ernest Chausson (1855–1899)				
B-flat Major, Op. 20	Paris Conservatory	Coppola	8	VM-261 (Alb.)
Composer: Anton Dvořák (1841–1904)				
No. 4, G Major, Op. 88	Czech Philharmonic	V. Talich	10	GM-248 (Alb.)
" " " " "	Symphony	Basil Cameron	8	B-9000-3
No. 5, E Minor, Op. 95 (*New World*)	Berlin State Opera	Kleiber	10	B-90150-4
" " " " " " "	Philadelphia	Stokowski	10	VM-273 (Alb.)
" " " " " " "	Hallé	Hamilton Harty	10	CM-77 (Alb.)
Composer: Edward Elgar (1857–1934)				
No. 1, A-flat Major, Op. 55	London Symphony	Elgar	11	VM-145 (Alb.)
No. 2, E-flat Major, Op. 63	London Symphony	Elgar	12	GM-42 (Alb.)

Composer: Cesar Franck (1822–1890)

Work	Orchestra	Conductor		Record
Symphony, D Minor	Lamoureux	A. Wolff	8	B-90197–200
" " "	Philadelphia	Stokowski	10	VM-22 (Alb.)
" " "	Paris Conservatory	P. Gaubert	11	CM-121 (Alb.)

Composer: Roy Harris (1898–   )

Work	Orchestra	Conductor		Record
Symphony, 1933	Boston Symphony	Koussevitzky	7	CM-191 (Alb.)

Composer: Franz Joseph Haydn (1732–1809)

Work	Orchestra	Conductor		Record
No. 45, F-sharp Minor (*Farewell*)	London Symphony	Henry Wood	6	CM-205 (Alb.)
No. 88, G Major	Vienna Philharmonic	Krauss	6	V-4189–91
No. 92, G Major (*Oxford*)	London Symphony	H. Weisbach	6	VM-189 (Alb.)
No. 94, G Major (*Surprise*)	Boston Symphony	Koussevitzky	6	VM-55 (Alb.)
" " "	Berlin State Opera	Leo Blech	6	G-D2040–2
" " "	Berlin Philharmonic	Horenstein	6	B-90358–60
No. 95, C Minor	London Symphony	Harty	4	D-K798–9
No. 97, C Major	London Symphony	Weisbach	6	VM-140 (Alb.)
No. 100, G Major (*Military*)	Symphony	Knappertsbusch	8	CM-189 (Alb.)
No. 101, D Major (*The Clock*)	N. Y. Philharmonic	Toscanini	7	VM-57 (Alb.)
" " "	Hallé Orchestra	Harty	7	CM-76 (Alb.)
No. 103, E-flat Major (*Drum Roll*)	St. Louis	V. Golschmann	6	CM-221 (Alb.)
No. 104, D Major (*London*)	Chamber Orchestra	J. Barbirolli	6	V-35981–3
Toy Symphony	Symphony	Weingartner	2	C-7242M
" "	Berlin State Opera	F. Weissmann	2	P-E10821

Composer: Vincent d'Indy (1851–1931)

Work	Orchestra	Conductor		Record
On a Mountain Song, Op. 25	Lamoureux	Albert Wolff	6	B-90270–2
" " " " "	Colonne	Paul Paray	6	CM-211 (Alb.)

Composer: Gustav Mahler (1860–1911)

Work	Orchestra	Conductor		Record
No. 2, C Minor (*Resurrection*)	Minneapolis	Ormandy	22	VM-256 (Alb.)
No. 5, C Minor (*Adagietto*)	Amsterdam Concertgebouw	Mengelberg	2	C-L1798

313

LIST OF PHONOGRAPH RECORDS OF SYMPHONIES (Continued)

Symphony	Orchestra	Conductor	No. of Sides	List Number
Composer: Felix Mendelssohn (Bartholdy) (1809–1847)				
No. 3, A Minor, Op. 56 (Scotch)	Royal Philharmonic	Weingartner	8	CM-126 (Alb.)
No. 4, A Major, Op. 90 (Italian)	Boston Symphony	Koussevitzky	6	VM-294 (Alb.)
" " " "	Hallé	Hamilton Harty	6	CM-167 (Alb.)
" " " "	La Scala	Ettore Panizza	7	VM-119 (Alb.)
Composer: Wolfgang Amadeus Mozart (1756–1791)				
No. 34, C Major, K. 338	Royal Philharmonic	Beecham	6	CM-123 (Alb.)
" " " "	Berlin State Opera	Leo Blech	4	G-EJ607-8
No. 35, D Major, K. 385 (Haffner)	N. Y. Philharmonic	Toscanini	5	VM-65 (Alb.)
" " " "	Hallé	Hamilton Harty	6	CM-42 (Alb.)
No. 36, C Major, K. 425	B. B. C. Symphony	Fritz Busch	6	VM-226 (Alb.)
No. 38, D Major, K. 504 (Prague)	Vienna Philharmonic	Kleiber	6	G-C1686-8
No. 39, E-flat Major, K. 543	B. B. C. Symphony	Bruno Walter	6	VM-258 (Alb.)
" " " "	Royal Philharmonic	Weingartner	6	CM-105 (Alb.)
" " " "	Berlin State Opera	Kleiber	6	V-9438-40
" " " "	Berlin State Opera	Knappertsbusch	6	P-E11003-5
No. 40, G Minor, K. 550	London Philharmonic	Koussevitzky	6	VM-293 (Alb.)
" " " "	Berlin State Opera	B. Walter	6	CM-182 (Alb.)
" " " "	Berlin State Opera	R. Strauss	7	B-90082-5
No. 41, C Major, K. 551 (Jupiter)	Chicago Symphony	F. Stock	6	VM-109 (Alb.)
" " " "	London Philharmonic	Beecham	7	CM-194 (Alb.)
" " " "	B. B. C. Symphony	Adrian Boult	7	VM-203 (Alb.)
Composer: Serge Prokofieff (1891–)				
Symphony (Classical) D Major, Op. 25	Boston Symphony	Koussevitzky	3	V-7196-7

Composer: Sergei Rachmaninoff (1873–   )

No. 2, E Minor, Op. 27	Minneapolis Symphony	Ormandy	12	VM-239 (Alb.)
" " " "	Cleveland Symphony	Sokoloff	12	B-50143-8

Composer: Nikolai Rimsky-Korsakoff (1844–1908)

No. 2, Op. 9 (*Antar*)	Paris Conservatory	P. Coppola	6	VM-210 (Alb.)
Symphonic Suite, Scheherazade, Op.35	Philadelphia Orchestra	Stokowski	12	VM-269 (Alb.)
" " " "	Berlin Philharmonic	O. Fried	11	B-90361-6
" " " "	Paris Conservatory	Ph. Gaubert	11	CM-136 (Alb.)

Composer: Albert Roussel (1869–1935)

No. 3, G Minor, Op. 42	Lamoureux Orchestra	Albert Wolff	6	PD-566126-8

Composer: Camille Saint-Saëns (1835–1921)

No. 3, C Minor, Op. 78	Symphony Orchestra	P. Coppola	8	VM-100 (Alb.)

Composer: Franz Schubert (1797–1828)

No. 3, D Major (*Excerpts*)	Berlin State Opera	Kleiber	2	P-E10974
No. 5, B-flat Major	Berlin State Opera	L. Blech	5	VM-170 (Alb.)
" " "	Berlin Philharmonic	Horenstein	5	PD-95402-4
No. 8, B Minor (*Unfinished*)	London Symphony	Henry Wood	6	CM-216 (Alb.)
" " " "	Berlin Philharmonic	Kleiber	6	T-E1777-9
" " " "	Cleveland Symphony	N. Sokoloff	6	B-50150-2
" " " "	Philadelphia	L. Stokowski	6	VM-16 (Alb.)
No. 10 (also known as No. 7 and No 9) C Major	B. B. C.	Adrian Boult	12	VM-268 (Alb.)
" " " " " "	Hallé Orchestra	H. Harty	14	CM-88 (Alb.)
" " " " " "	London Symphony	L. Blech	12	VM-33 (Alb.)

Composer: Robert Schumann (1810–1856)

No. 1, B-flat Major (*Spring*), Op. 38	Chicago Symphony	F. Stock	7	VM-86 (Alb.)
No. 2, C Major, Op. 61	Berlin State Opera	H. Pfitzner	10	B-90092-6

LIST OF PHONOGRAPH RECORDS OF SYMPHONIES *(Continued)*

Symphony	Orchestra	Conductor	No. of Sides	List Number
No. 3, E-flat Major (*Rhenish*) Op. 97	Paris Conservatory	Coppola	6	VM-297 (Alb.)
No. 4, D Minor, Op. 120	Minneapolis Symphony	E. Ormandy	6	VM-201 (Alb.)
" " " "	Mozart Festival Orchestra	B. Walter	8	CM-106 (Alb.)
Composer: Jean Sibelius (1865–)				
No. 1, E Minor, Op. 39	Minneapolis Symphony	Ormandy	10	VM-290 (Alb.)
" " " "	Symphony Orchestra	R. Kajanus	9	CM-151 (Alb.)
No. 2, D Major, Op. 43	Boston Symphony	Koussevitzky	11	VM-272 (Alb.)
" " " "	Symphony Orchestra	R. Kajanus	9	CM-149 (Alb.)
No. 4, A Minor, Op. 63	Philadelphia Orchestra	Stokowski	8	VM-160 (Alb.)
No. 5, E-flat Major, Op. 82	London Symphony	R. Kajanus		(In Sibelius Society Vol. 1: V-11503–6)
No. 6, D Minor, Op. 104	Finnish Nat'l. Orchestra	Georg Schneevoigt		(In Sibelius Society Vol 3: not available separately)
No. 7, C Major, Op. 105	B. B. C. Symphony	Koussevitzky		(In Sibelius Society Vol. 2: not available separately)
Composer: Igor Stravinsky (1882–)				
Symphony of Psalms	Symphony Orchestra	Igor Stravinsky	6	CM-162 (Alb.)
Composer: Peter Ilyitch Tschaikowsky (1840–1893)				
No. 3, D Major (*Polish*) Op. 29	London Symphony	Albert Coates	8	VM-166 (Alb.)
No. 4, F Minor, Op. 36	Amsterdam Concertgebouw	Mengelberg	10	CM-133 (Alb.)
" " " "	Philadelphia Orchestra	Stokowski	10	VM-48 (Alb.)

No. 5, E Minor, Op. 64	Philadelphia Orchestra	Stokowski	12	VM-253 (Alb.)
" " " " "	Amsterdam Concertgebouw	Mengelberg	13	CM-104 (Alb.)
" " " " "	Berlin State Opera	L. Blech	10	GM-140 (Alb.)
No. 6, B Minor (*Pathétique*), Op. 74	Charlottenburg Opera	A. Kitschin	11	PD-95956-61
" " " " "	Boston Symphony	Koussevitzky	10	VM-85 (Alb.)
" " " " "	Royal Philharmonic	O. Fried	10	CM-119 (Alb.)

Composer: Ralph Vaughan Williams (1872–   )

London Symphony	Queen's Hall Orchestra	Henry Wood	10	D-X114-8

317

FACTS ABOUT SYMPHONIC COMPOSERS

Abert, Johann Joseph, b. Kochowitz, Bohemia, 1832; d. Stuttgart, Germany, 1915. Double bass player and orchestral conductor, mostly at Stuttgart. Composed several operas. His orchestral works include six symphonies.

Albert, Eugene d', b. Glasgow, Scotland, 1864; d. Riga, 1932. Pianist and composer, best known by his operas, *Tiefland,* etc. Composed a symphony in F.

Alfven, Hugo, b. Stockholm, Sweden, 1872. Violinist, conductor and composer. His works include three symphonies and two symphonic poems.

Allen, Paul Hastings, b. Hyde Park, Mass., 1883. American composer, teacher, and radio musician. He wrote a symphony in E, 1912, and his orchestral works also include a *Serenade* (1927) and *Ex Nocte* (1930).

Antheil, George, b. Trenton, New Jersey, 1900. Notable American composer, now associated with motion pictures. He wrote a symphony in F (1926), and a second symphony has been announced as in preparation. His *Ballet Mécha-nique* caused a sensation, and he is credited also with a *Jazz Symphony* (1925), a Suite for Chamber Orchestra (1926), a Piano Concerto, etc.

Arensky, Anton Stepanovitch, b. Novgorod, Russia, 1861; d. Tarioki, Finland, 1906. Versatile and popular composer, with two symphonies to his credit, in a long list of vocal and instrumental works.

Ashton, Algernon, b. Durham, England, 1859. Critical writer, piano teacher and composer. His creative output includes at least five symphonies, mostly in manuscript.

Bach, Johann Sebastian, b. Eisenach, Germany, 1685; d. Leipzig, 1750. One of the greatest of all composers, and first of the "three B's" (later joined by Beethoven and Brahms). Trained as a violinist, and organist, he perfected himself in the technique of composition, often working through an entire night. He held various posts as musical director, and in 1723 became choirmaster and organist in the two principal churches of Leipzig, where he remained the rest of his life and composed his most important works. While the form of the symphony had not yet been established in the time of Bach, he wrote much instrumental music related to that style, and of influence in its later development (particularly the *Brandenburg Concertos* and various *Suites*). One of his compositions has the title of "symphony," and his orchestral concertos and suites are of symphonic proportions. Bach's mastery of the fugue, and of polyphonic music in general, created models for all succeeding composers.

Bach, Karl Philipp Emanuel, b. Weimar, Germany, 1714; d. Hamburg, 1788. Third son of Johann Sebastian Bach, and an important pioneer in the symphonic form. Eighteen of his orchestral works have been justly given the title of "symphonies," showing the early stages of sonata form, and definitely influencing Haydn in establishing the symphonic style. His development of instrumentation was also important. The younger Bach may fairly be called the first symphonic composer in the modern sense.

Bacon, Ernst, b. Chicago, Illinois, 1898. American composer and Pulitzer Prize winner in 1932, when he wrote his symphony in D minor (with piano). Other works (not yet published) include a *Symphonic Fugue* and *Hours with a Child.*

Balakirew, Mily, b. Novgorod, Russia, 1837; d. Leningrad (St. Petersburg), 1910. Founder and head of the group of five nationalistic composers who attempted to restore the folk elements in Russian music. (The others were Cui, Moussorgsky, Rimsky-Korsakoff and Borodin.) His works include two symphonies and two symphonic poems.

Banister, Henry Charles, b. London, England, 1831; d. Streatham, 1897. Composer of four symphonies and other works, besides a *Text-book of Music* and a number of critical and analytical treatises.

Bantock, Granville, b. London, England, 1868. Best known for his vocal music, but composer also of several symphonies, mostly of the program type, including the choral *Atalanta in Calydon* and *The Vanity of Vanities*, a *Hebridean Symphony*, and a festival symphony, *Christus;* also two suites and many other works.

Barber, Samuel, b. West Chester, Pa., 1910. Promising young American composer, winner of Prix de Rome and Pulitzer Prize, studying at the American Academy in Rome, where his first symphony was scheduled for a world premiere by the Augusteo Orchestra.

Bargiel, Waldemar, b. Berlin, Germany, 1828; d. there, 1897. A stepbrother of Schumann, and himself a highly respected musician in his day. His works include a symphony in C and other orchestral compositions.

Barlow, Samuel L. M., b. New York, 1893. American composer of songs, piano pieces, operas and orchestral works, including a piano concerto, *Ballo Sardo*, *Vocalise*, and the symphonic poem, *Alba*.

Barth, Hans, b. Germany, 1896. Pianist and composer, most of whose life has been spent in America. He is noted for his experiments with quarter tones. His works include a piano concerto, a suite for quarter tone strings, brass and tympani, a concerto for quarter tone strings and piano, and a *Pantomime Symphony* (in preparation).

Bax, Arnold E. T., b. London, England, 1883. Well known modern composer, whose works include two symphonies, in E-flat minor and E and C minor, several symphonic poems, and other orchestral music.

Beach, Mrs. H. H. A., b. Henniker, New Hampshire, 1867. America's leading woman composer, best known by her songs and choral works, but creator of a *Gaelic Symphony* in E minor, and other orchestral pieces in the symphonic style.

Beck, Franz, b. Mannheim, Germany, 1730; d. Bordeaux, France, 1809. Credited with twenty-four symphonies, in addition to operatic and ecclesiastical works.

Becker, Albert, b. Quedlinburg, Germany, 1834; d. Berlin, 1899. Gifted composer, whose works include a successful symphony in G minor.

Becker, John J., b. Henderson, Kentucky, 1886. American composer, credited with three symphonies, the first called *Étude Primitive* (1915), the second, *Fantasia Tragica* (1920), and the third, *Symphonia Brevis* (1929); also a *Concerto Arabesque*, for piano and orchestra (1930).

Becker, Reinhold, b. Adorf, Germany, 1842; d. Dresden, 1924. Violinist, conductor and composer, with a symphony in C and a symphonic poem included in a long list.

Beethoven, Ludwig van, b. Bonn, Germany, 1770; d. Vienna, Austria, 1827. Generally considered the greatest of symphonic composers, with nine immortal works in that form. (See pp. 61–132). His concertos (piano and violin) are also of symphonic proportions.

Bendel, Franz, b. Schoenlinde, Bohemia, 1833; d. Berlin, Germany, 1874. Pianist and composer, with some symphonies to his credit.

Benedict, Julius, b. Stuttgart, Germany, 1804; d. London, England, 1885. Conductor and composer of operas, with two symphonies in his list of works.

Bennett, Robert Russell, b. Kansas City, Missouri, 1894. Popular American composer and arranger, best known in the operatic field. He wrote an *Abraham Lincoln Symphony* (1929), a *Toy Symphony* (for five woodwinds, 1928), *Sights and Sounds*, a *Charleston Rhapsody*, and the opera, *Maria Malibran* (libretto by Robert Simon).

Bennett, William Sterndale, b. Sheffield, England, 1816; d. London, 1875. One of the leading English composers, best known for his piano compositions, but also creator of many orchestral works, including a symphony in G minor.

Berezowsky, Nicolai T., b. St. Petersburg (Leningrad), Russia, 1900. Composer now living in America, whose works include two symphonies (1925, 1929), a *Hebrew Suite, Russia*, a violin concerto, and a *Sinfonietta* (1931).

Berger, Wilhelm, b. Boston, Massachusetts, 1861; d. Jena, Germany, 1911. Teacher and composer, with two symphonies among his works.

Bergh, Arthur, b. St. Paul, Minnesota, 1882. Well known American composer, who has produced two orchestral melodramas, *The Raven* and *The Pied Piper of Hamelin*, and a symphonic choral work, *The Unnamed City*.

Berlioz, Hector, b. Grenoble, France, 1803; d. Paris, 1869. A brilliant but uneven composer in many forms, including several symphonies of a programmatic nature. The first of these was called *Fantastique*, with the subtitle, *Episode in the Life of an Artist* (1828). A sequel, *Lelio*, was less successful. He composed another program symphony, *Harold in Italy*, in 1834, and in 1839 the dramatic *Romeo and Juliet*, in which he added vocal soloists and a chorus to the orchestra. His works include also a *Grand Symphony* for military band, with strings and chorus ad lib. His best known work is the *Damnation of Faust*, in oratorio form, and he also composed operas and smaller orchestral works. His experiments in orchestration were important, and he added much to the life of the symphony through his attempts at dramatization, although his intentions frequently ran ahead of his inspiration.

SYMPHONIC COMPOSERS

Bizet, Georges, b. Paris, 1838; d. Bougival, France, 1875. Best known as the composer of the popular opera, *Carmen*, but with many orchestral works to his credit, including two movements of a symphony. His orchestral suite, *L'Arlesienne*, made up of incidental music to the Daudet play, has become almost as popular as his *Carmen*.

Bliss, Arthur, b. London, England, 1891. English composer, whose works include *Colour Symphony*, a suite from *Things to Come* (motion picture music), etc.

Bloch, Ernest, b. Geneva, Switzerland, 1880. One of the outstanding modern composers, particularly in the Jewish idiom. His symphonies include an early work in C-sharp minor, one in F, with the title *Israel*, an *Oriental Symphony*, on Hebrew themes, a "symphonic fresco," *Helvetia*, and the prize-winning *America* symphony, which contains choral passages. He has also written operas, chamber music, a symphonic poem, and other orchestral works (*Psalms, Schelomo,* etc.) of symphonic proportions.

Boccherini, Luigi, b. Lucca, Italy, 1743; d. Madrid, Spain, 1805. A prolific composer, mostly of chamber music, but with twenty symphonies and an orchestral suite to his credit. He is remembered to-day chiefly by his popular *Minuet*.

Boellmann, Leon, b. Ensisheim, Alsatia, 1862; d. Paris, 1897. Best known as a composer for the cello, in a rather popular style, but with a symphony in F listed among his works. His *Symphonic Variations for Cello and Orchestra* are familiar on concert programs.

Borch, Gaston, b. Guines, France, 1871. Composer of a symphony and three symphonic poems, *Genoveva, Quo Vadis* and *Frithjof*.

Bornschein, Franz Carl, b. Baltimore, Maryland, 1879. Outstanding American composer and critic. His works include a symphonic ballad for baritone and orchestra, *The Djinns*, an orchestral suite, *The Phantom Canoe*, and some symphonic poems.

Borodin, Alexander Porfirievitch, b. St. Petersburg (Leningrad), 1834; d. there, 1887. One of the nationalistic Russian group of five, and composer of many successful works, including the opera, *Prince Igor.* He wrote three symphonies (one unfinished), a symphonic poem, and other orchestral music.

Borowski, Felix, b. Burton, England, 1872. Well known teacher, composer and critic, living most of his life in Chicago. His works include an *Elégie Symphonique* (1916), a symphonic poem, *Eugene Onegin,* a piano concerto, and other orchestral pieces of symphonic proportions.

Brahms, Johannes, b. Hamburg, Germany, 1833; d. Vienna, Austria, 1897. The third of the "three B's," now recognized as the worthy successor of Bach and Beethoven in the field of absolute music. His four symphonies are rivalled only by the masterworks of Beethoven, and may be considered a climax in the symphonic style. His two piano concertos and violin concerto, as well as a double concerto for violin, cello and orchestra, are of symphonic proportions, and two *Serenades,* representing early studies in instrumentation, are generally classed also as symphonic music. (See pp. 185–215.)

Branscombe, Gena, b. Picton, Canada, 1881. Outstanding woman composer, most of whose life has been spent in the United States. She is best known for her songs, but has written a Symphonic Suite, *Quebec* (1928), a *Festival Prelude,* and other orchestral works.

Brockway, Howard, b. Brooklyn, N. Y., 1870. Outstanding American composer, whose works include symphonies in D and C major and a *Sylvan Suite* for orchestra.

Bruch, Max, b. Cologne, Germany, 1838; d. Berlin, 1920. A prolific and deservedly popular composer in the larger forms. His long list of works includes three symphonies and the same number of violin concertos, two of which are frequently heard on the concert platform.

Bruckner, Anton, b. Ansfelden, Austria, 1824; d. Vienna, 1896. An excellent organist and composer, largely self-taught, and strongly influenced by Wagner. His nine symphonies have been greatly admired, and efforts are being constantly made to arouse a more general appreciation of their beauties. Recently they have attained a fairly consistent success, under the leadership of distinguished conductors, although public opinion is still only mildly enthusiastic. The general feeling is that Bruckner's music is technically interesting, but mostly lacking in inspiration.

Buck, Dudley, b. Hartford, Connecticut, 1839; d. Orange, New Jersey, 1909. A prominent American composer, best known for his vocal works, largely of a sacred character, and as an organist. His works include a symphonic overture, *Marmion*.

Bungert, August, b. Muehlheim, Germany, 1846; d. Leutesdorf, 1915. A minor composer, whose conceptions surpassed his ability to express them. He composed two opera-cycles, *The Iliad* and *The Odyssey*, a *Symphonia Victrix*, and another symphony with the title *Zeppelin's First Great Voyage*.

Busch, Carl, b. Bjerre, Denmark, 1862. Generally regarded as an American composer, with particular interest in Indian themes, collected during a long residence in the West. His works include a symphonic prologue, *The Passing of Arthur*, a symphonic poem, *Minnehaha's Vision*, and other orchestral pieces of symphonic proportions.

Cadman, Charles Wakefield, b. Johnstown, Pennsylvania, 1881. One of America's leading contemporary composers, best known by his operas (*Shanewis*, etc.), and by such popular songs as *At Dawning, The Land of the Sky Blue Water*, etc. A specialist in American Indian music, he has composed the popular *Thunderbird Suite* (1914), an *Oriental Rhapsody* (1917), *To a Vanishing Race* (for strings) and an Orchestral Fantasy (with two saxophones, 1932).

Carpenter, John Alden, b. Park Ridge, Illinois, 1876. Highly successful American composer, consistently maintaining the true amateur attitude toward his work. His orchestral suite, *Adventures in a Perambulator,* is of symphonic proportions, an amusingly effective work. His ballets, *The Birthday of the Infanta* and *Skyscrapers,* are also orchestrally important.

Carter, Ernest, b. Orange, New Jersey, 1866. American composer of high standing. His most familiar composition is probably the Princeton *Step Song,* but he has written much good music in the larger forms, including a symphonic suite in D minor, for orchestra.

Casella, Alfredo, b. Turin, Italy, 1883. Prominent modern composer and pianist. He has written two symphonies and other orchestral music.

Chadwick, George Whitfield, b. Lowell, Massachusetts, 1854; d. Boston, 1931. One of America's greatest composers and teachers of music. His long list of important works includes three symphonies (in C, B-flat and F), a sinfonietta in D, three symphonic sketches for orchestra, (*Jubilee, Noël* and *A Vagrom Ballad*), a *Suite Symphonique,* and the symphonic poems, *Cleopatra* and *Aphrodite.*

Chaminade, Cecile, b. Paris, 1861. Generally considered the world's outstanding woman composer, although best known by her lighter works. She has written a ballet symphony, *Callirhoe,* a "lyric symphony," *Les Amazones,* two orchestral suites, and other compositions in the larger forms.

Charpentier, Gustave, b. Dieuze, France, 1860. Up to now, best known as composer of the opera *Louise* and by his orchestral suite, *Impressions of Italy,* he also wrote a "symphonic drama" (or concert-opera), *The Poet's Life,* a symphonic poem, *Napoli,* and other orchestral works.

Chasins, Abram, b. New York, 1903. Gifted American composer and pianist, whose orchestral works have been

performed by Toscanini. These include two piano concertos, *Parade* (1931) and three *Chinese Pieces* (1925).

Chausson, Ernest, b. Paris, 1855; d. Limay, France,
1899. Pupil of Cesar Franck, and a distinguished French
composer. His symphony in B-flat is important, and has
attained considerable popularity. His works include also
a symphonic poem, *Viviane*, the familiar *Poeme*, for violin
and orchestra, and other significant music.

Chavez, Carlos, b. Mexico City, 1899. Brilliant Mexican
composer and conductor, recently introduced to America.
His most important orchestral works are *H. P. Sinfonia
de Baile* (1926–27), and the Suite *Los Cuatros Soles* (1926).

Cherubini, Luigi, b. Florence, Italy, 1760; d. Paris,
France, 1842. One of the great composers of the world,
best known by his operas and church music. He wrote one
symphony, recently revived by Toscanini, whose charming music made a favorable impression, without endanger-
ing the reputations of the more familiar symphonic writers.

Clapp, Philip Greeley, b. Boston, Mass., 1888. American composer and pedagogue, associated with the Juilliard
Foundation and Iowa State University. He has written
three symphonies in A, E minor and E-flat major, besides
the tone poems, *Norge, A Song of Youth, In Summer*,
etc.

Clementi, Muzio, b. Rome, Italy, 1752; d. Evesham,
England, 1832. Celebrated pianist and composer, particularly known by his piano exercises. He wrote symphonies,
but they were overshadowed by those of Haydn, and are
now forgotten.

Coenen, Franz, b. Rotterdam, Holland, 1826; d. Leyden,
1904. Concert violinist and composer, with one symphony
listed among his works.

Coenen, Johannes Meinardus, b. The Hague, Holland,
1824; d. Amsterdam, 1899. Dutch conductor and composer, whose works include two symphonies.

Cole, Rosseter G., b. Clyde, Michigan, 1866. Distinguished American composer, whose works include a *Symphonic Prelude* (1915) and a *Pioneer Overture.*

Coleridge-Taylor, Samuel, b. London, 1875; d. Thornton Heath, 1912. Most distinguished of negro composers. Best known for his choral works, he also wrote a symphony in A minor and other orchestral music.

Converse, Frederick Shepherd, b. Newton, Massachusetts, 1871. Prominent American composer and teacher of music. His operas made his chief reputation, but he also wrote three symphonies, in D minor, E and C minor, the tone poems, *Ormazd, Flivver Ten Million, California,* and other orchestral works.

Copland, Aaron, b. Brooklyn, N. Y., 1900. Prominent American composer of the modern school. His works include a symphony for organ and orchestra (1924), an orchestral symphony of the same year, a *Dance Symphony* (1925), a piano concerto (1926) and a *Symphonic Ode* (1929).

Cowell, Henry Dixon, b. Menlo Park, California, 1897. Modern American composer, best known for his experiments with "tone clusters," and innovations of harmony. He wrote a symphony in 1918, a *Symphonietta* (chamber orchestra, 1928) and *Irish Suite,* a piano concerto (1929), an orchestral piece called *Synchrony* (1930), *Rhythmicana* (1931), and an orchestral suite is in preparation.

Cowen, Frederick Hymen, b. Kingston, Jamaica, 1852. Eminent English composer in a wide variety of forms, including six symphonies (*Scandinavian, Welch, Idyllic,* etc.) a sinfonietta in A, and three orchestral suites.

Czerny, Karl, b. Vienna, Austria, 1791; d. there, 1857. Best known as a teacher and composer of studies for the piano. His compositions include symphonies and considerable church music.

Damrosch, Leopold, b. Posen, 1832; d. New York, 1885. Father of Frank and Walter Damrosch, and an important pioneer in American music, particularly the development of opera. His compositions include a symphony in A, and other orchestral works.

David, Felicien, b. Vaucluse, France, 1810; d. St. Germain-en-Laye, 1876. Important French composer, best known by his operas. His early works include two symphonies.

David, Ferdinand, b. Hamburg, Germany, 1810; d. Klosters, Switzerland, 1873. Eminent violinist, teacher and composer, befriended and greatly respected by Mendelssohn, with whom he co-operated in his violin concerto. His own works include two symphonies.

Dawson, William L., b. Anniston, Alabama, 1899. Successful colored composer, conductor of the Tuskegee Choir. His *Negro Folk Symphony* was introduced by the Philadelphia Orchestra and made a deep impression.

Debussy, Claude, b. St. Germain-en-Laye, France, 1862; d. Paris, 1918. France's leading composer, generally recognized as the founder of the modern school. Best known by his songs and piano music, as well as the unique opera, *Pelleas and Melisande.* Some of his orchestral works are of symphonic proportions, particularly *La Mer, Iberia* and the three *Nocturnes.*

Delamarter, Eric, b. Lansing, Michigan, 1880. Distinguished American composer, organist, critic and conductor. Among other orchestral works, he has written a "jazz symphony" on American themes, which proved highly successful. The dates of his four symphonies are 1914 (D), 1926 ("after Walt Whitman"), 1931 and 1932.

Delaney, Robert Mills, b. Baltimore, Maryland, 1903. Composer of a *Don Quixote* symphony, 1927.

Ditters, Karl (von Dittersdorf), b. Vienna, Austria, 1739; d. Neuhaus, Bohemia, 1799. Prolific composer of operas (eclipsed by Mozart) and symphonies (eclipsed by Haydn and Mozart). His symphonies are remarkable as early examples of program music in this form. He wrote twelve on the *Metamorphoses of Ovid*. Forty-one symphonies remain in manuscript.

Dohnányi, Ernst, b. Pressburg, Hungary, 1877. Outstanding modern composer and pianist, well known in America, where he for a time conducted the Philharmonic Orchestra of New York. His first symphony, in F, won a prize in 1896. He has since written a second symphony, in D minor, and many other orchestral compositions of symphonic proportions.

Draeseke, Felix, b. Koburg, Germany, 1835; d. Dresden, 1913. Excellent composer, befriended by Liszt. His works include four symphonies.

Dubensky, Arcady, b. Viatla, Russia, 1890. Composer of a symphony in G minor (1916), another called *Russian Bells* (1928), an orchestral suite (1926), and an *ABC Suite*, for children.

Dukas, Paul, b. Paris, 1865; d. there, 1935. Distinguished modern French composer, best known by his popular orchestral piece, *The Sorcerer's Apprentice*. He wrote several operas and a symphony in C.

Dukelsky, Vladimir, b. Pskoff, Russia, 1903. Also known as Vernon Duke (as a popular composer). Gifted Russian American creator of music in many styles. His works include symphonies in F and D-flat.

Dunn, James P., b. New York, 1884; d. Jersey City, 1936. Well known American composer, whose works included a symphony in C (1929). He also wrote the symphonic poem, *We*, celebrating Lindbergh's flight, and another, *Annabelle Lee*, after Poe's poem. His songs are also well known.

Dvořák, Anton, b. Muehlhausen, Bohemia, 1841; d. Prague, 1904. Best known by his American symphony, *From the New World*, he has many other important works to his credit, including four other symphonies, a set of symphonic variations for orchestra, and a symphonic poem, *Heldenlied*. (See pp. 258–267).

Ehlert, Louis, b. Koenigsberg, Germany, 1825; d. Wiesbaden, 1884. Pupil of Schumann and Mendelssohn, and an excellent composer. Among other large works, he wrote a *Spring Symphony*.

Elgar, Edward, b. Broadheath, England, 1857; d. London, 1934. England's most important modern composer. Best known by his choral works (oratorios, etc.), he has several symphonies to his credit, as well as symphonic poems and smaller orchestral compositions. His *Enigma Variations* are also of symphonic significance.

Enesco, Georges, b. Cordaremi, Roumania, 1881. Distinguished violinist, conductor and composer, whose works include two symphonies and other orchestral pieces.

Eppert, Carl, b. Carbon, Indiana, 1882. American composer of orchestral works, including an *Arabian Suite*, a symphonic poem, *Wanderer's Night Song*, a symphonic epic, *The Argonauts of '49*, *The Pioneer*, *Traffic*, and *Symphony of the City*.

Faccio, Franco, b. Verona, Italy, 1840; d. Monza, 1891. Italian conductor and composer, who wrote a symphony in F and other works.

Farwell, Arthur, b. St. Paul, Minnesota, 1872. Distinguished American composer and teacher. He wrote a "symphonic hymn," *March, March* (1922), a *Symphonic Song on Old Black Joe* (1924), and a suite, *Gods of the Mountain* (1927).

Fauré, Gabriel, b. Pamiers. France, 1845; d. Paris, 1924. Outstanding among modern French composers, with operas, songs, chamber music and orchestral works to his credit, including a symphony in D minor.

Ferrata, Giuseppe, b. Gradoli, Italy, 1865. Talented Italian composer, who spent some time in America. His compositions include a choral symphony in D-flat.

Fétis, François Joseph, b. Mons, Belgium, 1784; d. Brussels, 1871. Famous musical scholar, critic and historian. His compositions include symphonies and other orchestral works.

Fibich, Zdenko, b. Seborsitz, Bohemia, 1850; d. Prague, 1900. Popular Czech composer best known in America by his *Poeme* for violin, which was turned into the popular song, *My Moonlight Madonna*. His works include three symphonies.

Foote, Arthur, b. Salem, Massachusetts, 1853. Outstanding American composer. His works include a symphonic prologue, *Francesca da Rimini*, some suites and other orchestral compositions, besides chamber music, songs and piano pieces.

Franck, Cesar, b. Liège, Belgium, 1822; d. Paris, 1890. Belgium's greatest composer, a pioneer in the modern French school. His one symphony, in D, is a universal favorite, and he also wrote several symphonic poems, a set of symphonic variations for piano and orchestra, oratorios, organ works and much chamber music of the highest type. (See pp. 216–221).

Gade, Niels Wilhelm, b. Copenhagen, Denmark, 1817; d. there, 1890. Founder of the Scandinavian school of music, and close friend of Schumann and Mendelssohn. A prolific composer, still widely played. He wrote eight symphonies, besides other works in the larger forms.

Ganz, Rudolph, b. Zurich, Switzerland, 1877. Distinguished pianist, teacher, conductor and composer, long resident in America. His first published work was a symphony in E, and he has written other orchestral works, as well as songs and piano pieces.

Gardner, Samuel, b. Elizabethgrad, Russia, 1892. Russian-American violinist and composer of marked ability. His Symphonic Rhapsody, *Broadway*, was introduced by the Boston Symphony Orchestra, and his tone poem, *New Russia*, has been played by leading orchestras.

He is best known by his popular violin piece, *From the Canebrake*, and has also written a successful piano quintet.

German, Edward, b. Whitchurch, England, 1862. Popular English composer, best known by his incidental music to *Henry VIII*. He wrote two symphonies, and other important orchestral works.

Gernsheim, Friedrich, b. Worms, Germany, 1839; d. Berlin, 1916. Eminent teacher and composer. His works include four symphonies.

Gershwin, George, b. New York, 1898. Popular American composer, best known for his light operas and songs. He has written three important orchestral works, the famous *Rhapsody in Blue* (1923), the Concerto in F (for piano, 1925), and *An American in Paris* (1928); also a second Rhapsody (1932) and a Rhumba. His suite from the opera, *Porgy and Bess* (1936) is of symphonic proportions.

Gilbert, Henry Franklin, b. Somerville, Massachusetts, 1868; d. Boston, 1918. Pupil of Macdowell and an outstanding American composer, with particular interest in Negro and Indian themes. His works include a symphonic poem, *The Dance in Place Congo* (produced as a ballet at the Metropolitan Opera House) and a symphonic prologue, *Riders to the Sea*, as well as other orchestral compositions.

Gilchrist, William Wallace, b. Jersey City, New Jersey, 1846; d. Philadelphia, Pa., 1916. Prominent American musician, working mostly in Philadelphia. He wrote two symphonies (in C and D) and much church music.

Giorni, Aurelio, b. Florence, Italy, 1895. Distinguished Italian-American pianist and composer. His works include a *Sinfonia Concertante* (1931) and the symphonic poem, *Orlando Furioso* (1926).

Glazounoff, Alexander, b. St. Petersburg (Leningrad) Russia, 1865; d. Paris, France, 1936. Famous Russian, composer, popularized in America largely by his ballet, *The Seasons*, and a violin concerto. He composed eight symphonies, several symphonic poems, and other large works for orchestra.

Glière, Reinhold, b. Kiev, Russia, 1875. Prominent composer, teacher and conductor of modern Russia. His works include three symphonies and some symphonic poems.

Glinka, Michail Ivanovitch, b. Smolensk, Russia, 1804; d. Berlin, Germany, 1857. Pioneer Russian composer, and founder of the nationalistic school, strongly influencing the later group of five. Best known by his operas, *A Life for the Czar* and *Russlan and Ludmilla*, he also produced many orchestral compositions, including two unfinished symphonies.

Godard, Benjamin, b. Paris, 1849; d. Cannes, 1895. Popular French composer of operas, songs and instrumental music. He wrote a symphony ballet (1882), a *Gothic Symphony* (1883), an *Oriental Symphony* (1884), and a *Legendary Symphony* (1886) with vocal soloists and chorus; also a symphony in B minor, a dramatic symphony, *Tasso*, with voices, and two orchestral suites.

Goetz, Hermann, b. Koenigsberg, Germany, 1840; d. Zurich, Switzerland, 1876. Talented composer, best known for his opera, *The Taming of the Shrew*, but also creator of a symphony in F and other orchestral works.

Goldbeck, Robert, b. Potsdam, Germany, 1839; d. St. Louis, Missouri, 1908. Pianist and composer, much of whose life was spent in America. He wrote both vocal and instrumental music, including a symphony, *Victoria*.

Goldmark, Karl, b. Keszthely, Hungary, 1830; d. Vienna, 1915. Popular composer, violinist and pianist. His overture, *Sakuntala*, and opera, *The Queen of Sheba*, made him famous. His orchestral works include a symphony in E-flat and the popular *Rustic Wedding Symphony*, as well as a symphonic poem, *Zriny*.

Goldmark, Rubin, b. New York, 1872; d. there, 1935. Nephew of Karl Goldmark, and a leader among American musicians. His works include a symphonic poem, *Samson*, a *Requiem*, and a *Negro Rhapsody*.

Goltermann, Georg, b. Hanover, Germany, 1824; d. Frankfort-on-the-Main, 1898. Best known as a cellist and composer for the cello, but with a symphony in A minor and other orchestral works to his credit.

Gottschalk, Louis Moreau, b. New Orleans, Louisiana, 1829; d. Rio de Janeiro, South America, 1869. Brilliant pianist and composer, with a special command of Creole music. Best known by his short piano pieces, he wrote also in the larger forms. His two symphonies are entitled *Night in the Tropics* and *Montevideo*.

Gounod, Charles François, b. Paris, 1818; d. there, 1893. Famous and popular composer, chiefly of operas and sacred music, best known by his *Faust* and *Romeo and Juliet* (also his *Redemption, Gallia, Ave Maria,* etc.). A symphony in E-flat is among his early works.

Granados, Enrique, b. Lerida, Catalonia, 1867; d. at sea (English Channel) 1916. Successful composer of Spanish music, remembered for his opera, *Goyescas*, and a familiar group of *Spanish Dances*. His works include two symphonic poems.

Grasse, Edwin, b. New York, 1884. Blind violinist and composer of note. His works include a symphony in G minor and an orchestral suite in C.

Gretchaninoff, Alexander, b. Moscow, Russia, 1864. Important composer, particularly of Russian church music. He wrote two symphonies (op. 6 and 27).

Grétry, André, b. Liège, Belgium, 1741; d. Paris, 1813. Best known as an operatic composer, but with six symphonies and other orchestral works to his credit.

Grieg, Edvard Hagerup, b. Bergen, Norway, 1843; d. there, 1907. Most popular of all Scandinavian composers.

Best known to-day by his songs and piano pieces, but his great concerto for piano and orchestra is of symphonic proportions, and he wrote other important orchestral music, including the two *Peer Gynt* suites, *Elegiac Melodies* (strings) and *Olav Trygvason* (with solo and chorus).

Griffes, Charles Tomlinson, b. Elmira, N. Y., 1884; d. New York, 1920. One of America's most important composers, whose tragically short life produced several fine orchestral works, including the symphonic poem, *The Pleasure-Dome of Kubla Khan*.

Griffis, Elliot. Gifted American composer, winner of a Pulitzer Prize. He has written a symphony in C minor, a symphonic poem, *Colossus*, and a ballade, *A Persian Fable*, besides chamber music, etc.

Gruenberg, Louis, b. Russia, 1884. Prominent Russian-American composer, best known by his opera, *The Emperor Jones*. He also wrote a *Jazz Suite* (1925), a symphony (1926) and the tone poem, *Enchanted Isle* (1927), besides other important orchestral works.

Guilmant, Alexandre, b. Boulogne, 1837; d. Paris, 1911. French organist and composer, mostly of organ music. His works include a symphony for organ and orchestra.

Hadley, Henry Kimball, b. Somerville, Mass., 1871. America's leading symphonic composer, prolific in many styles of music. His first symphony, *Youth and Life*, was composed in 1897. The second, *The Four Seasons*, dated 1901, won the Paderewski Prize and a prize from the New England Conservatory. His third symphony, in B minor, is dated 1906 and was first performed in 1907. Hadley's fourth symphony is called *North, East, South, West*. The key is D minor, and the date 1911. A fifth symphony is in manuscript, and there are also several symphonic poems and a number of other orchestral works in the extensive Hadley list. Henry Hadley is the founder and Honorary President of the National Association for American Composers and Conductors.

Hanson, Howard Harold, b. Wahoo, Nebraska, 1896. Important American composer with several symphonic works to his credit, as well as the successful opera, *Merry Mount*. At present head of the Eastman School of Music in Rochester. Hanson's compositions include the symphonic poems *Before the Dawn, Exaltation, North and West, Lux Aeterna, Pan and the Priest,* an *Organ Concerto,* a *Symphonic Rhapsody,* a *Symphonic Legend,* and two symphonies—the *Nordic* (1922) and the *Romantic* (1930).

Harris, Roy, b. Lincoln County, Oklahoma, 1898. A leader among modern American composers. He has written two symphonies (1929, 1933) and other important orchestral works, including an Andante, a Toccata, an Overture, a Concert Piece, some Suites, a Cello Concerto, etc.

Haydn, Franz Joseph, b. Rohrau, Austria, 1732; d. Vienna, 1809. The "Father of the Symphony," credited with establishing the permanent form of that type of composition, as well as the basic outlines of sonata form in general. Over one hundred symphonies by Haydn are listed, besides many other orchestral works, chamber music, sonatas, concertos, etc. His most important piece of vocal music is the dramatic oratorio, *The Creation,* rivalled by the less familiar *The Seasons.* He also wrote several operas, now forgotten, many songs, and a quantity of church music. Haydn was one of the most prolific and widely significant composers in the entire history of music. See pp. 1–36.

Hill, Edward Burlingame, b. Cambridge, Mass., 1872. Distinguished American composer and teacher of music at Harvard and elsewhere. His works include a Symphonic Pantomime, *Jack Frost* (1908), another called *Pan and the Star* (1914), a Symphonic Poem, *The Parting of Lancelot and Guinevere* (1915), four orchestral pieces under the title of *Stevensoniana* (1918), two Suites, and two Symphonies, the first in B-flat (1927) and the second in C (1929).

Hindemith, Paul, b. Hanau, Germany, 1895. Outstanding composer of the modern school. He has made a "symphony" of excerpts from his opera, *Mathis der Maler*, and is credited with other important orchestral works.

Hinton, Arthur, b. Beckenham, England, 1869. English composer, whose works include two symphonies, in B-flat and C minor.

Holst, Gustav, b. Cheltenham, England, 1874; d. London, 1934. Important modern composer. His first symphony, *Cotswolds* (1900), was followed by a symphonic poem and other orchestral works. His suite, *The Planets*, is of symphonic proportions, and has been widely played. Holst is also well known for his choral works.

Honegger, Arthur, b. Havre, France, 1892. Outstanding modernist, best known for his orchestral tone poem, *Pacific 231*. His *King David* is described by him as a "symphonic psalm," and his *Horace Victorieux* is called a "mimed symphony." He has written many other orchestral works.

Huettenbrenner, Anselm, b. Graz, Styria, 1794; d. there, 1868. Intimate friend of Beethoven and Schubert, and a composer of ability. He wrote five symphonies, in addition to a large amount of vocal music.

Indy, Vincent d', b. Paris, 1851; d. there, 1931. Outstanding French symphonic composer. His earliest symphonic work, op. 5, was called *Jean Hunyadi*. This was followed by two symphonic poems and a "symphonic trilogy," *Wallenstein*, op. 12. His "first" symphony, *On a French Mountain Song*, in G, with piano obbligato, is numbered opus 25, and the second, in B-flat, is op. 57. The Symphonic Variations, *Istar*, are generally regarded as a symphony, and widely played. Most of these compositions are programmatic.

Ippolitoff-Ivanoff, Mikail, b. Gatschina, Russia, 1859; d. Moscow, 1935. Prominent Russian composer, pupil of Rimsky-Korsakoff. His works include a symphony, a sinfonietta, and the popular *Caucasian Sketches*, for orchestra, which are of symphonic proportions. He also wrote several operas, and made a study of Grusinian folk-music.

Ives, Charles, b. Danbury, Conn., 1876. Modern American composer, who wrote two *Orchestral Sets* (1914–15) and a "third" and "fourth symphony" (1916).

Jacobi, Frederick, b. San Francisco, California, 1891. Popular American composer, chiefly in the lighter forms. He wrote a symphony in 1924, and also the orchestral tone poem, *Eve of St. Agnes.*

Jadassohn, Salamon, b. Breslau, Germany, 1831; d. Leipzig, 1902. Composer, teacher and writer on the theory of music. Among his compositions are four symphonies and other orchestral pieces.

James, Philip, b. New York, 1890. Prize-winning American composer and conductor, well known to radio listeners. His works include a symphonic poem, *Aucassin and Nicolette,* the *WGZBX Suite,* a *Kammer Symphonie,* and other major compositions for orchestra.

Jarecki, Tadeusz, b. Poland, 1889. Modern composer, whose works include a *Sinfonia Breve,* op. 20, a *Symphonic Suite,* op. 29, and a second symphony, op. 30 (1930).

Kallinikoff, Vassili, b. Voina, Russia, 1866; d. Jalta, 1901. Minor Russian composer, but with two symphonies to his credit, in G minor and A major.

Kelley, Edgar Stillman, b. Sparta, Wisconsin, 1857. Outstanding American composer in a variety of styles. His first symphony, op. 15, is called *Gulliver—His Voyage to Lilliput.* His second symphony, op. 33, has the title *New England.* Orchestral suites have been made of his *Ben Hur* and *Macbeth* music, and there is also an *Aladdin Suite* from his pen, besides other important orchestral works, songs, choral and chamber music.

Kramer, A. Walter, b. New York, 1890. Distinguished American composer, writer and editor, now also engaged in publishing music. His compositions, mostly in the smaller forms, include two *Symphonic Sketches*, op. 16, and a *Symphonic Rhapsody* for violin and orchestra, in F minor, op. 35. His songs are popular on the concert stage.

Kriens, Christiaan, b. Amsterdam, Holland, 1881; d. New York, 1934. Dutch-American composer and conductor. His long list of compositions includes two symphonies, in C and F, an orchestral suite, *In Holland*, and a symphonic poem, *Les Rois en Exile*.

Kurtz, Edward Frampton, b. Newport, Rhode Island, 1892. American composer of a symphony in A minor, 1927.

Lalo, Édouard, b. Lille, France, 1823; d. Paris, 1892. Popular French composer, best known by his *Symphonie Espagnole*, which is really a violin concerto. But he wrote an actual symphony in G minor, and other important orchestral works, as well as the opera, *Le Roi d'Ys*, whose overture is familiar.

Lassen, Eduard, b. Copenhagen, Denmark, 1830; d. Weimar, Germany, 1904. Minor composer of considerable popularity, whose works include two symphonies and other orchestral compositions.

Liszt, Franz, b. Raiding, Hungary, 1811; d. Bayreuth, Germany, 1886. Extraordinary pianist, and clever composer, chiefly noted for his technical feats. His compositions include a *Dante* symphony, a *Faust* symphony (in three movements, representing Faust, Marguerite and Mephistopheles), and a number of symphonic poems which are models of their kind, such as *Tasso, Les Preludes, Mazeppa*, etc. His piano music is outstanding, and he also wrote songs, choral music and sacred works.

Loeffler, Charles Martin, b. Muehlhausen, Alsace, 1861; d. Boston, 1935. Outstanding French-American composer of orchestral works and other important music. His symphony in one movement, *Hora Mystica*, for orchestra and men's chorus, was performed at the Norfolk Festival in

1916. He is also well known by his symphonic *Pagan Poem*, *The Death of Tintagiles*, *Vilanelle du Diable*, etc.

Macdowell, Edward, b. New York, 1861; d. there 1908. America's leading composer, best known by his songs and piano pieces, but with many orchestral works to his credit, including a symphony, *Roland*, the symphonic poems, *Hamlet*, *Ophelia*, *Lancelot and Elaine*, *Lamia* and the popular *Indian Suite*, *In October*, etc.

Maganini, Quinto, b. Fairfield, California, 1897. Well known American composer and conductor. He has written a symphony in G minor (1932), several Rhapsodies, and an *Ornithological Suite*.

Mahler, Gustav, b. Kalischt, Bohemia, 1860; d. Vienna, 1911. Distinguished composer and conductor, at one time leading the N. Y. Philharmonic Orchestra. He wrote nine symphonies, in D major, 1891; C minor, 1895; D minor, 1896; G major, 1901; D minor, 1904; A minor, 1906; E minor, 1908; E major, 1910 (with chorus and soloists, known as the *Symphony of a Thousand*); D major (posthumous). His work is characterized by greatness of conception and technical mastery, but has not yet proved sufficiently inspired to win general popularity. Mahler and Bruckner remain the most ambitious and least appreciated symphonic composers.

Mason, Daniel Gregory, b. Brookline, Mass., 1873. Outstanding American composer and teacher of music. His symphony in C minor, op. 11, was introduced in 1916 by the Philadelphia Orchestra. More recently he has written another symphony, in A, op. 30 (1930).

McDonald, Harl, b. Boulder, Colorado, 1899. Promising young American composer. His "program" symphony, *The Santa Fé Trail*, was introduced successfully by the Philadelphia Orchestra. He has also written a Symphonic Fantasy, *Mojave* (1922) and a Ballet Suite (1920).

Mendelssohn, Felix (Bartholdy), b. Hamburg, Germany, 1809; d. Leipzig, 1847. Gifted and popular composer of symphonic and other types of music. His *Midsummer Night's Dream Overture* was written when he was a mere boy. His *Songs without Words* are among the most familiar of piano compositions, and his *Elijah* ranks among the greatest of oratorios. He wrote four symphonies, the first, in C minor, op. 11, the second (*Scotch*) in A minor, op. 56, the third (*Italian*) in A major, op. 90, and the fourth (*Reformation*) in D, op. 107. His violin concerto is the most popular piece of that type. See pp. 174–184.

Miaskowski, Nikolai, b. Moscow, Russia, 1881. Interesting composer of modern music, with symphonic works to his credit.

Moore, Douglas Stuart, b. Cutchogue, N. Y., 1893. Eminent American composer and member of the musical faculty of Columbia University. His *Pageant of P. T. Barnum* is of symphonic proportions, and he has also written a *Symphony of Autumn* (1930).

Morris, Harold, b. San Antonio, Texas, 1890. One of the best of America's modern composers. He wrote a symphony in 1925, and also a piano concerto and other important orchestral works.

Mozart, Wolfgang Amadeus, b. Salzburg, Austria, 1756; d. Vienna, 1791. The "Wunderkind" of all composers, displaying amazing gifts from early childhood to the end of his tragically short life. He wrote over forty symphonies, of which the last three stand among the supreme masterpieces of music. Mozart was famous also for his operas (*Don Giovanni, The Marriage of Figaro, The Magic Flute,* etc.), chamber music, church music, songs, piano pieces, concertos, sonatas, etc., showing versatility, originality and musicianship, as well as apparently unlimited creative powers. See pp. 37–60.

Nicolai, Otto, b. Koenigsberg, Germany, 1810; d. Berlin, 1849. Best known for his opera, *The Merry Wives of Windsor* (especially the popular overture), but including a symphony and other orchestral numbers among his works.

Oldberg, Arne, b. Youngstown, Ohio, 1874. Distinguished American composer and teacher of music. His many orchestral works include symphonies in F minor, op. 23, and C minor, op. 34, both of which won prizes in national competitions. He has also composed much chamber music, concertos, sonatas, etc.

Ornstein, Leo, b. Krementchug, Russia, 1895. Pioneer among Russian-American modernists, and a concert pianist and teacher of high rank. He has written a symphony (with another in preparation), a symphonic poem, *The Fog*, a Suite from *Lysistrata*, a piano concerto, etc.

Paderewski, Ignace Jan, b. Kurilovka, Poland, 1860. Best known as a concert pianist and political leader, but also recognized as a distinguished composer, chiefly through his opera, *Manru*, and various piano pieces (of which the familiar *Minuet* is the most popular). Paderewski's works include a symphony in B minor, op. 24, first performed by the Boston Symphony Orchestra in 1909.

Paine, John Knowles, b. Portland, Maine, 1839; d. Cambridge, Mass., 1906. Pioneer among American composers and teachers of music, long on the Faculty of Harvard University, where he influenced many younger musicians. His symphony in C minor was first performed by Theodore Thomas and the Chicago Orchestra in 1876, and the same conductor introduced a second symphony, *Spring*, op. 23, in 1880. Paine also wrote symphonic poems (*An Island Fantasy, The Tempest*) and other important orchestral works, chamber music, an opera, songs, etc.

Parker, Horatio William, b. Auburndale, Mass., 1863; d. Cedarhurst, N. Y., 1919. An acknowledged leader among American composers, with significant works to his credit in many forms. His oratorio, *Hora Novissima*, is perhaps best known, and his operas, *Mona* and *Fairyland*, both won prizes of $10,000, the first from the Metropolitan Opera Company (1912) and the second from the National Federation of Music Clubs (1915). (Both librettos were by Brian Hooker.) Among Horatio Parker's orchestral works is a symphony in C minor, op. 7 (manuscript), performed in Munich in 1885, a *Scherzo* in G, a symphonic poem, etc. He also wrote songs, chamber music and choral works of high quality.

Parry, Charles Hubert, b. Bournemouth, England, 1848; d. Rustington, 1918. Eminent English composer in various forms. His works include five symphonies. The first is in G (1882); the second in F (1883); the third in C (1889); the fourth in E minor (1889) and the fifth in B minor (after 1900). Parry also wrote much vocal music, particularly part-songs in the old English style, which proved highly successful.

Pimsleur, Solomon, b. Paris, France, 1900. French-American composer of considerable creative activity, appearing also as pianist and lecturer. His *Symphonic Ballade*, op. 18, no. 5, has been performed by the N. Y. Philharmonic and other orchestras. There is also a *Symphonic Suite*, op. 33, completed in 1935, and a *Symphonic Ode and Peroration*, op. 35, dated 1936. Other orchestral works by Pimsleur are the tone poem, *Miracle of Life and the Mystery of Death*, op. 32, a *Partita* for strings, several Overtures and a *Meditative Nocturne*.

Piston, Walter, b. Rockland, Maine, 1894. Eminent modern American composer. His works include a *Symphonic Piece* (1927) and a Suite (1929).

Powell, John, b. Richmond, Virginia, 1882. American pianist and composer of high rank, who has made a special study of negro and mountain music. His *Negro Rhapsody*, for piano and orchestra, is of symphonic proportions, and he has written concertos for the piano and the violin, and other works in the larger forms.

Pratt, Silas Gamaliel, b. Addison, Vermont, 1846; d. Pittsburgh, Pa., 1916. American composer and pianist, with a number of orchestral works to his credit, including a symphony (*The Prodigal Son*), two symphonic poems, two suites, etc.

Prokofieff, Serge, b. Ekaterinoslav, Russia, 1891. Brilliant Russian composer of the modern school. He has written four symphonies (*Classical*, etc.) and many other orchestral works, besides concertos, piano pieces, chamber music, etc.

Rachmaninoff, Sergei V., b. Onega, Russia, 1873. Generally regarded as Russia's leading musician of modern times, and one of the greatest of living composers. His first symphony, op. 13, was written in 1895; the second, op. 27, appeared in 1907. His choral cantata, *The Bells* (after Poe's poem) was first called Symphony no. 3, op. 35 (1912), but recently he has completed a purely orchestral symphony which is now known as his third. Rachmaninoff has also written four piano concertos, a symphonic poem, *The Island of the Dead* (after Boecklin's famous picture), many songs, piano pieces, sacred music, etc. It is unfortunate that he should still be best known to the general public by his youthful and now hackneyed *Prelude in C-sharp minor.*

Raff, Joseph Joachim, b. 1822, Lachen, Switzerland; d. Frankfort, Germany, 1882. A minor German composer, whose symphonies at one time attained considerable popularity. He wrote eleven symphonies altogether, besides a sinfonietta for wind instruments, several suites, concertos and other orchestral works. The programmatic symphony, *Im Walde* (*In the Forest*), is still frequently played. Raff's *Leonore* symphony contains a familiar march tune, which was publicized in a sentimental musical novel called *The First Violin.* His best known work is still the melodious little *Cavatina*, played by every violinist.

Reger, Max, b. Brand, Germany, 1873; d. Jena, 1916. Scholarly composer, both prolific and versatile, whose works include orchestral pieces of symphonic proportions. His *Variations* on themes by Hiller and Mozart are well known on concert programs, and he is also credited with a *Symphonic Prologue to a Tragedy*, a sinfonietta, an orchestral serenade, several tone poems, suites, concertos, etc.

Reinecke, Karl, b. Altona, Germany, 1824; d. Leipzig, 1910. Excellent composer, pianist and teacher, with many works to his credit, including three symphonies, ten overtures and other orchestral music.

Reznicek, Emil Nicolaus, b. Vienna, Austria, 1861. Minor composer of operas and instrumental music, including two symphonies, *Tragic*, in D minor and *Ironic*, in E major, a symphonic poem, *Peter Schlemihl*, two symphonic suites, etc.

Ries, Ferdinand, b. Bonn, Germany, 1784; d. Frankfort, 1836. A piano pupil of Beethoven and later a prolific but uninspired composer. His works include six symphonies and other orchestral compositions, besides much chamber music, etc.

Rimsky-Korsakoff, Nikolai A., b. Tikhvin, Russia, 1844; d. Leningrad (then St. Petersburg), 1908. One of the famous Russian group of five, particularly associated with Moussorgsky, some of whose work he completed. Rimsky is probably best known by the light *Song of India*, from his opera *Sadko*, and by the symphonic suite, *Scheherazade*, which has found a regular place on symphony programs (see pp. 248–257). His opera, *Le Coq d'Or*, has also become popular, and his use of the Oriental idiom is almost unique in music. He has three actual symphonies to his credit, the first in E minor, the second a programmatic work with the title *Antar*, and the third in C major. There is also a sinfonietta in A minor and other orchestral material of symphonic proportions, including the overture, *Russian Easter*, a *Spanish Caprice*, etc.

Rogers, Bernard, b. New York, 1883. Composer of a symphony (1929) and an orchestral work called *Japanese Landscapes* (1925).

Roussel, Albert, b. Tourcoing, France, 1869. Minor French composer, whose works include two symphonies and a Symphonic Prelude, *Resurrection*.

Rubinstein, Anton G., b. Wechwotynecz, Russia, 1830; d. Peterhof, 1894. Famous pianist and composer, unfortunately best known to the general public by his hackneyed *Melody in F* and *Kammenoi-Ostrow.* He wrote six symphonies, of which the one called *Ocean,* op. 40, has six movements, to which he later added a seventh. Rubinstein composed much orchestral and chamber music, several successful operas, songs, etc.

Saint-Saëns, Camille, b. Paris, 1835; d. there, 1921. Outstanding composer of modern France, prolific in many styles. The general public probably knows him best by an aria from his oratorio-opera, *Samson and Delilah,* the cello solo, *The Swan,* from his *Carnival of Animals,* and the tone poem, *Danse Macabre.* But Saint-Saëns wrote five symphonies (one with organ), several important symphonic poems, suites, concertos and other large orchestral works, besides chamber music, songs, piano pieces, sacred music and operas.

Saminsky, Lazare, b. Odessa, Russia, 1883. Distinguished Russian-American composer, best known for his sacred music. He has written five symphonies, as follows: No. 1, *Of the Rivers,* 1914; no. 2, *Of the Summits,* 1918; no. 3, *Of the Seas,* 1924; no. 4, 1927; no. 5, *Jerusalem* (with chorus), 1932.

Schelling, Ernest, b. Belvedere, New Jersey, 1876. American pianist, composer and conductor, specializing in children's concerts. His *Morocco* is called a "symphonic tableau." Other orchestral works, such as the *Impressions of an Artist's Life* (1913), his violin concerto (1916) and *A Victory Ball* (1923) are of symphonic proportions.

Schubert, Franz Peter, b. Lichtenthal, Austria, 1797; d. Vienna, 1828. One of the great musicians of all time, perhaps the most extraordinary natural composer that ever lived. See pp. 133–150.

Schumann, Robert Alexander, b. Zwickau, Germany, 1810; d. Bonn, 1856. One of the leaders of Romanticism in music, with a high rank among the great composers of the world. See pp. 151–173.

Scriabine, Alexander N., b. Moscow, Russia, 1872; d. there, 1915. One of the most important of modern composers, influenced by Chopin, and himself affecting the work of many of his contemporaries and followers. His three symphonies include *The Divine Poem*, op. 43, while his *Prometheus* (with color organ) and *Poem of Ecstasy* are also of symphonic proportions. He wrote much other orchestral music, significant piano pieces, etc.

Sessions, Roger, b. Brooklyn, N. Y., 1896. A leader among American modernists in music. He wrote a symphony in 1927, and his Suite from *The Black Maskers* (1928) is also important. A violin concerto appeared in 1926, and there are other orchestral works to his credit, including another symphony, chamber music, etc.

Shepherd, Arthur, b. Paris, Idaho, 1880. American composer and musical scholar. Among his orchestral works is a *Choreographic Suite* (1931) and a tone poem, *Horizons*.

Shostakovitch, Dimitri, b. Leningrad, Russia, 1906. Most spectacular of the modern Russian composers, whose opera, *Lady Macbeth of Msensk*, created a sensation. He has written three symphonies (with a fourth now under way) and other orchestral works, besides composing for the motion pictures.

Sibelius, Jean, b. Tavastehus, Finland, 1865. Probably the greatest modern symphonic composer, with eight important symphonies to his credit, mostly in a definitely modern and individual style. He has also written such symphonic poems as *The Swan of Tuonela* and the popular *Finlandia*, suites and other orchestral works, an opera, choral works, chamber music, etc. The symphonies of Sibelius are listed as follows: No. 1, E minor, op. 39; no. 2, D major, op. 43; no. 3, C major, op. 52; no. 4, A minor, op. 63; no. 5, E-flat major, op. 82; no. 6, D minor, op. 104; no. 7, C major, op. 105.

Sinding, Christian, b. Kongsberg, Norway, 1856. Popular Scandinavian composer, who spent some time in America as teacher of composition at the Eastman School, Rochester, N. Y. His works include two symphonies and other orchestral compositions.

Skilton, Charles Sanford, b. Northampton, Mass., 1868. American composer and teacher, specializing in Indian music, and long a member of the Faculty of Kansas University. His *Suite Primeval* and *Indian Dances* are of symphonic proportions.

Smetana, Friedrich, b. Leitomischl, Bohemia, 1824; d. Prague, 1884. Outstanding Czech composer, best known for his opera, *The Bartered Bride*, but with a *Triumphal Symphony* to his credit, various symphonic poems, chamber music, etc.

Smith, David Stanley, b. Toledo, Ohio, 1877. Prominent American composer and teacher of music, long a member of the Yale Faculty. His works include three symphonies, in F minor, op. 28, in D, op. 42, and in C minor, op. 60, the symphonic poems, *Darkness and Dawn* and *Prince Hal,* overtures and other orchestral works, chamber music, etc.

Somervell, Arthur, b. Windermere, England, 1863. Distinguished English composer, whose works include a symphony and a set of symphonic variations.

Sowerby, Leo, b. Grand Rapids, Michigan, 1895. Outstanding American composer, with three symphonies to his credit, as well as a Suite from *The Northland* (1923) and a symphonic poem, *The Prairie* (1929).

Spelman, Timothy Mather, b. Brooklyn, N. Y., 1891. American composer of orchestral music, including two suites, *Barbaresque* and *Saints' Days,* and a symphonic poem.

Spohr, Ludwig, b. Brunswick, Germany, 1784; d. Cassel, 1859. Violinist, conductor and composer of note. He wrote nine symphonies, as follows: No. 1, E-flat, op. 20; no. 2, D minor, op. 49; no. 3, C minor, op. 78; no. 4, F major, op. 86 (*Consecration of Tone*); no. 5, C minor, op. 102; no. 6, G major, op. 116 (*Historical*); no. 7, C major (for two orchestras), op. 121; no. 8, G minor, op. 137; no. 9, B minor (*The Seasons*), op. 143. Spohr also composed ten operas, a number of violin concertos (generally considered his best works), sacred and chamber music, smaller orchestral pieces, etc.

Stamitz, Johann, b. Deutsch-Brod, Bohemia, 1717; d. Mannheim, 1757. A pioneer in orchestral composition, generally recognized as a forerunner of Haydn, and credited with fifty symphonies, although these were far from the formal outlines later established.

Stanford, Charles Villiers, b. Dublin, Ireland, 1852; d. London, 1924. Distinguished composer in many styles. His works include seven symphonies, of which the *Irish*, op. 28, is best known, five operas, and much music in the smaller orchestral forms, including a popular *Irish Rhapsody* and a set of *Irish Dances*.

Still, William Grant, b. Woodville, Mississippi, 1895. Outstanding colored composer in the modern style. He wrote an *Afro-American Symphony* (1931), and such tone poems as *Africa, Puritan Epic,* etc.

Stock, Frederick A., b. Duelich, Germany, 1872. German-American conductor and composer (Chicago), whose works include a symphony in C minor.

Stoessel, Albert, b. St. Louis, Mo., 1894. Distinguished American conductor, violinist, teacher and composer, long associated with the Juilliard Faculty in New York. He has written a "symphonic portrait," *Cyrano de Bergerac*, a *Hispania Suite*, and other large orchestral works.

Stojowski, Sigismond, b. Strelzy, Poland, 1870. Eminent composer, pianist and teacher of music. His works include a symphony in D minor, op. 21, awarded a prize in

Leipzig, a *Symphonic Rhapsody*, op. 23, for piano and orchestra, several concertos, besides songs, piano pieces and chamber music.

Strauss, Richard, b. Munich, Germany, 1864. A leader among modern composers, best known by his operas (*Rosenkavalier, Elektra, Salome*) and his symphonic poems (*Don Juan*, op. 20, 1889; *Tod und Verklaerung*, op. 23, 1890; *Macbeth*, op. 24, 1891; *Till Eulenspiegel*, op. 28, 1895; *Also sprach Zarathustra*, op. 30, 1896; *Don Quixote*, op. 35, 1898; *Ein Heldenleben*, op. 40, 1899). Strauss is also one of the great song-writers of all time, following the tradition of Schubert, Schumann and Brahms. His *Sinfonia Domestica*, op. 53, 1904, created a sensation because of its detailed musical program of domestic events, including a baby's bath. He also wrote a symphony in F minor, op. 12, and another called *Alpensinfonie* (1915), several concertos, chamber music, etc.

Stravinsky, Igor, b. St. Petersburg (now Leningrad), 1882. Important modern composer, best known by his ballets (*Petrouschka, L'Oiseau de Feu, Le Sacre du Printemps*, etc.). Outstanding among his more recent works is a *Symphony of Psalms*, and he has two other significant symphonies to his credit. Stravinsky was long considered the most extreme of the modernists, and is still recognized as a revolutionist in the field of music.

Stringfield, Lamar, b. Raleigh, N. C., 1897. American composer specializing in the mountain music of the South. His works include a suite, *From the Southern Mountains* (1927), a "symphonic ballet" (1929), a "symphonic fantasy," *At the Factory* (1929), and a "symphonic patrol," *A Negro Parade* (1931).

Stringham, Edwin John, b. Kenosha, Wisconsin, 1890. Eminent American composer. His first symphony, in B-flat minor, is called *Italian* (1929-30). He has also written the symphonic poems, *The Phantom, Visions*, and *The Ancient Mariner*, and a Suite, *Danses Exotiques*.

Strube, Gustav, b. Ballenstedt, Germany, 1867. Distinguished composer, conductor, violinist and teacher. He has composed two symphonies, two symphonic poems, a suite and other important orchestral works, as well as concertos, chamber music, etc.

Svendsen, Johann Severin, b. Christiania, Norway, 1840; d. Copenhagen, Denmark, 1911. Eminent Scandinavian composer, whose works include two symphonies, four *Norwegian Rhapsodies*, and other orchestral material.

Szymanowski, Karol, b. Timoshovka, Poland, 1883. Impressionistic composer in the modern style, writing mostly for the piano, but with two symphonies to his credit, besides other orchestral works, chamber music and songs.

Taneieff, Sergei Ivanovitch, b. Vladimir, Russia, 1856; d. Moscow, 1915. Nephew of an older composer of the same name, pupil of Rubinstein and Tschaikowsky, teacher of Scriabine and Rachmaninoff. His compositions include four symphonies and other orchestral works, chamber music, etc.

Taylor, Deems, b. New York, 1885. Popular and successful American composer, best known by his operas, *The King's Henchman* and *Peter Ibbetson*, produced at the Metropolitan Opera House. His *Siren Song*, a symphonic poem, won the orchestral prize of the National Federation of Music Clubs in 1912. His *Jurgen* and the Suite *Through the Looking Glass* are also of symphonic significance.

Thompson, Randall, b. New York, 1899. Eminent American composer, whose two symphonies have made a deep impression when played in New York and elsewhere. He has recently done research work in the music of American colleges, and meanwhile developed his creative work in many directions.

Thomson, Virgil, b. Kansas City, Mo., 1896. American composer best known for his music to Gertrude Stein's *Four Saints in Three Acts.* He has to his credit two symphonies, the first *On a Hymn Tune* (1928), the second dated 1931, as well as other orchestral works.

Toch, Ernst, b. Vienna, Austria, 1887. Composer of a symphony, *An mein Vaterland*, with vocal soloists, chorus and organ, also a chamber symphony, sonatas, concertos, string quartets, piano and violin music and other works.

Tschaikowsky, Peter Ilyitch, b. Votkinsk, Russia, 1840; d. St. Petersburg (now Leningrad), 1893. Most popular of Russian composers. See pp. 222–248. His works include six symphonies: No. 1, G major, op. 13; no. 2, C minor, op. 17; no. 3, D major, op. 29; no. 4, F minor, op. 36; no. 5, E minor, op. 64; no. 6, B minor (*Pathétique*), op. 74. Also a *Manfred Symphony*, op. 58, six orchestral suites (of which the *Nutcracker* is most popular), orchestral fantasies and symphonic poems, among which his *Romeo and Juliet* and *Francesca da Rimini* are most important, ten operas (*Eugen Onegin, Pique Dame*, etc.), concertos, chamber music, songs, etc.

Van der Stucken, Frank, b. Fredericksburg, Texas, 1858. Distinguished American composer and conductor (Cincinnati Orchestra and Conservatory, etc.). His works include a Symphonic Prologue, *William Ratcliff*, a *Festival March* and other orchestral pieces.

Verdi, Giuseppe, b. Roncole, Italy, 1813; d. Milan, 1901. One of the greatest of all operatic composers (*Aïda, Falstaff, Otello, Il Trovatore, La Traviata, Rigoletto, Un Ballo in Maschera, La Forza del Destino*, etc.), but with many orchestral works to his credit, including two symphonies.

Vogrich, Max, b. Hermannstadt, Austria, 1852; d. New York, 1916. Eminent pianist and composer. His works include two symphonies, in E minor and A minor, as well as concertos, operas, piano music, etc.

Volkmann, Robert, b. Lommatsch, Germany, 1815; d. Buda-Pesth, Hungary, 1883. Excellent teacher of music and composer of two symphonies, in D minor, op. 44, and

B-flat, op. 53, as well as other orchestral works, chamber music, etc.

Wagenaar, Bernard, b. Arnhem, Holland, 1894. Distinguished Dutch-American composer. He has written two symphonies (1926 and 1930), besides a *Sinfonietta, Divertimento,* etc.

Wagenseil, Georg Christoph, b. Vienna, Austria, 1715; d. there, 1777. Music teacher of the Empress Maria Theresa, and a pioneer composer of note. He is credited with thirty "grand symphonies" for orchestra, as well as ten "symphonies" for harpsichords, two violins and cello, besides concertos, sonatas, etc.

Wagner, Richard, b. Leipzig, Germany, 1813; d. Venice, Italy, 1883. The world's greatest composer of music-drama (*Lohengrin, Tannhaeuser, Die Meistersinger, Parsifal, Tristan und Isolde, Das Rheingold, Die Walkuere, Siegfried, Goetterdaemmerung*). He wrote a symphony in C major in 1833, and his overtures and other orchestral works are of symphonic proportions.

Weingartner, Felix, b. Zara, Dalmatia, 1863. Distinguished conductor and composer. He has to his credit three symphonies, as well as other orchestral works, operas, chamber music, etc.

Wessel, Mark, b. Coldwater, Michigan, 1894. Composer of a symphony (1932), and a *Symphonie Concertante* (for horn and piano).

White, Paul, b. Bangor, Maine, 1895. Young American composer whose first symphony recently won a marked success.

Whithorne, Emerson, b. Cleveland, Ohio, 1884. Prominent American composer, a leader in the modern movement. His first symphony was written in 1929. He has also composed a violin concerto and a popular suite, *New York Days and Nights.*

Whiting, Arthur, b. 1861; Cambridge, Mass., d. New York, 1936. Scholarly American composer, pianist and lecturer on music, with several works in the larger forms, including a Suite for horns and strings, a *Concert Overture*, a piano concerto and a Fantasie for piano and orchestra.

Widor, Charles-Marie, b. Lyons, France, 1845. Distinguished organist and composer. He wrote two orchestral symphonies, and other works in similar form for the organ.

Williams, Ralph Vaughan, b. Down Ampney, England, 1872. Outstanding English composer, best known by his *London Symphony*, (1912–13). He also wrote a *Pastoral Symphony*, a *Sea Symphony*, for baritone, soprano, chorus and orchestra, a "symphonic impression," *In the Fen Country*, three *Norfolk Rhapsodies*, a *Bucolic Suite*, and other orchestral works.

Wilson, Meredith. Young American composer, whose symphony, *San Francisco*, made an excellent impression when broadcast during a performance in the city which it celebrates.

Zemlinsky, Alexander von, b. Vienna, Austria, 1872. Modern composer, whose works include three symphonies.

INDEX

Absolute Music, 168–9, 185
Adagio, 26, 87, 88, 126, 166, 247
Allegretto, 110, 117
Allegro, 23, 24, 51, 54, 96, 105, 142, 162, 212, 245
Alsace, 72
Andante, 42, 48, 65, 146, 177
Arabian Nights, 250, 252
As You Like It, 106

Bach, J. S., 58, 59, 62, 175, 176, 215
Bag-pipe, 15
Banjo, 230
Baritone, 129
Bass (*passim*)
  Bass Drum, 30, 32; Bass Viol, 127, 128, 129, 135
  Bass Voice, 131
Bassoon, 5, 20, 28, 64, 178, 202, 203, 224, 229, 253
Beethoven, L. van, xi, 45, 47, 51, 53, 54, 59, 61–133, 134, 144, 147, 150, 158, 175, 185, 186, 192, 195, 200, 201, 206, 215, 217, 224, 226, 247, 263
  First Symphony, 53, 62–70; Second Symphony, 70–76, 126; Third Symphony (*Eroica*), 76–85, 98, 122, 201, 202; Fourth Symphony, 85–91; Fifth Symphony (*Fate*), xi, 45, 51, 53, 80, 86, 91–101, 103, 121, 122, 158, 186, 192, 195, 206, 226, 247; Sixth Symphony (*Pastoral*), 101–107, 195; Seventh Symphony (*Dance*), 107–114, 115, 122; Eighth Symphony, 114–121, 122; Ninth Symphony (*Choral*), 115, 121–132, 144, 147, 150, 192; *Fidelio,* 62; *Leonore Overture, no. 3,*

86; *Missa Solemnis,* 121; *Prometheus,* 83
Birch Tree, The (Folk-song), xi, 232–3
Bizet, G., 30 (*Carmen*)
Brahms, J., xii, 53, 62, 134, 151, 160, 185–215, 216, 217, 224
  First Symphony, 53, 186–194; Second Symphony, 194–201; Third Symphony, 201–208, 210; Fourth Symphony, 208–215; *Sapphische Ode,* 195–6; *Zigeunerlieder,* 198
Brass, 30, 84, 130, 137, 194, 221, 230, 231, 233, 241, 244
Bruckner, A., xii
Bugle, 78

Cadenza, 132, 158, 253
Cantata, 26
Caro mio ben, 88
Cello (Violoncello), 29, 71, 77, 94, 110, 136, 137, 190, 197, 199, 203, 204, 206, 211, 242
Chaconne, 214, 237
Chamber Music, 38, 62, 217, 223, 258
Chant, 76
Chopin, F., 151
Chorale, 194, 211
Chorus, 58, 59, 121, 129, 131, 185
Chromatic Scale, 34, 164, 218, 225, 227
Clarinet, 13, 71, 95, 105, 106, 112, 115, 135, 138, 148, 177, 191, 202, 229
Classicism, 150, 151
Coda, 19, 24, 25, 32, 36, 59, 65, 66, 69, 72, 73, 76, 79, 84, 87, 88, 90, 94, 95, 100, 104, 106, 109, 112, 113, 114, 116, 120, 123, 127, 131, 137, 138, 141, 143, 145, 150, 154, 158, 162,

INDEX

359

INDEX

241; Sixth Symphony (*Pathétique*), 241–248; *Marche Slav,* 223; *Nutcracker Suite,* 223; *Overture 1812,* 223; *Romeo and Juliet,* 223

Variations, 7, 83, 84, 95, 111, 199, 214, 233, 239
Viola, 94, 110, 197
Violin, 4, 10, 20, 35, 37, 58, 62, 66, 67, 71, 89, 90, 105, 108, 109, 112, 120, 124, 134, 138, 165, 174, 176, 195, 197, 214, 217, 221, 223, 250, 251
Violoncello (See cello)

Wagner, R., 62, 64, 87, 106, 107, 126, 158, 163, 169, 170
Flying Dutchman, 163; *Meistersinger,* 126; *Nibelungen Ring,* 169; *Prize Song,* 126; *Rheingold,* 171; *Tristan und Isolde,* 106; *Walkuere,* 64, 87
Wagon Wheels, 261
Waltz, 238, 239
Watts, Isaac, 72, 73
Weber, C. M. von, 109
Westminster Chime, 193–4
Wieck, Clara (Schumann), 152
Wind Instruments, 45, 47, 67, 112, 127, 193, 232
Wood-wind, 5, 15, 27, 29, 41, 49, 54, 71, 87, 89, 93, 95, 124, 125, 128, 129, 137, 145, 199, 202, 203, 213, 219, 225, 227, 229, 230, 231, 251, 257

Yankee Doodle, 266

For your complete enjoyment of this book we recommend that you listen to the many excellent recordings of the musical score of these famous compositions.

Below is a suggested list of recordings which are available.

BACH, JOHANN CHRISTIAN
Sinfonia in B Flat Major—1st Move.—Allegro assai; 2nd Move.—Andante
Mengelberg—Philharmonic-Symphony Orch. of N. Y.
7483
Sinfonia in B Flat Major—3rd Move.—Presto
Philharmonic Symphony Orch.
7484
BACH, KARL PHILIPP EMANUEL
Symphony No. 3, in C Major
NBC String Symphony Orchestra
Inc. in Album M-390 (12091–12097) DM (12863–12869).
BEETHOVEN
Symphony No. 1, in C Major (Op. 21)
Toscanini—B. B. C. Orchestra
Album M-507 (15383–15387) DM (16179–16183).
Symphony No. 1, in C Major (Op. 21)
Ormandy–Philadelphia Orch.
Album M-409 (14691–14694) DM (16508–16511).
Symphony No. 2, in D Major (Op. 36)   Serge Koussevitzky–Boston Symphony Orchestra
Album M-625 (15771–15774-S) DM (15979-S–15982).
Symphony No. 3, in E Flat Major ("Eroica") (Op. 55)   Coates–Symphony Orchestra
Album G-2 (36251–36256).
Symphony No. 3, in E Flat Major ("Eroica") (Op. 55).
Serge Koussevitzky–London Philharmonic Orchestra
Album M-263 (8668–8673) DM (16663–16668).
Symphony No. 3, in E Flat Major ("Eroica") (Op. 55)   Toscanini–NBC Symphony Orch.
Album M-765 (17852–17858-S) DM (17866-S–17872).
Symphony No. 4, in B Flat Major (Op. 60)   Ormandy–Minneapolis Symphony Orchestra
Album M-274 (8747–8751) DM (16994–16998).
Symphony No. 4, in B Flat Major (Op. 60)   Toscanini–B. B. C. Symphony Orchestra
Album M-676 (16325–16328) DM (16333–16336).
Symphony No. 5, in C Minor (Op. 67)   Toscanini–NBC Symphony Orchestra
Album M-640 (15827–15830) DM (15965–15968).
Symphony No. 5, in C Minor (Op. 67)   Koussevitzky–London Philharmonic Orchestra
Album M-245 (8508–8512) DM (16635–16639).
Symphony No. 5, in C Minor (Op. 67)
Berlin Philharmonic Orchestra, conducted by Wilhelm Furtwängler
Album M-426 (14793–14797-S) DM (16456-S–16460).
Symphony No. 5—1st Movement (Abridged)
and Symphony No. 8 (Schubert) (Inc. in G-15)   Victor Symphony Orch.
36329
Symphony No. 6, in F Major ("Pastoral") (Op. 68)
Toscanini–British Broadcasting Co. Symphony Orchestra
Album M-417 (14707–14711) DM (16472–16476).
Symphony No. 7, in A Major (Op. 92)   Leopold Stokowski–Philadelphia Orchestra
Album M-17 (6670–6674) DM (17268–17273).
Symphony No. 7, in A Major (Op. 92)
Arturo Toscanini–Philharmonic-Symphony Orchestra of N. Y.
Album M-317 (14097–14101) DM (16732–16736).
Symphony No. 8, in F Major (Op. 93)   Serge Koussevitzky–Boston Symphony Orchestra
Album M-336 (14257–14259) DM (16745–16747).
Symphony No. 9, in D Minor ("Choral") (Op. 125)   Leopold Stokowski–Philadelphia Orchestra
Album M-236 (8424–8432-S) DM (16621-S–16629).
BERLIOZ
Symphonie Fantastique (Op. 14)   Bruno Walter–Paris Conservatory Orch.
Album M-662 (12692–12697) DM (12704–12709).
BIZET
Symphony No. 1, in C Major   Goehr–London Philharmonic Orchestra
Album M-721 (13501–13504) DM (13509–13512).
BORODIN
Symphony No. 2, in B Minor   Albert Coates–London Symphony Orchestra
Album M-113 (11163–11165) DM (13235–13237).
BRAHMS
Symphony No. 1, in C Minor   Leopold Stokowski–Philadelphia Orchestra
Album M-301 (8971–8975) DM (16712–16716).
Symphony No. 1, in C Minor (Op. 68)   Walter–Vienna Philharmonic Orchestra
Album M-470 (12264–12268) DM (12781–12785).
Symphony No. 1, in C Minor—4th Move. (Abridged)
and Symphony in D Minor (Franck) (Inc. in G-15)   Victor Symphony Orchestra
36331
Symphony No. 2, in D Major (Op. 73)   Stokowski–Philadelphia Orchestra
Album M-82 (7277–7282).
Symphony No. 2, in D Major (Op. 73)   Eugene Ormandy–The Philadelphia Orchestra
Album M-694 (17302–17307) DM (17314–17319).
Symphony No. 3, in F Major (Op. 90)   Leopold Stokowski–Philadelphia Orchestra
Album M-42 (6962–6966) DM (17258–17262).
Symphony No. 3, in F Major (Op. 90)   Walter–Vienna Philharmonic Orchestra
Album M-341 (12022–12025) AM (12026–12029) DM (12897–12900).

Symphony No. 3, in F Major (Op. 90).   Kindler-National Symphony Orch.
    Album M-762 (17888–17891) DM (17896–17899).
Symphony No. 4, in E Minor (Op. 98)   Koussevitzky-Boston Symphony Orchestra
    Album M-730 (17514–17518-S) DM (17524-S-17528).
Symphony No. 4, in E Minor   Stokowski-Philadelphia Orch.
    Album M-185 (7825–7829).
Symphony No. 4, in E Minor   Walter-B. B. C. Symphony Orchestra
    Album M-242 (11734–11738) DM (12883–12887).
Symphony No. 4, in E Minor (Op. 98)   Abendroth-London Symphony Orchestra
    Album G-7 (36273–36278).
BRUCKNER
Symphony No. 3, in D Minor—Scherzo   Vienna Symphony Orchestra
                                                            11726
Symphony No. 4, in E Flat Major ("Romantic")   Karl Böhm-Saxonian State Orchestra
    Album M-331 (14211–14218) DM (16867–16874).
Symphony No. 5, in B Flat Major (Bruckner-Orig. Score)   Saxonian State Orchestra
    Album M-770 (17921–17925) DM (17939–17943).
    Album M-771 (17926–17929) DM (17944–17947).
Symphony No. 7, in E Major   Eugene Ormandy-Minneapolis Symphony Orchestra
    Album M-276 (8770–8777-S) DM (16983-S–16990).
Symphony No. 9, in D Minor (Original Edition)   Hausegger-Munich Philharmonic Orchestra
    Album M-627 (15784–15790) DM (15972–15978).
Symphony in D Minor (The Posthumous "Youth")—Scherzo   Zaun-Berlin State Opera Orchestra
                                                            11726
CHAUSSON
Symphony in B Flat Major (Op. 20)   Piero Coppola-Paris Conservatory Orchestra
    Album M-261 (11783–11786) DM (13168–13171).
DVOŘÁK
Symphony No. 2, in D Minor (Op. 70)   Vaclav Talich-Czech Philharmonic Orchestra
    Album M-663 (12710–12714) DM (12720–12724).
Symphony No. 4, in G Major (Op. 88)   Talich-Czech Philharmonic Orchestra
    Album M-304 (11899–11903) DM (13154–13158).
Symphony No. 5, in E Minor ("From the New World") (Op. 95)
                                 Leopold Stokowski-Philadelphia Orchestra
    Album M-273 (8737–8741) AM (8742–8746) DM (16684–16688).
Symphony No. 5, in E Minor ("From the New World") (Op. 95)
                     Czech Philharmonic Orchestra, cond. Georg Szell
    Album M-469 (12254–12258) AM (12259–12263) DM (12786–12790).
Symphony No. 5, in E Minor—2nd Move. (Abridged)
    and Symphony No. 4 (Tschaikowsky) (Inc. in G-15)   Victor Symphony Orchestra
                                                            36330
FRANCK
Symphony in D Minor   Leopold Stokowski-Philadelphia Orchestra
    Album M-300 (8959–8964) DM (16706–16711).
Symphony in D Minor—2nd Move. (Abridged)
    and Symphony No. 1 (Brahms) (Inc. in G-15)   Victor Symphony Orchestra
                                                            36331
Symphony in D Minor   Pierre Monteux-San Francisco Symphony Orchestra
    Album M-840 (18246–18250) DM-840 (18251–18255).
GLIERE
Symphony No. 3, in B Minor ("Ilia Mouromets")   Stokowski-Philadelphia Orchestra
    Album M-841 (18262–18267) DM-841 (18268–18273).
HANSON
Symphony No. 2 ("Romantic") (Op. 30)   Hanson-Eastman-Rochester Symphony Orchestra
    Album M-648 (15865–15868) DM (15953–15956).
HARRIS
Symphony for Voices on Poems of Walt Whitman
            The Westminster Choir, conducted by John Finley Williamson
    1st Movement—Song for All Seas, All Ships
    2nd Movement—Tears
    3rd Movement—Inscription—Parts 1 and 2
    Album M-427 (14803–14804).
Symphony No. 3   Serge Koussevitzky-Boston Symphony Orchestra
    Album M-651 (15885–15886).
HAYDN
Symphony No. 67, in F Major   Orchestra of New Friends of Music
    Inc. in M-536 (15336–15340-S) DM (16164-S–16168).
Symphony No. 80, in D Minor (Edited by Alfred Einstein)
                     Orchestra of New Friends of Music, Fritz Stiedry, conductor
    Album M-536 (15336–15340-S) DM (16164-S–16168).
Symphony No. 86, in D Major   Bruno Walter-London Symphony Orchestra
    Album M-578 (12461–12463) DM (12675–12677).
Symphony No. 88, in G Major (Old B. & H. No. 13)   Toscanini-NBC Symphony Orch.
    Album M-454 (14928–14930) DM (16370–16372).
Symphony No. 88, in G Major (Old B. & H. No. 13)
    Part 1—1st Movement—Adagio—Allegro
       and Part 2—1st Move.—Allegro (conc.)   Vienna Philharmonic Orchestra
                                                              4189
    Part 3—2nd Move.—Largo   and Part 4—Vienna Philharmonic Orchestra
                                                                  4190
    Part 5—3rd Movement—Menuetto—Allegretto—Trio and Part 6
    —4th Move.—Finale—Allegro con spirito   Vienna Philharmonic Orchestra
                                                              4191
Symphony No. 88, in G Major—Finale—Allegro con spirito (B. & H. No. 13)
                               Koussevitzky-London Philharmonic Orchestra
                                                                  8512

(Included in Album M-245)
Symphony No. 92, in G Major ("Oxford")   Walter–Paris Conservatory Orchestra
  Album M-682 (12974–12976) DM (12980–12982).
Symphony No. 94, in G Major ("Surprise")   Koussevitzky–Boston Symphony Orchestra
  Album M-55 (7058–7060) DM (16766–16768).
Symphony No. 97, in C Major (Salomon Set)   Weisbach–London Symphony Orchestra
  Album M-140 (11317–11319) DM (13218–13220).
Symphony No. 100, in G Major ("Military")   Walter–Vienna Philharmonic Orchestra
  Album M-472 (12274–12276) DM (12778–12780).
Symphony No. 101, in D Major ("The Clock") (Old B. & H. No. 4)
        Arturo Toscanini–Philharmonic-Symphony Orchestra of N. Y.
  Album M-57 (7077–7080) DM (16769–16772).
Symphony No. 102, in B Flat Major   Serge Koussevitzky–Boston Symphony Orchestra
  Album M-529 (15304–15306) DM (16173–16175).
Symphony No. 104, in D Major ("London")   Edwin Fischer's Chamber Orchestra
  Album M-617 (12512–12514) DM (12636–12638).
Symphony No. 104, in D Major ("London") (Old B. & H. No. 2)
  Part 1—1st Movement—Adagio—Allegro and
    Part 2—1st Move. (conc.)—2nd Move.—Andante   Barbirolli's Orchestra
           35981

KALINNIKOV
Symphony No. 1, in G Minor   Indianapolis Symphony Orchestra, Fabien Sevitzky, Cond.
  Album M-827 (18187–18190) DM-827 (18191–18194) Four 12 inch Records.
MAHLER
Symphony No. 2, in C Minor   Eugene Ormandy–Minneapolis Symphony Orchestra
  Album M-256 (11753–11763) DM (13172–13182).
Symphony No. 5, in C Minor—Adagietto   Walter–Vienna Philharmonic Orchestra
           12319
Symphony No. 9   Vienna Philharmonic Orch., cond. by Walter
  Album M-726 (13522–13531) DM (13542–13551).
McDONALD
Rhumba Symphony—Rhumba   Stokowski–Philadelphia Orchestra
           8919
Fourth Symphony—Cakewalk (Scherzo)
  and Amelia Goes to the Ball—Overture   Ormandy–Philadelphia Orchestra
           15377
MENDELSSOHN
Symphony No. 4, in A Major ("Italian") (Op. 90)   Panizza–Members of La Scala Orch., Milan
  Album G-8 (36279–36282).
Symphony No. 4, in A Major ("Italian") (Op. 90)   Serge Koussevitzky–Boston Sym. Orch.
  Album M-294 (8889–8891) DM (16703–16705).
MOZART
Symphony No. 28, in C Major (K. 200)   Berlin College of Instrumentalists
  Album M-502 (12322–12323).
Symphony No. 29, in A Major (Mozart, K. 201)   Koussevitzky–Boston Symphony Orch.
  Album M-795 (18063–18067-S) DM (18073-S-18077).
Symphony No. 32, in B Flat Major (K. 319)   Fischer's Chamber Orchestra
  Album M-479 (15043–15045) DM (16300–16302).
Symphony No. 34, in C Major (Mozart, K. 338)   Koussevitzky–Boston Symphony Orchestra
  Inc. in Album M-795 (18063–18067-S) DM (18073-S-18077).
Symphony No. 35, in D Major ("Haffner") (K. 385)
        Arturo Toscanini–Philharmonic-Symphony Orchestra of N. Y.
  Album M-65 (7136–7138) DM (16558–16560).
Symphony No. 36, in C Major (K. 425)   Fritz Busch–B. B. C. Symphony Orchestra
  Album M-266 (11802–11804) DM (13165–13167).
Symphony No. 38, in D Major ("Prague") (K. 504)   Walter–Vienna Philharmonic Orchestra
  Album M-457 (12239–12241) DM (12810–12812).
Symphony No. 39, in E Flat (K. 543)   Walter–B. B. C. Symphony Orchestra
  Album M-258 (11775–11777) DM (12888–12890).
Symphony No. 40, in G Minor (K. 550)   Serge Koussevitzky–London Philharmonic Orchestra
  Album M-293 (8883–8885) DM (16700–16702).
Symphony No. 40, in G Minor (K. 550)   Frederick Stock–Chicago Symphony Orchestra
  Album G-3 (36257–36259).
Symphony No. 40, in G Minor (K. 550)   Arturo Toscanini–NBC Symphony Orchestra
  Album M-631 (15753–15755) DM (15969–15971).
Symphony No. 41, in C Major ("Jupiter") (K. 551)
        Vienna Philharmonic Orchestra cond. by Bruno Walter
  Album M-584 (12467–12470-S) DM (12649-S-12652).
PROKOFIEFF
Classical Symphony, in D Major (Op. 25)   Serge Koussevitzky–Boston Symphony Orchestra
           7196
           7197
RACHMANINOFF
Symphony No. 2, in E Minor (Op. 27)   Ormandy–Minneapolis Symphony Orchestra
  Album M-239 (8463–8468) DM (17057–17062).
RIMSKY-KORSAKOV
Symphony No. 2 ("Antar") (Op. 9)   Paris Conservatory Orchestra
  Album M-210 (11671–11673) DM (13199–13201).
SAINT-SAENS
Symphony No. 3, in C Minor (Op. 78) with Organ   Coppola–Symphony Orchestra
  Album M-100 (9908–9911) DM (13238–13241).
SCHUBERT
Symphony No. 4, in C Minor ("Tragic")
        Philharmonic-Symphony Orch. of N. Y., conductor, John Barbirolli
  Album M-562 (15426–15429) DM (16128–16131).

Symphony No. 5, in B Flat   Dr. Leo Blech–Berlin State Opera Orchestra
   Album M-170 (11476–11478) DM (13205–13207).
Symphony No. 8, in B Minor ("Unfinished")   Koussevitzky–Boston Symphony Orchestra
   Album M-319 (14117–14119) DM (16737–16739).
Symphony No. 8, in B Minor ("Unfinished")   Stokowski–Philadelphia Orchestra
   Album M-16 (6663–6665) DM (16760–16762).
Symphony No. 8, in B Minor ("Unfinished")   Walter–Vienna Philharmonic Orchestra
   Album G-9 (36248–36250).
Symphony No. 8, in B Minor—1st Move. (Abridged)
   and Symphony No. 5 (Beethoven) (Inc. in G-15)   Victor Symphony Orchestra
                                                36329
Symphony No. 9, in C Major (B. & H. No. 7)   Bruno Walter–London Symphony Orchestra
   Album M-602 (12498–12503) DM (12629–12644).

SCHUMANN
Symphony No. 1, in B Flat Major ("Spring") (Op. 38) Koussevitzky–Boston Symphony Orch.
   Album M-655 (15895–15898) DM (15903–15906).
Symphony No. 2, in C Major (Op. 61)   Philadelphia Orchestra, cond. Eugene Ormandy
   Album M-448 (14885–14889) DM (16401–16405).
Symphony No. 3, in E Flat ("Rhenish") (Op. 97) Piero Coppola–Paris Conservatory Orchestra
   Album M-237 (11706–11708) DM (13183–13185).
Symphony No. 4, in D Minor (Op. 120) Eugene Ormandy and the Minneapolis Symphony Orch
   Album M-201 (7982–7984) DM (17105–17107).

SIBELIUS
Symphony No. 1, in E Minor (Op. 39)   Eugene Ormandy–Minneapolis Symphony Orchestra
   Album M-290 (8873–8877) DM (16692–16696).
Symphony No. 2, in D Major (Op. 43)   Koussevitzky–Boston Symphony Orchestra
   Album M-272 (8721–8726-S) DM (16678-S–16683).
Symphony No. 3, in C Major (Op. 52)   London Symphony Orch., conducted by Robert Kajanus
   Included in Album M-394 (12113–12116, 14552–14554) DM (12856–12859, 16545–16547).
Symphony No. 4, in A Minor (Op. 63)
          The London Philharmonic Orchestra, conducted by Sir Thomas Beecham
   Album M-446 (12215–12221) DM (12818–12824).
Symphony No. 4, in A Minor (Op. 63)   Stokowski–Philadelphia Orchestra
   Album M-160 (7883–7886) DM (17172–17175).
Symphony No. 5, in E Flat Major (Op. 82)   Koussevitzky–Boston Symphony Orchestra
   Album M-474 (15019–15023) DM (16308–16312).
Symphony No. 6, in D Minor (Op. 104)   Finnish Nat'l Orch., cond. by Georg Schneevoigt
   Inc. in M-344 (14386–14392) DM (16844–16850).
Symphony No. 7, in C Major (Op. 105)   British Broadcasting Co.
           Symphony Orch., conducted by Serge Koussevitzky
   Album M-394 (12113–12116, 14552–14554) DM (12856–12859, 16545–16547).

STRAUSS, RICHARD
Symphonia Domestica (Op. 53)   Eugene Ormandy–Philadelphia Orchestra
   Album M-520 (15225–15229) DM (16227–16231).

SZOSTAKOWICZ
Symphony No. 1 (Op. 10)   Leopold Stokowski–Philadelphia Orchestra
   Album M-192 (7884–7888-S) DM (16601-S–16605).
Symphony No. 5 (Op. 47)   Leopold Stokowski–Philadelphia Orchestra
   Album M-619 (15737–15742) DM (15995–16000).

TSCHAIKOWSKY
Symphony No. 2, in C Minor ("Little Russian") (Op. 17)
                   Goossens–Cincinnati Symphony Orchestra
   Album M-790 (18035–18038) DM (18043–18046).
Symphony No. 3, in D Major ("Polish") (Op. 29) Nat'l Symphony Orch., cond. by Kindler
   Album M-747 (17710–17714) DM (17720–17724).
Symphony No. 3, in D Major (Op. 29)   Coates–London Symphony Orchestra
   Album M-166 (11459–11462) DM (13211–13214).
Symphony No. 4, in F Minor   Leopold Stokowski–Philadelphia Orchestra
   Album M-48 (6929–6933) DM (17251–17255).
Symphony No. 4, in F Minor   Koussevitzky–Boston Symphony Orchestra
   Album M-327 (14185–14189) DM (16740–16744).
Symphony No. 4, in F Minor—3rd Move. (Abridged)
   and Symphony No. 5 (Dvořák) (Inc. in G-15)   Victor Symphony Orchestra
                                                36330
Symphony No. 5, in E Minor—2nd Move. (Abridged)
   and Scheherazade–Festival at Bagdad (Inc. in G-15)   Victor Symphony Orchestra
                                                36332
Symphony No. 5—Andante Cantabile (Op. 64) and Love Theme from
   "Romeo and Juliet"—Overture (Inc. in P-15)   Victor Salon Orchestra
                                              26488
Symphony No. 5, in E Minor (Op. 64)   Stock–Chicago Symphony Orchestra
   Album G-4 (36260–36265).
Symphony No. 5, in E Minor   Leopold Stokowski–Philadelphia Orchestra
   Album M-253 (8589–8594) DM (16647–16652).
Symphony No. 5, in E Minor (Op. 64)   The Philadelphia Orchestra, Eugene Ormandy, Cond.
   Album M-828 (18177–18181) DM-828 (18182–18186). Five 12 inch Records.
Symphony No. 6, in B Minor ("Pathétique") (Op. 74) Serge Koussevitzky–Boston Sym. Orch.
   Album M-85 (7294–7298) DM (16565–16569).
Symphony No. 6, in B Minor ("Pathétique") (Op. 74) Eugene Ormandy–Philadelphia Orch.
   Album M-337 (14264–14268) DM (16748–16752).
Symphony No. 6, in B Minor ("Pathétique") (Op. 74) Furtwängler–Berlin Philharmonic Orch.
   Album M-553 (15395–15400) DM (17561–17566).

WILLIAMS
Symphony in F Minor   B. B. C. Symphony Orchestra, conductor, Vaughan Williams
   Album M-440 (12182–12185) DM (12833–12836).